on track ...
The Hollies

every album, every song

Andrew Darlington

sonicbondpublishing.com

Sonicbond Publishing Limited
www.sonicbondpublishing.co.uk
Email: info@sonicbondpublishing.co.uk

First Published in the United Kingdom 2021
First Published in the United States 2021

British Library Cataloguing in Publication Data:
A Catalogue record for this book is available from the British Library

ISBN 978-1-78952-159-7

Typeset in ITC Garamond & ITC Avant Garde
Printed and bound in England

Graphic design and typesetting: Full Moon Media

For Catherine,
Who shared the whole strange trip

Would you like to write for Sonicbond Publishing?

We are mainly a music publisher, but we also occasionally publish in other genres including film and television. At Sonicbond Publishing we are always on the look-out for authors, particularly for our two main series, On Track and Decades.

Mixing fact with in depth analysis, the On Track series examines the entire recorded work of a particular musical artist or group. All genres are considered from easy listening and jazz to 60s soul to 90s pop, via rock and metal.

The Decades series singles out a particular decade in an artist or group's history and focuses on that decade in more detail than may be allowed in the On Track series.

While professional writing experience would, of course, be an advantage, the most important qualification is to have real enthusiasm and knowledge of your subject. First-time authors are welcomed, but the ability to write well in English is essential.

Sonicbond Publishing has distribution throughout Europe and North America, and all our books are also published in E-book form. Authors will be paid a royalty based on sales of their book. Further details about our books are available from www.sonicbondpublishing.com. To contact us, complete the contact form there or email info@sonicbondpublishing.co.uk

on track ...
The Hollies

Contents

Introduction

The road is long, with many a winding turn, that leads us to who knows where? Who knows where?

Everyone loved The Hollies. They were the 'group's group'. Never confrontational or rebellious, always smartly suited, always smiling. With an unbroken run of immaculate pop singles which, while they seldom had that must-buy factor of the latest Rolling Stones or Beatles record, were hallmarked by tight harmonies and unfailing chart sensibility. Throughout the sixties and well into the seventies, everyone had – own up – at least one or two Hollies singles in their collection. When Tony Hicks' mouths 'Hello Mum' as the *Top of the Pops* cameras pan past him, even normally-disapproving parents were charmed. No one begrudged The Hollies their hits.

When 'He Ain't Heavy, He's My Brother' and 'Long Cool Woman In A Black Dress' became global million-sellers, The Hollies were inducted into *The Rock 'n' Roll Hall of Fame*. Graham Nash – by then deep into his second career as part of Crosby, Stills, Nash & Young, was reunited with other members of the outfit, Allan Clarke, Bernard 'Bernie' Calvert, Eric Haydock, and Terry Sylvester – although significantly without either Bobby Elliott or Tony Hicks, all on stage together in the March 2010 ceremony.

Rock History tells how the origins of The Hollies can be traced back to post-war Manchester, and two gawky five-year-old pupils at Ordsall Board Primary School. Born within two months of each other, Allan Clarke (born 5 April 1942 in Salford, one of six children) and Graham Nash (2 February 1942) started out as school friends. Hanging out together as fourteen-year-olds, they bought their first guitars inspired by the Skiffle fad. Although born in Blackpool, Graham spent much of his childhood within 1 Skinner Street, Salford, a now-demolished back-to-back *Coronation Street* terraced house with outside lav. 'I have so many great memories of growing up in Salford' he told me. 'And first being turned on to the magic of music in Salford. I didn't leave Salford until I was eighteen. So I have lots of great memories of the struggles and the joys and the heartaches of doing something that was different from anything any of your family had done. Nobody in my family had been in a band before. Ever.'

When his parents gifted him with a Dansette record player as a reward for passing his eleven-plus exam, Graham's first purchase was Gene Vincent's 'Be-Bop-a-Lula' on a big old 78rpm disc; 'I wanted that, and from that moment wanted nothing else.' Meanwhile, Allan failed that same exam but recalled amiably, 'I was working six days a week and getting £1-19s-11d, then going out at weekends and getting five quid for singing four songs'. For the two friends were by then serving their musical apprenticeship together by playing local dates on the Manchester club circuit as The Two Teens. Then they were The Ricky & Dane Young duo, and briefly, they were also The Guytones – a play on the name of their Japanese guitars. Caught up in the generational energy-wave of Rock 'n' Roll, they were performing Lonnie Donegan, Everly Brothers and early-Cliff Richard covers, so hungry to play they'd have done it for free but enjoying the as-yet-slight financial rewards too.

Competing in a pre-*X-Factor* talent contest, they played the Art Deco Hippodrome Theatre on Wednesday 19 November 1958, in competition with Liverpool's Johnny & The Moondogs. 'Johnny' Lennon later went on to greater things! Allan and Graham became half of The Fourtones, then through a torturous process, pacting eventually with Eric Haydock (born Eric John Haddock, 3 February 1943 in Stockport) and drummer Donald Rathbone (born October 1942 in Wilmslow) as The Deltas, until – with Fender guitarist Vic Steele (born 8 May 1945), they finally evolved into The Hollies. It was for a December 1962 gig at the 2Js that The Deltas rebranded themselves with a name not entirely unconnected with their taste for the songs of another formative influence – 'Buddy Holly didn't swivel his hips or grease his hair, he wore glasses, he was one of us.' (Allan)

Thereby hangs a tale. Along with Buddy Holly, The Everly Brothers were vocal models for the burgeoning Hollies sound. A vital influence, there's an argument that Everly harmonies also template those of Simon & Garfunkel, Status Quo and many others. And before The Hollies even got together, Graham and Allan managed to see the brothers when they played the Manchester Free Trade Hall on Wednesday 13 February 1957, as part of a UK tour. They even waited outside their Hotel at 2:30 am to catch a glimpse of the duo. 'We idolised them', Allan tells me. 'We tried to work out where they'd be staying. We decided it must be the Grand, which was the poshest place to stay (Graham recalls it was the Midland Hotel). So we went there and hung around on the pavement outside. Eventually, they came out and chatted to us. They must have stopped talking with us for about twenty-five minutes.' Graham takes up the tale: 'they came out of a Night Club, slightly inebriated, and instead of patting us on the head and signing an autograph, they talked to me and Allan for twenty-eight minutes… it changed my life.' Sure it did, six years later Don & Phil came calling, and the two Manchester graduates wound up writing eight of the twelve tracks for the Evs' May 1966 album *Two Yanks in London*. Phil Everly was also the first artist to record Albert Hammond's 'The Air That I Breathe', which The Hollies lifted for their own number 2 hit in 1974.

Manchester has an important niche in pop history. There was a healthy club scene, with the Twisted Wheel, the 2Js (later the Oasis) and the Bodega. In that first wave of Beat Groups, as well as The Hollies, there was Freddie & The Dreamers (with former-Fourtone Derek Quinn) and Herman's Hermits. Later there were the Factory years of Joy Division and New Order, plus The Smiths, then The Stone Roses and the Madchester exploits of Happy Mondays, before the all-conquering 1990s Britpop of Oasis.

The Hollies started out as very much part of the Beat Boom's first wave when even the idea of the Beat-Group as a self-contained writing-singing-playing musical unit was still a novelty. There had been The Crickets, The Shadows, Johnny Kidd & The Pirates, but it was the advent of The Beatles that normalised the idea that a group could be a magical auditory Lego as unique as a retinal-print, each member an integral component playing interactionally to create a whole greater than the sum of its parts. But before they broke into chart-dom, they were sitting up there in Manchester reading the Music Press – just as I was, and imagining themselves on its pages. 'That's what you did. You imagined yourself on those pages, ' Graham told me. 'Yeah, every time you'd get *Disc* or *New Musical Express*, you could picture that's what you could do. And you dreamed, and you'd pull yourself towards that dream, and it happened with me. I was fortunate to have it all come true....'

The face of music was about to undergo a seismic lurch, and there was an urgent need to be a part of that newness. 1962 closed with business as usual – Elvis Presley enjoyed a run at number 1 with 'Return to Sender', but way down beneath him, the world was shifting, as The Beatles made their very modest chart debut with 'Love Me Do' up to a high of number 17 (27 December). Into the New Year, there was 'Please Please Me', and nothing would ever be the same again. For British teens, 1963 was when everything changed. Throughout that year, the Beat Boom was strictly a local UK phenomenon. This was a special time. It would never come again. For US teens, that firebreak in history didn't happen until The Beatles appeared on *The Ed Sullivan Show* with 'I Want To Hold Your Hand' in 1964.

But first, the relentlessly London-based music industry was shocked out of its complacency, sending talent-scouts and A&R men scuttling up to the sudden Pop gold-mines of the dark industrial north-west of England in search of the next Fab Four. Things were starting to fall into place. Tommy Sanderson worked at music publishers Francis Day & Hunter; he had his ear to the ground. He was given a nudge by a Manchester radio producer. As a result, as early as January 1963, he and Parlophone's staff producer Ron Richards – George Martin's primary assistant – headhunted The Hollies when they played a lunchtime stint at *The Cavern Club*. 'Every time we played there, it seemed we would have something stolen', laughs Bobby Elliott. 'One time, we had a Vox amp stolen. Given the fact that there was only one exit to the club, it amazes me how they even got the stuff out!'

Ron Richards was so impressed with what he saw that he invited The Hollies to audition in London. Guitarist Vic Steele didn't want to risk turning professional, so group manager Allan Cheetham invited Tony Hicks (born 16 December 1943, in Nelson) to audition instead. Tony had started out playing with the local group Les Skiflettes, who graduate into Ricky Shaw & The Dolphins when Tony was still just fourteen. They had 'three Truvoice amps and wore pale blue jackets and black trousers, white shirts and red ties. Cliff Richard & The Shadows were obviously an influence, as was Eddie Cochran' (according to Bobby Elliott's autobiography). By the time Bobby joined on drums (30 September 1961), with Bernie Calvert on bass, they were simply called The Dolphins. Bobby recalls those memories in his 2010 song 'Then, Now, Always (Dolphin Days)', as sung by Tony: 'We sure knew how to cut it, back in Dolphin days.' So why did Tony quit The Dolphins? Because The Hollies had the major-label contract. That was the lure.

Destined to be the longest-serving band member, Tony joined The Hollies line-up in time for their EMI Studio test recordings. They were signed by The Beatles label, Parlophone and assigned Ron Richards as producer. Born Ronald Richard Pratley (22 January 1929), Ron had worked his way up through the industry as a Tin Pan Alley song-plugger for Chappell Music, as EMI promotions' manager, and then assistant to George Martin. When he discovered singer Jerry Lordan and produced his 1960 hit singles 'I'll Stay Single' (number 26) and 'Who Could Be Bluer' (number 17), he'd begun forging his own distinctive path. Although he continued working with George Martin on Beatles sessions, he retained The Hollies as his own personal project.

It was under Ron's production guidance that The Hollies first entered the charts the week 'From Me to You' was number 1. Their Famous Five Adventure was underway. 'It's been a long strange trip,' Graham tells me, 'remind me to tell you some time...'.

1963 and 1964

'(Ain't That) Just Like Me' (Earl Carroll and Billy Guy) b/w 'Hey What's Wrong With Me' (Nash, Clarke)

Personnel:
Allan Clarke: vocals, harmonica
Graham Nash: vocals, rhythm guitar
Eric Haydock: bass guitar
Tony Hicks: vocals, lead guitar
Don Rathbone: drums
Released: May 1963, Parlophone R 5030

For the first Hollies recording session on the evening of 4 April, they repeat a song they'd done at their test recording, but couldn't recapture the audition 'sparkle', so used the test version for their debut single instead, a revival of The Coasters '(Ain't That) Just Like Me', written by Earl Carroll and Billy Guy. It lifts the old Nursery Rhyme format as used by Johnny Preston for 'Cradle of Love', and was explored in a comic way by Anthony Newley with 'Pop Goes the Weasel'. In a maybe patronising way, it introduces the reassuring familiarity of 'Mary had a little lamb' and 'Hey Diddle Diddle the cat and the fiddle' into adolescent romance. According to cynical marketing logic, it was just throwaway pop, targeted at fickle pubescent teens. In a slightly more raucous way, the song was also recorded by the high-profile Searchers, on their November 1963 *Sugar and Spice* album. But the single does the trick for The Hollies; it cracks the chart and reaches a respectable UK number 25 (27 June) during a ten-week run. It made them part of the First Wave of the New Thing, in a summer Hit Parade topped by Brian Epstein's Gerry & The Pacemakers ('I Like It' at number 1), Freddie & The Dreamers ('If You Gotta Make a Fool of Somebody' at number 3) and The Beatles ('From Me to You' dropping to number 4).

The driving B-side, 'Hey What's Wrong With Me', is a 1:53-minute original song credited to Nash-Clarke recorded at the same session, with a Buddy Holly catch, and incorporating the 'Twist and Shout' ascending-voices break. With the group's initial intuitive Allan-Graham duo chemistry enriched by Tony's third strand voice, enabling a greater range of harmony trickology, all The Hollies ingredients are there, even though they're in a raw, unpolished form.

'Searchin'' (Leiber, Stoller) b/w 'Whole World Over' (Nash, Clarke)

Personnel:
Allan Clarke: vocals, harmonica
Graham Nash: vocals, rhythm guitar
Eric Haydock: bass guitar
Tony Hicks: vocals, lead guitar
Bobby Elliott: drums

plus Tommy Sanderson: piano
Released: August 1963, Parlophone R 5052

'Searchin'' is a revival of another Leiber-Stoller Coasters oldie, which The Beatles had done as part of their failed Decca audition of 1 January 1962. Although ragged when compared to what's to come, The Hollies effectively play off Graham's gum-shoe drawl against Allan's lead – his talking-break, 'well, Sherlock Holmes and ole' Sam Spade got nothin', child, on me', rises into 'gonna walk right down that street, like Bulldog Drummond', adding half-recited humour above the piano-led backing (with that same Tommy Sanderson adding piano). It received a unanimous thumbs-down review on BBC-TV's *Juke Box Jury*, with panellist Pat Boone advising viewers to go out and buy the original version instead. The single nevertheless spent fourteen weeks on the chart and reaches number 12 (number 10 in *NME* chart on 18 September), boosted by a live slot on the BBC radio *Pop Goes The Beatles* show, and mimed on ITVs *Ready Steady Go!* (11 October 1963). The romantic Nash-Clarke 'Whole World Over', with distinctive Everly Brothers harmonies and guitar changes, 'gonna search the whole world over, gonna find the one I love, even though it takes a hundred years', had been recorded at the earlier 4 April session, and is slower, with keening harmonica.

By then (July), Don Rathbone had moved from drums to join the group's management structure before returning home to Stoke-on-Trent. As Oasis were to discover in years to come, five friends sitting around a pub table dreaming 'in my mind my dreams are real... tonight I'm a Rock 'n' Roll star', when that dream begins to turn into reality, friendship is not always enough. 'He was good for roadwork', explains Allan, 'but when we got in the studio, he just didn't come up to scratch'. He was 'a lovely, sensible bloke', agrees Bobby, but 'technically he struggled to give the band the emphatic foundation that was needed to elevate their music onto the world stage'.

So Don was replaced by Bobby Elliott (born in Burnley, 8 December 1942). The first record Bobby ever bought – from the Electron Record Shop in Burnley – was the Benny Goodman EP 'Sing Sing Sing' featuring drummer Gene Krupa. He'd started out drumming with Gerry Storm & The Falcons, and was essentially self-taught, but like Krupa, when Bobby jackhammers the drumkit, he transfered both energy and muscle power with precision. He'd dated Tony Hicks' sister Maureen while they were both colleagues in The Dolphins, although more recently Bobby had turned pro when he was recruited into Shane Fenton and The Fentones, beating a young Keith Moon at the audition. There were other connections. Tommy Sanderson managed Shane Fenton, whose records were also produced by Ron Richards.

Speaking the same musical language, this is the first classic Hollies line-up that toured extensively in the UK, building a solid fan base. Both 'Searchin'' and the follow-up 'Stay' are featured on the 1976 LP *Hits of the Mersey Era: My Generation* (EMI NUT1).

'Stay' (Williams) b/w 'Now's the Time' (Clarke, Nash)

Personnel:
Allan Clarke: vocals, harmonica
Graham Nash: vocals, rhythm guitar
Eric Haydock: bass guitar
Tony Hicks: vocals, lead guitar
Bobby Elliott: drums
Released 15 November 1963, Parlophone R5077

Tony Hicks and Bobby Elliott were browsing in a Scottish junk shop when they discovered a copy of the original Maurice Williams and The Zodiacs record – which had been a UK number 14 as recently as January 1961. They pay 'three and six' (three shillings and six-pence) for it, a good value purchase because their revival becomes not only The Hollies third single but the group's first top ten hit, peaking at number 8 (16 January 1964, during a sixteen-week run). It comes in the new tight hard Beat-group guise, needing just two studio takes, with Tony playing a different solo each time, which engineer Peter Brown skilfully spliced together into the completed master. Working around its riffing 'your Momma don't mind (bopbop-showaddywaddy), and your Poppa don't mind (bopbop-showaddywaddy)', they mime 'Stay' as the fourth act to appear on the first edition of BBC-TVs *Top of the Pops*, broadcast on New Year's Day from 'this old church on Dickenson Road in Manchester' according to Bobby Elliott. 'Clarkie (Allan Clarke) had come up by train from London, and had shared a compartment with Brian Jones of the Stones, who were also on.' Jackson Browne later took the same song and slowed it down into an audience sing-along that made the American Top 20 in 1978, but The Hollies version retains the definite edge.

When The Hollies first arrived in London from Manchester, they played two auditions, their Parlophone test recordings with Ron Richards, and a screen-test for the De Laine Lea Company, which resulted in the Clarke-Nash penned B-side bearing the credit 'From the film *It's All Over Town*'. The movie was a light low-budget Lance Percival and Willie Rushton musical comedy featuring Frankie Vaughan, with The Springfields and Acker Bilk added to the cast for dubious teen appeal. Recorded on 15 May 1963, the song is the closest The Hollies get to capturing The Beatles feel – maybe it's the descending lines of 'Misery' plus the 'oh yeah' from 'I'll Get You'. No fade; there's an upbeat crash finish.

By 15 December, the upwardly-mobile Hollies joined a package tour headlined by Bobby Rydell and Helen Shapiro. In the Vocal Group Section of the years-end *New Musical Express* annual poll, they score eleventh place, and appear at the poll concert at the Wembley Empire Pool (26 April 1964) with Freddie & The Dreamers, new heavyweights The Dave Clark Five, The Rolling Stones, and others.

Stay With The Hollies

Personnel:
Allan Clarke: vocals, harmonica
Graham Nash: vocals, rhythm guitar
Eric Haydock: bass guitar
Tony Hicks: vocals, lead guitar
Bobby Elliott: drums except on 'Little Lover'
Don Rathbone: drums on 'Little Lover'
Produced at EMI Studios 15 May-11 December 1963 by Ron Richards.
Released: 7 February 1964, Parlophone PMC 1220
Running time: 33:42
Highest chart position: UK: 2

Unlike later decades where the album had become the primary product, with
strategic spin-off singles used as promotional tools with tie-in high-budget
videos to maximize sales potential, the music industry functioned in a different
way in 1964. Before venturing into long-play territory, the band – or group as
it was then – had first to prove its marketability by establishing its name with
hit singles. Then the album that would eventually emerge might not feature
any of the singles at all. The 45rpm market and the 33-&-a-third market were
considered as separate entities. The irresistible single-on-single rise of The
Hollies chart positions meant that sessions for their first album were recorded
across the two days of 29 October and 11 December. A straight transcript of
the way they'd been doing the material live, they grab nothing of available
studio potential. Tagged for ease of recognition after their first top ten hit, *Stay
With the Hollies* boasts a generous fourteen tracks – despite a playing time
of just 33:42-minutes. To a later *Record Collector* magazine reviewer, it is 'an
enthusiastic beat and Rock 'n' Roll collection that catches the group before
they had sorted out the finer points of their harmonic blend; but it offers a
guide to how they must have sounded in Manchester's Beat Clubs, thanks to its
collection of the group's favourite cover versions.'
   The Hollies on this album are, with descriptions from a fan magazine:

Tony Hicks: 5' 11", lead guitar, an ex-electrician who enjoys driving and chicken
curry. He likes making models, watching TV and chess, but hates snobs.

Eric Haydock: 5' 8", bass guitar, former toolmaker, a Ray Charles fan who
drinks milk and dresses casual. He gets a kick out of football.

Bobby Elliott: 5' 11", drums, Bobby was a mining engineer who enjoys Ten Pin
Bowling and good Modern Jazz, he would like to be the greatest drummer in
Europe, and retire at forty-five.

Allan Clarke: 5' 10", vocalist who also plays harmonica, has worked as a
millhand, silkscreen printer and salesman, he collects matchbox tops, and his
ambition is to be a millionaire. He says 'my bank manager is my best friend'.

Graham Nash: 5' 11", plays guitar and sings, he's a one-time assistant manager in a gent's outfitters (the Toggery in Stockport, owned by The Hollies first manager Michael Cohen). He likes smart suits, cider and steak, but can't stand white shoes.

The album was rewarded by a satisfying 25 weeks on the UK album chart, peaking at number 2 – beneath *With The Beatles*. It was later reissued in stereo, on CD by the Beat Goes On label (BGOLP4) in October 1987.

'Talkin' 'Bout You' (Charles)
Drawing heavily on their rough-&-tumble live set, built up from a wide range of Blues and R&B covers, side one opens with this slick and unmistakably Hollies take on Chuck Berry's interpretation of the Ray Charles rocker. There were two attempts at nailing the track, one with Don Rathbone drumming, the other with the incoming Bobby Elliott, but whichever, anchored in tight drums and bass, with Tony Hicks channelling Chuck Berry guitar, it's topped off by shrill Allan-led harmony vocals with a few high-voice 'ah-ha-ha's thrown in to add to the excitement factor.

'Mr Moonlight' (Johnson)
This Blues song was originally done by Dr Feelgood & The Interns in 1962 and was also covered by The Merseybeats. With Graham's voice to the fore, it anticipates the John Lennon-fronted *Beatles For Sale* version by eleven months! Although Lennon's vocal lead and song arrangement serves only to emphasise the distance The Hollies have yet to make up, or maybe it's just by comparison that The Hollies sound unfocused here?

'You Better Move On' (Alexander)
Born in Sheffield, Alabama, Arthur Alexander was the first artist to emerge from Rick Hall's famous Muscle Shoals studios with this seminal hit. He went on to write 'Anna', which The Beatles cover on their debut *Please Please Me* album. The Hollies jog-through of the R&B song was released in January 1964 in direct competition to the simultaneously-issued Rolling Stones EP track. The Hollies adopt a more plaintively endearing close-harmony approach, which lacks The Stones' more emotionally-charged dramatic depth. Lyrically, when faced with a more wealthy rival for his woman's affections, he pleads, 'that's up to her, yes and the Lord above'. As Bill Wyman's *Stone Alone* (1990) autobiography recalls, Graham and Allan had joined The Stones on 4 February 1964 at Regent Sound Studios, with Gene Pitney and Phil Spector, during sessions for The Rolling Stones' first album, playing tambourine, maracas, and banging coins on empty bottles to percussive effect for at least three tracks, 'Little by Little', 'Can I Get a Witness', and the spontaneous jam 'Now I've Got a Witness' (just as Graham with David Crosby would later add harmonies to Jefferson Starship's extravagant 1970 *Blows Against the Empire* album).

'Lucille' (Little Richard with Al Collins)

From Macon, Georgia, 'Little' Richard Penniman – who described himself as The Quasar of Rock – was the most outrageously flamboyant of all the 1950s performers, with a string of nuclear-powered rock classics to his name, frequently covered but never equalled, including an iconic appearance in the Jayne Mansfield movie *The Girl Can't Help It* (1956). Opening Little Richard's 'Lucille' with an Allan Clarke shriek, The Hollies reach back into Rock 'n' Roll history for this Beat-Group standard, which also titled a Beatles EP with Paul McCartney taking vocals. Although they're obviously having fun, there's just a suspicion that maybe true uninhibited wildness is not a natural fit for The Hollies.

'Baby Don't Cry' (Hiller, Ford)

'Dance a little, shake a little, you can even twist and shout', an inconsequential throw-away song by jobbing writers Anthony Toby Hiller – later joint-composer of 'Save Your Kisses for Me' for Brotherhood of Man with Perry Ford of The Ivy League. Although The Hollies give it their best shot, it's essentially juvenile pop, fleshed out by Tony's guitar, and leading into a 'One, Two, Three, Four!' close at the 2:07-minute mark.

'Memphis' (Berry)

Another competent run-through of a song that formed part of every sixties beat group's repertoire and which had already been a top twenty hit for Sheffield artist Dave Berry. The Hollies were always more about precision than they were about unrestrained wildness, although there are shrieks thrown in to simulate those energies here, carrying the loping rhythms through to Chuck's dubious closing joke about 'Marie is only six years old'. The public was less aware of paedophilia in 1964 than it is now.

'Stay' (Williams)

The singles hit that provides the album title; it still sounds compulsively tight.

'Rockin' Robin' (Leon René under the pseudonym 'Jimmie Thomas')

A crowd-pleasing part of their live repertoire, The Hollies staccato beat and nasal delivery opens side two by chirping 'tweet tweet twiddley-dee' into the chorus of Bobby Day's erstwhile novelty hit. This catchy cover precedes Michael Jackson's single by some considerable time. Tony's concise solo and third-part harmonies prove just how integrated the group sound has become in such a brief space of time.

'Watcha Gonna Do 'Bout It?' (Carroll, Payne)

Originally recorded by Doris Troy under Artie Ripp's supervision for Atlantic Records (and briefly in the UK chart at number 37 in December 1964), The

16

Hollies take the song at an easy loping pace, 'our love, yeah yeah, is slowly going on the rocks, yeah yeah yeah'. They do it faster paced when they perform it live for various radio broadcasts at the time, with Allan singing the 'tell me Sugar-Pie' line with a smile of wry humour. Born in New York in 1937, Doris Payne had been spotted by James Brown while she was working as an usherette at the Apollo Theatre, and signed to Atlantic as Doris Troy, where she quickly scored with her own co-composition, 'Just One Look'. Later, she relocated to England as a prolific session singer for Apple Records for Dusty Springfield ('In the Middle of Nowhere'), for Pink Floyd's *Dark Side of the Moon*, and The Rolling Stones 'You Can't Always Get What You Want'.

'Do You Love Me' (Gordy)
The Hollies' playful cover of the Twist and Mashed Potato dance song leads in with an unconvincing talking introduction and adds a 'bom-bom-bom b-bom-bom-bom' break. A Contours Gordy-label song, it was also the subject of a chart battle between the pounding gravity of the burgeoning Dave Clark Five and the twinkling silliness of Brian Poole & The Tremeloes, who took it all the way to number 1. The Hollies version of 'Candy Man' also precedes The Tremeloes' hit cover.

'It's Only Make Believe' (Twitty, Nance)
Conway Twitty's country-pop 1958 hit, which the teenage duo of Allan and Graham had once performed as part of a talent competition at 'The Towers Holiday Camp'. It has a unique song construction that consists of the same line repeated at steadily ascending pitch. In a change of pace, Allan and Graham channel their Everly Brothers mode to give it an impassioned close-harmony make-over. This Hollies track precedes a 1964 UK number 10 hit version for Billy Fury. On an album of incisive bite-size tracks, at 3:13 minutes, this is the longest.

'What Kind of Girl Are You' (Charles)
Recorded during the album's second sessions, on Wednesday 11 December 1963. Piercing stratospherically-high voices, set off by counter-harmonies, whoops, and quite complex vocal changes, lead into an elongated 'I wanna know-woe-woe-ooh, ooh-ooh-yeah'. It's difficult to think of another group of the era attempting such contortions! Tony's solo, kicked by Bobby's consummate percussive input, drives the track through to its guitar-crash finale.

'Little Lover' (Nash, Clarke)
For the album's only self-penned track – recorded 15 May 1963 – Don Rathbone plays drums on Clarke/Nash's typically raw Merseybeat 'C'mon c'mon, c'mon little lover'. According to Tony, their approach at the time was

simply to 'get hold of a song, or write one, and then rehearse it on the road and then come into the studio and do it in one go'. Recording was essentially to tape a live performance, leaving the technical tweaks to Ron Richards and his sound crew, Pete Brown and engineer Ken Townsend. This balance would tilt as they became more familiar with studio work, but these were their first steps. They were learning the game.

'Candy Man' (Neil, Ross)

This is another competent, regulation cover, simultaneously on the charts by an uninspired Brian Poole & The Tremeloes, although songwriter Fred Neil – who had served his time at the famous Brill Building – was a respected Greenwich Village folkie who would write 'Everybody's Talkin', famous for its inclusion on the *Midnight Cowboy* (1969) movie soundtrack and 'Other Side of This Life', released by both Jefferson Airplane and The Lovin' Spoonful. Recorded at The Hollies' 11 December session, there was a harmonica overdub added at the album's final mix.

Related Releases

Here I Go Again (Imperial LP-12265)

Because things were different elsewhere, there were other album editions. American marketing strategy operated on alternate principles. A pop album might be built around two singles; each side led off by an instantly-recognisable hit song, plus the B-sides, padded out with a selection of covers and fillers. Issued for the US market by Imperial, *Stay With the Hollies* was retitled and slimmed down to a more parsimonious twelve tracks. The American listing is:

'Here I Go Again', 'Stay', 'Lucille', 'Memphis', 'You Better Move On', 'Talkin' 'Bout You', 'Just One Look', 'Keep Off That Friend of Mine', 'Rockin' Robin, 'Do You Love Me', 'What Kind of Girl Are You', 'It's Only Make Believe'

'Just One Look' (Troy, Carroll) b/w 'Keep Off That Friend of Mine' (Hicks, Elliott) (21 February 1964, Parlophone R5104)

Their significant breakthrough came with this breezily sleek cover, a drum-kick introduction to a joyously celebratory revival of Doris Troy's R&B hit, its shining harmonies carried on the energy-rush of first love. Listen to Doris Troy's original, which is looser and warmer; The Hollies take it harder, tighter, faster, with Graham rising into near-falsetto middle-eight vocal lines, 'I thought I was dreamin', but I was wrong, yeh yeh yeah...' into the chorus. It soars to their highest chart placing yet – number 2 (26 March 1964, on a thirteen-week chart run), peaking one place behind Billy J Kramer & The Dakotas' 'Little Children', and one place above The Rolling Stones' 'Not Fade Away'. In fact, the *NME* chart published 14 March 1964 with 'Just One Look' at number seven, was significant in another way. It was the first time that every record in the top ten was British – with British records at number 11 and number 12 too, while number 13, Gene Pitney's 'That Girl Belongs to Yesterday', was an American artist benefitting from an early Mick Jagger & Keith Richard composition.

'Just One Look' reached number 20 in Australia, while it also became the group's first US chart entry, at number 98 (during May). With first-time writer credits going to Tony Hicks and Bobby Elliott, the B-side is a jumpy appealing warning that 'she's lost her smile, she's not so gay'. According to Bobby, producer Ron double-tracked the three-way harmony, and 'at the press of a button, we became choir-like!' With the songwriting chores – and lucrative royalties – increasingly gravitating around the Hicks-Clarke-Nash axis, Bobby's writing contributions would subsequently be marginalised. 'Keep Off That Friend of Mine' makes its album debut on the American *Here I Go Again* edition.

Meanwhile, from 28 March, the Hollies opened *Pop Around*, a series of Radio Luxembourg programmes.

The Hollies EP (June 1964, Parlophone GEP 8909)

A neat little 45rpm package taking 'Rockin' Robin' and 'Watcha Gonna Do 'Bout It' from the LP, but tacking on two new tracks recorded 2 March, 'What Kind of Love' (Clarke, Hicks, Nash), and 'When I'm Not There' (Tony Hicks), two attacking punchy tracks with raw guitar solos at 1:43 and 1:47-minutes apiece, making this a sought-after item. All the bands around them were drawing on essentially the same pool of R&B and Rock 'n' Roll songs, adapting them to taste and style, but that source was not inexhaustible. If the band was to survive, it was necessary for them to write their own songs. Even though these early attempts were purpose-built, they show that, even when operating on cruise control, The Hollies were never less than proficient.

'Here I Go Again' (Shuman, Westlake) b/w 'Baby That's All' (Chester, Mann) (15 May 1964, Parlophone R5137)

Writing in *Disc*, reviewer Don Nicholl headlines 'Hollies Sound Is Even BETTER!', saying that 'they achieve a striking sound on the title phrase and are going to catch plenty of ears with this'. On *Juke Box Jury*, it was voted 'Hit' by all four panellists. Posing the existential question 'what can I do when there's nothing I can do?', it's a new song written with The Hollies specifically in mind by American Mort Shuman, who had written hits for Elvis Presley ('Viva Las Vegas'), with lyrics by Welsh-born Clive Westlake (who wrote 'I Close My Eyes and Count to Ten' for Dusty Springfield). Drawn by the inexorable magnetism of a doomed love – 'try as I may, and I do', took The Hollies back up to a UK number four (18 June 1964) and stayed on the chart for twelve weeks. Although it stalled at a humble Number 107 in America, it also reached number 14 in Australia. No fade; it closes with an instrumental crash. The 2:15-minute B-side, written by the Chester-Mann team, is equally strong, with Bobby's chiming Paiste 602 cymbal with its bifurcated rivets and three-way harmonies wrapped tightly around a romantic lyric, with lusciously elongated phrasing. It would later be gathered onto their 1978 *The Other Side of The Hollies* compilation. At this time, the label of the Parlophone single was black with the circled £ logo, a big 45rpm to the right of the press-out centre, and credits in silver lettering. It was issued in a plain green bag, long before the picture sleeve became standard.

Just One Look EP (July 1964, Parlophone GEP 8911)

A compilation of previously-issued tracks with both sides of the single 'Just One Look' (Payne and Carroll), and its B-side 'Keep Off That Friend of Mine', plus 'I'm Talking About You' and 'Lucille' from the album.

'We're Through' (Ransford) b/w 'Come On Back' (Ransford) (11 September 1964, Parlophone R5178)

By the end of 1964, the pressure for regular hit singles was relentless. A career could stand or fall on a chart position. As familiar faces on TV Pop shows, The Hollies were no longer new kids on the block. There were newer, louder and hairier groups making their debut, The Kinks, The Animals, and The Pretty Things, while many of the other first wave beat groups were already failing, such as The Fourmost, The Swinging Blue Jeans, and The Merseybeats. There was a need to move on, to advance upwards. They played a 'Big Star Parade' summer season at the Weymouth 'Gaumont Theatre' twice-nightly for four weeks from Monday 27 July to Saturday 22 August 1964 – with seats priced at 9/6d, 7/6d in the stalls, 9/6d and 5/6d in the circle. Allan and Graham were both newly-married, Allan to Jeni née Bowstead (March 24), and Graham to Rose (24 May). It was time for them to be together. The residency also allowed them beach-time during the day, and 'I suppose it was the lazy atmosphere that induced Allan to write 'We're Through'', suggests Bobby Elliott. Less frenetic than before, yet sweetly melodic, its beautiful acoustic descending guitar line leads into distinctive Hollies harmonies, hinting that there's much promise yet to come. Intended as an album track, and initially visualised with a Latin Bossa Nova flavour which 'got lost somewhere', it turned out so well that, having proved themselves with covers, producer Ron Richards relented and gave way to their desire for it to become the group's first self-penned A-side. Issued as by Clarke, Hicks and Nash under the alias 'L Ransford', it hit number 7 (29 October 1964) during a chart run of eleven weeks. A French-language version was recorded 22 February 1966, which remained unissued until the 2011 CD box-set *The Hollies: Clarke, Hicks and Nash Years*. Much later, in the third episode of the Netflix superhero series *The Umbrella Academy* (February 2019), Klaus listens to 'We're Through' on his headphones.

Another L Ransford effort, 'Come On Back', makes for an equally strong pairing. There are drum crashes and shrill 'gob-iron' harmonica, but already the harmonies are tight. There's a Graham Nash-sung middle-eight and an artful pause in the build. Allan claims that some of The Hollies B-sides were good enough to be A-sides in their own right; this is a case in point.

Here I Go Again EP (October 1964, Parlophone GEP 8915)

Another attractively packaged EP combines both sides of the single 'Here I Go Again' and 'Baby That's All' with two album tracks, 'You Better Move On' and 'Memphis'. In September, The Hollies joined a nationwide tour supporting fellow Manchester headliners Freddie & The Dreamers, with ex-Searcher Tony Jackson's Vibrations, plus Marianne Faithfull, all travelling in a big Timpsons coach. It was followed by a tour with The Dixie-Cups, Heinz, with a young Ritchie Blackmore, The Tornados, and Jess Conrad. The pace was relentless, although Graham confided to journalist Joe Smith, 'I can't remember much pressure with The Hollies. We were having too good a time. Music saved our ass.' (In *Off The Record*, Pan Books, 1990.) The Hollies toured through October as part of a Larry Parnes package with Millie, Lulu, and The Jimmy Nicols Shubdubs, opening at Finsbury Park 'Astoria' (17 October) through to the Rochester 'Odeon' (31 October).

In The Hollies Style

Personnel:
Allan Clarke: vocals, harmonica
Graham Nash: vocals, rhythm guitar
Eric Haydock: bass guitar
Tony Hicks: vocals, lead guitar
Bobby Elliott: drums
Produced at EMI Studios 13 April-25 August 1964 by Ron Richards
Released: November 1964, Parlophone PMC 1235
Running time: 29:08
No chart places

The EMI Recording Studios, not yet named after its Abbey Road address in St John's Wood, was a grand and imposing edifice with a history extending back at least to 1931. It was an intimidating prospect for five young hicks from the sticks. Staff were expected to dress formally in suit and tie, while sound engineers wore the white coats of laboratory assistants. Familiar with recording classical music and dance bands, it was a place where the more disreputable upstart of Rock 'n' Roll had made its debut as recently as 1958 when surly young rebel Cliff Richard & The Drifters cut 'Move It' in Studio Two.

It's not clear whether The Hollies used that same studio when, encouraged by the success of the first album, recordings for a follow-up commenced 13 and 27 April 1964. With twelve tracks, seven originals stacked up against just five covers, the playing time runs to 29:08-minutes. The cover art shows the group, with Tony Hicks and Allan Clarke seated, Graham Nash standing centre behind them, and Eric Haydock and Bobby Elliott standing left and right. They are posed beneath a painting in what seems to be a stately home – an allusion to 'style', with the album title in a complementary script flourish. Yet once released, the album didn't actually chart. Although there was a Canadian edition (Capitol Records T6143), curiously, it was never released in the USA.

'Nitty Gritty/Something's Got a Hold on Me' (Chase, James, Kirkland, Woods)
With a call-and-response 'let's... get... right on down, to the REAL nitty-gritty', they move into mod soul territory, smoothly eliding Shirley Ellis and Etta James together into a 4:08-minute medley bridged by a sharp 1-2-3-4 count-in. Recorded on 25 August 1964, there's a later version done live for BBC Radio (broadcast 7 June 1965, Whit Monday), where Bobby describes this as 'one of our more classical titles'.

'Don't You Know' (L Ransford)
Drum-shot play-in to a high Beatles-style cross between 'All My Lovin'' and 'Tell Me Why', 'don't you know what I know, don't you feel what I feel'. On 25 June

1965, Dick James Publishing sets up 'Gralto' – for the Graham, Allan, Tony writer-triumvirate, as a company to publish their own compositions. Allan tells me 'the record company said that Clarke-Nash-Hicks was too long, and we had to come up with another name. So 'L Ransford' was one of Graham's ideas. It was the name of his grandfather or something. I always thought the B-sides we wrote together were good enough to be singles in their own right, but our producer, Ron Richards, thought better of it. He preferred to go with covers or songs by other writers.'

'To You My Love' (L Ransford)
Recorded during the 25 August session that produced the final version of the single 'We're Through', this sweetly melodic early classic is to Graham Nash what 'Yesterday' is to Paul McCartney, emphatic evidence of uniquely evolving and blossoming skills that hint at the group's power still to come. It would not be out of place on a Crosby, Stills, Nash & Young album or on one of Graham's later solo projects.

'It's In Her Kiss' (Clark)
Also known as 'The Shoop Shoop Song', and a US hit for Betty Everett, it had already been covered by The Searchers on their April 1964 *It's The Searchers* LP, and would be a massive number 1 for Cher in 1990. The Hollies spin their magic by dispensing with the shoop-shoop backing in favour of a call-and-response group chant-back to Allan's question 'is it in her eyes? is it in her sighs?'. There's even a bass-guitar solo break. The Swinging Blue Jeans issued their own version as part of their 1998 compilation *At Abbey Road: 1963-1967*.

'Time for Love' (L Ransford)
Acoustic strum and harmonica break, with Graham taking prominent vocals on the shining harmonies, it's time to tell the world about their secret love. The track betrays an increasingly sophisticated sound, as Eric Haydock's bass and Bobby Elliott's drums underscore with a steady rhythmic propulsion. Recorded on 13 April 1964, with 'Don't You Know', these were the first two tracks recorded for the album, although both 'Here I Go Again' and 'Baby That's All' were cut at the same productive session.

'What Kind of Boy' (Irwin)
One of the album's standouts, performed on radio promo slots, there's a pleasing mix of moods and pace with Allan's solo voice, matched to clean clear harmony passages that flow like honey from a spoon. Big Dee Irwin, who once recorded a single called 'Happy Being Fat', had his biggest success with 'Swinging on a Star' as a duet with Little Eva. As mentioned earlier, The Hollies had topped 'The Big Star Parade' bill in Weymouth, where the 295 lb six-footer Big Dee closed the first half of the show. It seems likely The Hollies first

heard the song there. Shane Fenton & The Fentones also appear in the show's second half – the future Glam-Rock star Alvin Stardust – with comedy duo Little & Large (billed as Syd & Eddie).

'Too Much Monkey Business' (Berry)
Without Charles 'Chuck' Edward Anderson Berry, the story of Rock 'n' Roll would be very different. It's he who took Chess R&B and astutely shifted its focus towards the white teenage market, bringing in bobbysoxer themes of schooldays, dancing to the jukebox, cruising in Cadillacs, and big shiny guitars. Elvis sang Chuck Berry. George Harrison sings 'Roll Over Beethoven' on *With The Beatles*. The Beach Boys stole the tune of 'Sweet Little Sixteen' for 'Surfin' USA'. The Rolling Stones' first single was Chuck Berry's 'Come On'. 'Too Much Monkey Business' is the song structure Bob Dylan borrows for the scrambled word-tumble of 'Subterranean Homesick Blues'. The Hollies' energetic treatment of the song has a distinctly Berry-style Tony Hicks guitar solo, with Tony, Graham and Allan trading vocal lines and verses.

'I Thought of You Last Night' (Freed)
High-flying duo harmonies in The Hollies' Everly Bros-style, with the slow-paced folk-soft sensitivity of Simon & Garfunkel, employed on this sentimental torch song. There seems to be a shot at mainstream sophistication at work here, similar to Paul McCartney doing the standard 'Till There Was You' on *With The Beatles*. Originally done by Jeri Southern, the group might have heard this lush jazz chanteuse on the BBC Light Programme's *Jack Jackson's Record Round Up* or *Forces Favourites* as they were growing up through the late 1950s.

'Please Don't Feel Too Bad' (L Ransford)
Growing up in public on a fast learning curve, they were rapidly becoming a prolific writing team, going from the basic verse-chorus-verse-middle eight-instrumental break-verse-chorus-close format, clearly betraying their models The Beatles, Buddy Holly and The Everly Brothers, but throwing in original curves and novel twists towards a distinctive collective identity of their own. Each new song pushes them a little further. Sure, here there's an occasional Beatles 'I Want To Hold Your Hand' tone to the smoothly rising harmony breaks, but the song was considered strong enough to be covered by German group The Space-Makers in 1965 (Sonet T-7213-B), and in 1966 by South African group The Vedettes (HMV 45-SAB 2074).

'Come On Home' (L Ransford)
Fast-paced with harmonica break, at an economical 1:44-minutes, this represents a reversion to the primal near-punk beat-group sound they were already accelerating away from. 'I've been told many times about you, about

your life', he sings, yet he still wants her back. For these recording sessions, the group are set up in a circle in the studio, facing one another, so the energy flows directly, as Graham takes a solo line to add contrasting vocal colour.

'You'll Be Mine' (L Ransford)

He's made up his mind not to be 'left on the shelf', which was a sad euphemism for the terrible fate of remaining unmarried, or at least not being part of a committed relationship. These were less liberated days. But Allan's plaintive lead voice is enlivened by unexpected chord changes, while the chugging beat-group backing takes off into tasty mandolin-style acoustic guitar soloing from Tony in the instrumental break and fade.

'Set Me Free' (L Ransford)

According to the studio log, The Hollies did preliminary work on a track called 'Party Line' on 13 July 1964, although there's no evidence of it ever being completed. Surely it's too early to have been a version of Ray Davies *Face to Face* Kinks album track? Instead, they close the album by looking back at the rough harmonica edge and manic drum-breaks of their early R&B repertoire, with what Bobby Elliott calls 'our early bluesy busker'. They recorded this song, along with 'Here I Go Again', on 28 September, plus 'Something's Got a Hold on Me' the day after, for the BBC Light Programme's *Saturday Club*. The trio of tracks were later gathered onto the May 2012 compilation CD *Radio Fun* (EMI 440 7702).

Related Releases

We're Through EP (December 1964, Parlophone GEP 8927)

Combining both sides of the single 'We're Through' and 'Come On Back' with two album tracks, 'What Kind of Boy' and 'You'll Be Mine'. By the year's end, The Hollies played the Liverpool Odeon as part of the Brian Epstein promoted 'Gerry's Xmas Cracker' with Gerry & The Pacemakers, The Fourmost, plus ballad-crooner Danny Williams, while The Hollies moved up to eighth position in the annual *NME* poll.

'Yes I Will' (Goffin, Titelman) b/w 'Nobody' (Ransford) (22 January 1965, Parlophone R5232)

The Gerry Goffin-Russ Titelman A-side would later be recorded by the Monkees for their debut album, as a vocal showcase for Manchester-born Davy Jones as 'I'll Be True to You'. For The Hollies, it assumes a romantic lilt, erupting into a powerful harmony chorus, playing vocal strengths against each other, with a strong guitar break; yet it hits no higher than a UK number 9 (18 March 1965), despite staying in the chart thirteen weeks. Working from a demo acetate 'that featured Carole King's distinctive voice', they had two shots at recording the song. An earlier rejected studio take (recorded 15 December 1964) with more prominent acoustic guitars was later included on the mono version of their August 1968 *Hollies Greatest* number 1 album. Also taking a pledge, Eric Haydock wedded Pamela in Stockport on 22 January 1965. B-side 'Nobody' is a Hollies original that revisits their early sound, with glass-sharp harmonica. On Tuesday 2 February, 11:31 am, The Hollies sing 'Nobody', and the Larry Williams song 'She Said Yeah' on the BBC Light Programme's *Delaney's Delight* with Mark Wynter and Linda Saxone as guests of bandleader Eric Delaney. Recorded on 26 January, both tracks were collected onto the *Radio Fun* CD compilation.

Through March, The Hollies tour the UK as 'special guests' on a bill with The Rolling Stones, Dave Berry & The Cruisers and Goldie & The Gingerbreads. 'We all travelled around in a Ford Thames van. Our equipment went in this van, which was quite small' Bobby Elliott recalls, 'we just had a drumkit, a bass amplifier for Eric Haydock and an amp for Tony Hicks, who would play both the rhythm and lead guitar parts at the same time. That was his style of playing. Graham Nash would be playing an acoustic guitar that plugged in. Matter of fact, it didn't even have a jack on it. We were young and enthusiastic and never had much time to think about being uncomfortable, cold and hungry' (to *DISCoveries* magazine, November 1989).

Then through April, they make the US for the first time, playing the New York Broadway Paramount on a 'Soupy Sales' bill, witnessing an explosive altercation with Little Richard, then performing 'Yes I Will' with Go-Go dancers on NBC-TVs 'Hullabaloo', introduced by George Hamilton (27 April 1965). Bobby took time out to see his jazz-drummer idol Gene Krupa play at the Times Square 'Metropole Café', while the group also found time to record three 'Ransford' tracks at the New York Bell Studios – the studio Buddy Holly had used to record 'Rave On'. The tracks were 'Listen Here to Me', 'So Lonely', and 'Bring Back Your Love to Me', which would remain unissued until the 2003 *The Long Road Home* CD box-set.

On return from the USA., on 5 May, they record 'I'm Alive' at Abbey Road studios in St Johns Wood.

In The Hollies Style EP (April 1965, Parlophone GEP 8934)

Four tracks were lifted from the previous album; 'Too Much Monkey Business' and 'What Kind of Boy', plus two L Ransford titles ,'To You My Love' and 'Come On Home'. 'On this EP, Ron Richards has reproduced the unique and exciting sound of the Hollies,' says David Block's liner notes.

1965-1966

'I'm Alive' (Ballard) b/w 'You Know He Did' (Ransford) (21 May 1965, Parlophone R5287)

Allan Clarke became defensive when I suggested that, for The Hollies, there was no Big Bang moment. No 'House of the Rising Sun' or 'My Generation' moment. 'Well, we were always top twenty', he argued, 'we had around eighteen top ten and thirty top forty hits'. Yes, but it was more a gradual growth, with each single charting a little higher in a kind of evolutionary growth; until the pause defined by 'We're Through' and 'Yes I Will'. When 'I'm Alive' became their first chart-topper, it was less of a surprise and more an inevitability. A deserved reward for two year's hard work. A hit record depends on all manner of random factors, not all of which have to do with quality; being heard at the right time, being on the right radio slot; being seen to advantage on TV; a catchy hook that ear-worms its way into your head. Or simply, the fan having the available pocket money as they stroll past the record store.

Can it be that 'I'm Alive' is in any way superior to the Hollies singles that preceded it? Written by Clint Ballard Jr – who wrote 'The Game of Love' for Manchester's Wayne Fontana & The Mindbenders – it certainly has an upbeat, positive joy, a tuneful energy-burst that's instantly arresting. But no, I think not. Yet it's on the chart fourteen weeks, nudges Elvis Presley's 'Crying in the Chapel' off the number 1 spot (8 July 1965), and tops the UK chart for three weeks. They mime it on the 100th edition of *Top of the Pops*, before it's deposed by the Byrds 'Mr Tambourine Man' – featuring Graham Nash's future colleague David Crosby. And no one begrudges The Hollies the success. It also reaches number 16 in Germany, number 13 in Holland, and number 11 in Australia, despite stalling at a lowly US number 103.

L Ransford's B-side takes the 'Louie Louie' riff, complete with a yea-yea-yea echo from 'Whatcha Gonna Do 'Bout It', into places it's seldom been, with Allan's keening harmonica adding edge. The conversational emphasis 'you know he did' adds an inviting colloquial hook. A French-language version was recorded on 22 February 1966, which remained unissued until the 2011 CD Box-set *The Hollies: Clarke, Hicks and Nash Years*.

Further American dates were put on hold in order to concentrate on promotion, but on 30 July, The Hollies film inserts for US TV shows *Shindig* and the *Red Skelton Show*.

'Look Through Any Window' (Gouldman) b/w 'So Lonely' (Ransford) (27 August 1965, Parlophone R5322)

Manchester's Graham Gouldman was building a reputation as a writer of fine songs with a unique Northern slant. 'No Milk Today' sets its simple heartbreak message to the milkman in 'a terraced house in a mean street back of town', which must have confused Herman's Hermits' US fans! Although Graham never achieved a hit song with his own group, The Mockingbirds – he would have to wait until 10cc to do that – he provided The Yardbirds with classic singles ('For Your Love', 'Heart Full of Soul' and 'Evil-Hearted You'), and wrote this charming song for The Hollies, taking the title suggested by his co-manager, Charles Silverman. With cascading Tony Hicks guitar and racing harmonies, they see 'the drivers on the roads, pulling down their heavy loads', see 'little children all around' and 'the little ladies in their gowns'. It stayed on the charts for eleven weeks, and peaked at number four (30 September 1965), then climbing to US number 32 (Imperial 66134), boosted by an appearance on *Hullabaloo* introduced by Frankie Avalon, and by a full-page *Billboard* ad. They also played a seventeen-day American tour from 17 September, including a Chicago concert with The Animals. A rejected French-language version – 'Regardez Par Des Fenetres' – was later included on the *Rarities* compilation, with the lyrics learned phonetically, 'we could have been singing in Swahili for all we knew' recalled Allan, 'and apparently, the French felt the same!' The single hit number 10 in Denmark and number 12 in Holland.

A strong guitar figure propels the moody 'So Lonely', with Graham and Allan trading vocal lines, adopting a kind of 'You've Lost That Lovin' Feelin'' feel to its ambitious vocal interchanges. Initially tried out in a more raw blueprint take at the New York Bell Studios on 27 April 1965, this is a second more fully realised shot at recording the song on 13 July 1965.

Everyone wanted The Hollies. Even boy's action-comic the *Eagle* carried an enthusiastic Hollies feature in their 7 August 1965 issue. And during the first week of January 1966, The Barron Knights comedy-spoof 'Merry Gentle Pops' stood at number 10 on the *New Musical Express* chart, celebrating the Pop Stars Christmas Party by reconfiguring the lyric into 'Jump Through Any Window', adding the carol 'The Hollies and The Ivy League, they are both well-known'.

I'm Alive EP (September 1965, Parlophone GEP 8942)
The most commercially successful of The Hollies seven EPs, it collects the hit title track, plus 'You Know He Did' and 'Mickey's Monkey', as well as the previously-unreleased 'Honey and Wine', a slinky Gerry Goffin-Carole King song with bluesy Tony Hicks guitar solo, recorded 7 April 1965. The song was also done, less effectively, by Wayne Fontana & The Mindbenders. Three weeks of Hollies live dates were cancelled from 24 October, when Allan is hospitalised for tonsillectomy, resuming tonsil-free in November for shows in Sweden and Denmark. 'Five guys sporting two Vox amps and a drum kit', according to Bobby, 'we had to thrash and strain to be heard'.

The Hollies (Parlophone PMCS 309)
This is a curious 'Greatest Hits' LP compilation issued in Sweden – which shows just how far The Hollies have come in such a short period of time. It gathers:

'Look Through Any Window', 'Baby That's All', '(Ain't That) Just Like Me', 'Searchin'', 'What Kind of Love', 'Here I Go Again', 'Yes I Will'' 'I'm Alive', 'Nobody', 'Hey, What's Wrong With Me', 'Just One Look', 'When I'm Not There', 'So Lonely', 'We're Through'.

In The Hollies Style
There was no US edition, and this reconfigured Canadian edition did not emerge until October 1965:

'I'm Alive', 'You Know He Did', 'Honey and Wine', 'Mickey's Monkey', 'Come On Back', 'We're Through', 'Yes I Will', 'Don't You Know', 'To You My Love', 'Time for Love', 'What Kind of Boy', 'Too Much Monkey Business'.

Hollies

Personnel:
Allan Clarke: vocals, harmonica
Graham Nash: vocals, rhythm guitar
Eric Haydock: bass guitar
Tony Hicks: vocals, lead guitar
Bobby Elliott: drums
plus James Stroud: vocals, guitar
Alan Hawkshaw: piano on 'Put Yourself in My Place'
Produced at EMI Studios 10 November 1964-13 July 1965 by Ron Richards.
Released: 10 September 1965, Parlophone PMC 1261
Running time: 28:36
Highest chart position: UK: 8

The sixties – as England began to swing – are frequently seen as simpler days. Unlike the situation in the USA., the UK formed a tight self-contained market, dominated by a handful of major record labels. There was no thriving Indie sector. The artist had no visibility if they were not signed to one of the majors, with no access to a mass audience. But once they were signed, and once they'd achieved at least a modest chart position with early singles, the promotional machinery was in place. And the record industry had evolved a sophisticated logistics of delivery. The arrival of the 45rpm mini-groove single had made the old highly-breakable 78rpm shellac obsolete. The twelve-inch record album was a more expensive luxury purchase, making the neat four-track EP package an affordable compromise. No cassettes, obviously, although parents or schools might have a big table-top reel-to-reel tape recorder. The only way to hear that hit tune on-demand was to buy that black vinyl disc.

The lucrative sixties music explosion accelerated the cosy, insular industry into overdrive. From the pressing plant, the records were transported, as physical products, to a network of individual record stores the length and breadth of Britain. Some were boutique high street shops with browser boxes to flip through album-sleeves, with listening booths where potential purchasers could listen to a track or two on the pretext of maybe buying. Others were enclaves in electrical retailers where you could also buy front room prestige radiograms, or teen-friendly Dansette portables, while others like Brian Epstein's NEMS were snuck into department stores.

The new release was supported by an equally sophisticated backup promotion. The weekly music press reviewed as many of them as space allowed – *New Musical Express*, *Melody Maker* and *Record Mirror* trailed by other titles such as *Disc*, *Music Echo*, the glossy *Pop Weekly* and the *Rave* colour monthly. A favourable review could tip the hit/miss balance and send fans scurrying with their 6s 8d in their hands to be the first one on their block. Radio was restricted to the BBC Light Programme, where air-time on Brian Matthews' *Saturday Club* could prove crucial. Radio Luxembourg carried a solid, pop content after 6 pm, but reception was increasingly poor the greater the distance from the south coast the listener happened to be. As the decade progressed, there was also Pirate Radio, forcing the BBC to eventually restructure and offer Radio One. A TV appearance was even better. ITV had *Thank Your Lucky Stars*, and then *Ready Steady Go*, while BBC had *Juke Box Jury*, on which a celebrity panel would deliver their verdict on the latest chart contenders, and then *Top of the Pops*, which became the shop-window of choice for new acts.

Once on that treadmill, with a couple of hits to provide recognition-factor, the press reviews would be afforded more space, and their *Top of the Pops* appearance followed inevitably. On 19 November 1965, there was a 'Glad Rag Ball' held at the Wembley Empire Pool, where – for just a 30 shilling ticket – fans could see The Kinks, The Who, Georgie Fame & The Blue Flames, Wilson Pickett, The Golden Apples of the Sun ... and The Hollies. The Hollies were now in that fantabulous position. The onus was on them to maintain that status.

The third studio album was originally issued simply in mono format. The title was 'HOLLIES' in red lettering, on a cover showing monochrome wedges of each of the five group members. The reverse was given over to a single atmospheric shot of the group gathered around the microphone in the studio. Issued on 1 September 1965, it stayed on the UK album chart for fourteen weeks, peaking at number 8. Confusingly, the stereo version was not issued until November 1969 and then on the Starline label, where it was retitled *Reflection* (SRS 5008).

'Very Last Day' (Stookey, Yarrow)

Featured live during their set on The Rolling Stones tour, where the programme described The Hollies as 'one of the outstanding vocal-instrumental aggregations ever to arrive on the music scene in the Beat Era', this track was issued as a single in Scandinavia, backed with 'Too Many People', where it became a considerable success. It's a Gospel-tinged Peter Paul & Mary song from the trio's breakthrough third album, *In the Wind*, with a vague egalitarian subtext, albeit wrapped up in Biblical references. Tony plays banjo, with Graham on acoustic guitar.

'You Must Believe Me' (Mayfield)

The Hollies tended to exercise good taste when it came to covers. Curtis Mayfield always managed to inject a soulful Gospel feel into his Impressions songs with high falsetto vocals and subtle horns, a feel that comes across strongly even when The Hollies accelerate the tempo through simpler beat-group instrumentation. They'd already premiered this song on a BBC *Top Gear* session recorded 19 February 1965, which was later collected onto the *Radio Fun* compilation.

'Put Yourself in My Place' (L Ransford)

This is one of the first Hollies compositions to be covered by another high-profile act. In January 1966, Episode Six received high-rotation plays on pirate radio when they recorded the song as their debut single. The group features

Ian Gillan and Roger Glover – later of Deep Purple – and their take on it has a plaintive edge. The Hollies original is delivered with a harder thrust, showing their increasing sophistication and assurance both in the studio and as songwriters.

'Down the Line' (Orbison)

Texan, Roy Orbison – the Big 'O' – left an indelible imprint on rock history with his big, dramatic near-operatic ballads, but he'd started his career as a rockabilly rocker on the yellow 'Sun' record label with this moody composition – the B-side of his debut single 'Ooby Dooby' – recorded by him with The Teen Kings when it was still titled 'Go Go Go'. It was re-titled 'Down the Line' by Jerry Lee Lewis when he recorded it and took it into the US charts in 1958. The song had also been admirably covered on a 1959 EP by Cliff Richard & The Drifters. Now it gives The Hollies the opportunity to do some authentic Rock 'n' Roll ... in The Hollies style. Roy himself revived the song for his celebrated 1989 come-back *Black & White Night* with Elvis Costello, James Burton and Bruce Springsteen.

'That's My Desire' (Loveday, Kresa)

This track serves the same function as 'I Thought of You Last Night' on *In the Hollies Style*. A 1931 'Great American Songbook' item that had amassed an extensive catalogue of earlier versions, from Frankie Laine to Doo-Wop vocal groups, from Eddie Cochran to Buddy Holly, it was also done by Cliff Richard on a 1959 album. Here, it finds The Hollies in a slow romantic mood. Another shot at mainstream sophistication.

'Too Many People' (L Ransford)

Hollies is a transitional album, glancing back over their collective shoulder to their origins with 'Lawdy Miss Clawdy', while taking a step forward towards more ambitious material with 'Too Many People'. 'This ain't no story, no fairy-tale', Allan cautions. This is no straightforward boy-girl love-you lost-you lyric; it's a serious attempt to grapple with issues. Too many people have died, first in plagues or in wars. There's a move into 'Protest' territory. Issued as a Scandinavian single, it became a considerable hit for them in Sweden.

'Lawdy Miss Clawdy' (Price)

An early New Orleans R&B hit for Specialty Records with a Dave Bartholomew arrangement and Fats Domino on piano; it became popular with rock 'n' rollers, including Elvis Presley, who cut his own version. Following Army service in Korea, Lloyd Price then had a run of UK hits in 1959 with 'Stagger Lee' (number 7), 'Where Were You (On Our Wedding Day)?' (number 15), and 'Personality' (number 9). For The Hollies, this is a straight beat-group run-through, delving back into their old club repertoire.

'When I Come Home To You' (L Ransford)

Allan and Graham swap verses then harmonise the chorus with sweet vocal chimes and rippling guitar runs. There's something of 'I'm Alive' in its forceful instrumentation and something John-&-Paul about the way the rhyming voices merge. Many years later, ABC would hymn Smokey Robinson as a purveyor of 'the slyest rhymes, the sharpest suits'; and as rock became wilder around them, The Hollies were never less than immaculately professional and sharply suited as a walking product placement for their manager's 'Toggery' chain of Gent's Outfitters! Because The Fab Four had the round-neck collarless Beatles-jackets, there was a brief attempt at a square-collar Hollies uniform – 'like a girl's gymslip top', according to Bobby Elliott – which were soon discarded in favour of silver-grey Tonic suits with black-edged jackets and velvet collar trim... again, tailored by Michael Cohen's family business.

'Fortune Teller' ('Naomi Neville', aka Allen Toussaint)

A song featured by – and already recorded by – a number of beat groups, including The Merseybeats in 1963, and by former-Searcher Tony Jackson with The Vibrations in 1965. The Hollies retain the rawness of their early performances in this fun story where the singer goes to get his fortune read, then ends up marrying the Fortune Teller. And when they hit those harmonies, they hit them hard.

'So Lonely' (L Ransford)

As the B-side of 'Look Through Any Window', this constitutes the album's only previously released track. The Hollies workmanlike methodology, with four songs nailed in a three-hour session, vindicates their assurance in capturing the song in one or two takes. Driven by Bobby Elliott's drums, they maintain unequalled levels of spontaneity and energy.

'I've Been Wrong' (L Ransford)

Performed live on *The Brian Matthews Radio Show*, with a sharp, stabbing vaguely-Kinks guitar riff with high keening harmonies, this is a concise 1:56-minutes but needs no more. It's one of the songs chosen by The Everly Brothers for their *Two Yanks in London* album and forms the A-side of their 1966 single b/w 'Hard Hard Year' (WB 5754). The duo tighten the urgent pleading delivery in a master-class demonstration of just where The Hollies style had begun. The song was also covered by the Norwegian group Firestones.

'Mickey's Monkey' (Holland, Dozier, Holland)

A lively Northern Soul-slanted Bobby Elliott-led percussive cover of a 1963 Motown dance-hit for The Miracles, which cashes in on yet another short-lived dance-fad, 'monkey see, monkey do'. Recorded on 1 March 1965 as part of the same session as 'Very Last Day' and 'That's My Desire', The Hollies omit Smokey Robinson's talk-in 'Alright, is everybody ready?', and plunge directly into the 'lum de lum de lai-ai' chant. It sounds like they had fun recording it, and Tony's guitar solo is raw.

Related Releases
'If I Needed Someone' (Harrison) b/w 'I've Got a Way of My Own' (Ransford) (3 December 1965, Parlophone R5392)
The Beatles cover had always been something of a poisoned chalice and something The Hollies had successfully steered away from. So far. Each Beatles album had spun-off hits for other artists from the very start, with 'Do You Want To Know a Secret' from their debut album igniting a run of hits for Billy J Kramer & The Dakotas. *With The Beatles* gifted The Rolling Stones with their top twenty breakthrough, 'I Wanna Be Your Man'. But when The Naturals covered 'I Should Have Known Better' from *A Hard Day's Night*, or The Overlanders took the *Rubber Soul* song 'Michelle' all the way to number one, neither led to a career beyond that one bright moment. With The Hollies by now established in their own right, at George Martin's suggestion, they recorded 'If I Needed Someone', not a Lennon-McCartney song, but George Harrison's contribution to *Rubber Soul*. George sings, 'but you see now I'm too much in love', which The Hollies amend to 'can't you see how I'm too much in love?', apart from which the arrangements are essentially similar. The Beatles a little tighter, The Hollies a tad looser. But, less than happy with their treatment, George Harrison himself publicly denounces The Hollies version as 'soulless'. It stayed on the charts for nine weeks, but halted at number 20 (13 January 1966), the same week that saw The Beatles 'We Can Work It Out' b/w 'Day Tripper' at number 1. for The Hollies. It represents a considerable fall from their previous standard, charting only marginally higher than their debut '(Ain't That) Just Like Me'. The B-side is an equally strong original composition, driven by Allan's Echo Vamper harmonica, but smoother and adeptly delivered, with a lyrically urgent plea for change, 'why they deny me the right to start living, I'll never know'. Pop, but with an edge. The year closes with Graham making a brief acting appearance in Rediffusion-TV's *For Older Children* play 'Stage One Contest', a winning episode called 'The Party', written by Beverley Williams.

Hear! Here! (January 1966, Imperial LP-9299)
Prompted by The Hollies first American Top Forty hit with 'Look Through Any Window', this fix-up album dressed in Woody Woodward cover-art made the US number 145. From 27 March, The Hollies jet across the Atlantic for a support six-week tour, plagued by TV bans due to union problems. A follow-up tour in June was scrapped due to trouble with work permits. Meanwhile, the album tracklist is:

'I'm Alive', 'Very Last Day', 'You Must Believe Me', 'Put Yourself in My Place', 'Down the Line', 'That's My Desire', 'Look Through Any Window', 'Lawdy Miss Clawdy', 'When I Come Home to You', 'So Lonely', 'I've Been Wrong, 'Too Many People'

'I Can't Let Go' (Taylor) b/w 'Running Through The Night' (Ransford) (18 February 1966, Parlophone R5409)

Around the corner from Denmark Street's 'Tin Pan Alley', Tony Hicks listened to demos at Dick James Music in the music publisher's Charing Cross office. He passed over John Phillips 'California Dreamin'' and zeroed in on this classic song. Chip Taylor is not only actor Jon Voight's brother but the author of 'Wild Thing'. And for me, this is the best Hollies single so far. It opens with a deeply compulsive naggingly-insistent guitar throb used as an assault weapon, before Allan leads in with the opening phrases, until it explodes into the jangling lead guitar, and an awesome mix of dexterous harmonies, multi-layered with a precision worthy of Brian Wilson; harmonies and counter-harmonies unfurl, rising against each other through a strafing guitar-break, with Graham's high falsetto riding the grid of interweaving voices, until a dramatic 'Hey'. It stops, after which it drops back to the bass run and opens again from the start, roaring into a perfect guitar solo. When the art of the 45rpm single is properly employed, it can be devastating, with energy, innovation and imagination compressed into a precise 2:24-minute package. It stayed on the chart for ten weeks and hit the UK number two (17 March 1966), where it stayed for three weeks, unable to dislodge the Walker Brothers 'The Sun Ain't Gonna Shine Anymore' from the top slot (except in *NME* where it peaks at Number 1 for the single week of 12 March 1966). Equally impressive when done live on the German TV *Beat Club* (8 May), it hit number 31 there, number two in Denmark, and number 27 in Holland. The playful 'L Ransford' B-Side, 'Running Through the Night', has a curious country sway to it, with the interplay of vocal chemistry at its most volatile. A tie-in EP titled 'I Can't Let Go' (June 1966, Parlophone GEP 8951) was the last of the fine run of Hollies extended-play packages, adding 'Look Through Any Window', 'I've Got a Way of My Own' and 'So Lonely'. By May, 'I Can't Let Go' was also climbing the American charts, peaking at a high of number 42. Much later, 'I Can't Let Go' was featured on the multi-artist compilation *The History of British Rock* (1974 Double vinyl, Sire SAS 3702).

Two Yanks in London by The Everly Brothers (July 1966, Warner Bros Records WS 1646) No chart placings.

The English Invasion had shaken the American music scene to its core, toppling the careers of many, and overnight making others seem old-fashioned and obsolete. Meanwhile, The Beatles kept raising the bar with each new release. Brenda Lee rose to the challenge by flying to London in the hope of catching some of that Swinging London stardust, and stormed back with a

John Carter-Ken Lewis rocker 'Is It True', with Jimmy Page on guitar, which placed her firmly back on-trend and into the Top Twenty as early as September 1964. Failed US Rocker P.J. Proby – previously both James Marcus Smith and Jet Powers – hopped the transatlantic jet to England where he reinvented himself into controversial stardom, as hit-maker and friend of The Fab Four, who gifted him with an original song – 'That Means a Lot', a number 30 hit in September 1965. So Allan Clarke, Tony Hicks and Graham Nash were invited by The Everly Brothers to submit songs for an LP they intend to record in London. There's an intuitive logic to the connection. After a day sifting material at the London Mayfair Hotel, The Hollies join Don and Phil at the Pye studio in Great Cumberland Place for recording sessions held between 16 May and 2 June 1966. 'That was wonderful; that was one of the biggest things that I ever did', Allan enthused to me. 'I'll always remember that. There was one time we were together in the vocal booth and Don turns to me and says 'how do I sing this, Al?'' (Alan assumes an appropriate, and uncannily accurate Everly accent). Session musicians also include Jimmy Page, John Paul Jones and, it is claimed, Reg Dwight, before he switched names to Elton John. The full album track list is:

'Somebody Help Me' (Jackie Edwards), 'So Lonely' ('L Ransford'), 'Kiss Your Man Goodbye' (Don and Phil), 'Signs That Will Never Change' ('L Ransford'), 'Like Every Time Before' ('L Ransford'), 'Pretty Flamingo' (Mark Barkan), 'I've Been Wrong Before' ('L Ransford'), 'Have You Ever Loved Somebody' ('L Ransford'), 'The Collector' (Don and Phil with Sonny Curtis), 'Don't Run and Hide' ('L Ransford'), 'Fifi the Flea' ('L Ransford'), 'Hard Hard Year' ('L Ransford')

'After the Fox' (Bacharach) b/w 'The Fox Trot' (Bacharach) (15 September 1966, United Artist UP1152)

Goodness Gracious Me, the sixties was a crazy time, with the music scene open to every kind of novelty. While The Hollies were stuck at number 20 with 'If I Needed Someone', a few slots above them at number 15 was another even more bizarre Beatles cover-version, Peter Sellers' Shakespearian comic-rendition of 'A Hard Day's Night'! Not that the actor was new to the charts. He was part of The Goons, whose manic 'Ying-Tong Song' confused and mind-boggled record-buyers back when discs spun at 78rpm. Sellers also had duo chart romps with Sophia Loren, oddities that were the brain-spawn of a tyro George Martin long before his days with The Beatles.

Meanwhile, tacking a pop 'name' to the soundtrack of a mainstream movie was long seen as a cunning marketing ploy to seduce teen appeal. And it frequently worked. It worked for Lulu in *To Sir With Love* (1967). It worked for The Seekers with *Georgy Girl* (1966). Manfred Mann worked on the *Up the Junction* (1968) soundtrack. Now those various strands came together on 10 May when The Hollies recorded the theme for the Peter Sellers crime-caper

heist movie *After the Fox* at Abbey Road studios – '(Burt) Bacharach forced
The Hollies through dozens of takes before being restrained by the group's
producer, Ron Richards. Then Peter Sellers arrived, 'killed' the piano with a
pretend karate chop, and proceeded to add his vocal responses in one of his
most devilish accents', with Sellers doing spoken-word parts and The Hollies
adding call-and-response. 'Who is the Fox?' – 'I am the Fox'. 'Why do you
steal?' – 'So I be rich'. 'Why not work?' – 'Ah, work is hard'. You'll be caught!'
– 'I never fail'. The track is played over the animated *Pink Panther*-style credit
sequence and sets the tone for the movie, with its English-language screenplay
by Neil Simon.

For a London 'Palladium' show (14 May), Klaus Voorman deputised for an
'ill' Eric Haydock ('Klaus wanted too much money' jokes Allan, 'we couldn't
afford him'). Then Bernie Calvert stood in for Eric during a three-week
European tour, joining in time for gigs in Sweden, although Eric returns to
promote 'Bus Stop'. But after missing several gigs, unhappy with touring,
Eric was finally asked to leave The Hollies in July. 'After all' said Graham with
breathtaking insensitivity, 'the bass player does the least work in the group'!
Between bassists, they recruited session player Jack Bruce to stand in for the
'After the Fox' session, while the track's composer Burt Bacharach tinkles
piano. Although the track is featured on the soundtrack LP (United Artists SULP
1151), the B-side, 'The Fox Trot', is credited to Burt Bacharach himself, and is
not by The Hollies. The single was not considered a regular part of The Hollies
discography, not even on their usual label, and was not heavily promoted. So,
although it was no real surprise when it failed to chart, it's still an amusing and
entertaining track, well worth searching out.

Eric, meanwhile, took his Fender six-string VI bass to form Haydock's
Rockhouse. The new group issued a revival of Sam Cooke's 'Cupid' b/w 'She
Thinks' (November 1966, Columbia DB 8050), and then John Sebastian's
Lovin' Spoonful song 'Loving You' b/w 'Mix-a-Fix' (February 1967, Columbia
DB 8135). There are problems – and litigation – over venues using the word
'Hollies' prominently to advertise Haydock's Rockhouse gigs, although that's
more down to promoters intent on selling tickets rather than Eric himself. But
the road is long with many a winding turn, and in the fullness of time, Eric
would briefly become a Hollie again in time for 'Holliedaze'.

Would You Believe?

Personnel:
Allan Clarke: vocals, harmonica
Graham Nash: vocals, rhythm guitar
Eric Haydock: bass guitar
Tony Hicks: vocals, lead guitar
Bobby Elliott: drums
Produced at EMI Studios by Ron Richards, 14 September 1965-25 March 1966.
Released: 1 June 1966, Parlophone PMC 7008
Running time: 29:26
Highest chart position: UK: 16

Frank Sinatra had returned to the charts with 'Strangers in the Night', his run at the number 1 spot bookended by The Rolling Stones 'Paint It Black' and The Beatles 'Paperback Writer'. The Kinks, Animals, Troggs, Yardbirds and Merseys were all quickening the pulse of the top ten. It's into this vibrant Pop scene that The Hollies released their fourth album, with an effectively arty cover drawn by Jennifer Sebley and sleeve notes by Andy Wickham. It meant a return to Abbey Road's EMI Studios with Ron Richards again taking production credits, but with the band gained a more assured confidence when it came to input and experiment. The first track to be laid down was the group arrangement of the traditional song 'Stewball' on 14 September 1965. They return on 13 October to record 'I've Got a Way of My Own'. After a gap, they returned to record the single 'I Can't Let Go', cutting 'Don't You Even Care' during the same session. There were more recordings scattered across the next two months, with the final two tracks – 'Sweet Little Sixteen' ('one of the group's stage favourites' points out one reviewer helpfully), and 'one-time single hope' 'I Am a Rock', completed on 25 March. 'This set has enormous concentrated feeling and should at long last dispel thoughts and ideas that The Hollies are still waiting for recognition. They aren't!' said *New Musical Express*. The album peaked at number 16 and remained on the album chart for eight weeks. It was reissued in October 1974 on the budget Music for Pleasure label as *I Can't Let Go* (MFP 50094), and later on CD by Beat Goes On (BGOLP24).

'I Take What I Want' (Porter, Hodges, Hayes)

A Sam & Dave song, covered on EP by The Artwoods in a raw swaggering strutting Mod make-over. Allan Clarke makes a less convincing bad, bad go-getter, as Tony Hicks' nagging curling guitar riff sets off their smoother, more slick but punchy up-tempo reading. Introduced by Brian Matthews on *The Top of the Pops Radio Show*, Brian decides to interview Eric Haydock – 'the quiet one of the group', only to be interrupted by Allan and Graham, to comic effect.

'Hard, Hard Year' (L Ransford)

This is one of the songs chosen by The Everly Brothers for their album, and B-side of their US 1966 single 'Somebody Help Me', then later revived by Indie group The Bevis Frond on the 2013 Hollies tribute album *Re-Evolution*. The Hollies' own interpretation starts with strummed guitar and simple tambourine percussion for a look on 'the bad side of life', broken by Tony's startling fuzz-guitar interlude. The lyrics document blue-collar hard-times, 'first month, snows came, put me in bed, couldn't work the same, job's gone, bills are here', leaving him with 'bad times, something's wrong, money's gone, I'm on my own'. It's an impressive flaunting of the group's new maturity.

'That's How Strong My Love Is' (Jamison)

Although this pleading Roosevelt Jamison love-pledge song is mostly associated with the Otis Redding talk-singing reading, it was also done by The Rolling Stones on their *Out of Our Heads* album, and by The In Crowd (an early line-up of Tomorrow), as well as this one. Given a typically Hollies three-part harmony make-over, Graham plus Tony, with Allan to the fore, it smoothly and seamlessly transfigures into part of their repertoire. They recorded a BBC radio session for *Saturday Club* (23 March 1966), including this and 'I Take What I Want', both included on the CD *Radio Fun*.

'Sweet Little Sixteen' (Berry)

Yet more Chuck Berry; the fourth cover of his songs across four albums. Because The Hollies were never big enough to define the decade, in the way that The Beatles or The Rolling Stones do, they were nevertheless woven into the tapestry of the sixties by reflecting – rather than determining – each nuance and shift of the times. And this album is one that shows them gradually altering and finding wriggle-room within that status. From raw R&B to a touch of new Mod, a taste of Folk-Rock, a hint of Protest… yet all melded through their own unique filter.

'Oriental Sadness' (L Ransford)

Wrapped in a beguiling interplay of harmonies, with Tony's guitar swerving into the slight suggestion of oriental colouring, warning voices talkback beneath the main theme that 'she'll never trust in anybody no more', before closing with the flourish of a shimmering gong. As the *Record Collector* review points out, this album 'finds the band straddling British R&B, Folk-Rock and the tentative signs of a distinct songwriting style', as evidenced here.

'I Am a Rock' (Simon)

As a messed-up adolescent myself, this Paul Simon song seemed to express the angst at the deep core of my confused soul. Paul Simon first recorded it with aching bedsitter sincerity on his solo acoustic *The Paul Simon Songbook* (1965) album, then recorded it again as part of the electric Simon & Garfunkel *Sounds of Silence* LP (1966) spun off as the duo's third charting single. So, although it was not quite a case of The Hollies doing what The Byrds had done to Bob Dylan's 'Mr Tambourine Man', their 'I Am a Rock' uses a fast smooth-harmony arrangement. There's an argument that Paul Simon's hesitant opening guitar phrases and stripped-back instrumentation catch the dysfunctional misfit outsider isolation exactly, 'hiding in my room, safe within my womb', whereas The Hollies arrangement alters the phrasing and lifts it into slickly-targeted pop (nervously substituting the overly-gynaecological 'womb' into a repetition of 'room'), yet there's sufficient empathy in their close-harmony voices to save the message. And why simply replicate? Covering a song should also personalise it in new ways.

The Hollies' eventful USA tour gave evidence of their rising status, playing shows and dates from 28 March 1966 – including rehearsals for *Hullabaloo*. They played as opening act at Murray The K's new Long Island club from 1-3 April, while they grabbed the opportunity of attending a Simon & Garfunkel recording session in New York. They're also there at a studio session for The Mamas and the Papas on 28 April, where Bobby got to meet legendary session drummer Hal Blaine. This was around the time that Graham met Mama Cass Elliott, who would later introduce him to David Crosby and Stephen Stills. By 30 April, The Hollies had played Tucson, Arizona, and on 6 May performed two shows thirty miles apart in Sacramento! They closed the tour on 7 May 1966 by playing Pismo Beach.

'Take Your Time' (Holly, Petty)
During his brief career, Buddy Holly wrote some of the most melodic love songs of the early Rock 'n' Roll era and was a major formative influence. The Beatles expertly replicate his 'Words of Love' on *Beatles for Sale*. The Rolling Stones kick off their career with Buddy's 'Not Fade Away'. When The Hollies opt for the 1958 'Rave On' B-side, they delete Buddy's squeaky organ figure in favour of glittering guitar, and acquit themselves well. They would return to Buddy Holly with a full album of covers later in their career.

'Don't You Even Care' (Ballard)
Recorded after a three-month pause, 13 January 1966, they recommence sessions with this Northern Soul song formerly cut by Leslie Uggams. There is jabbing Tony Hicks guitar and the kind of attractively-involved song construction familiar from Clint's 'I'm Alive'. Ballard also wrote hits for Wayne Fontana & The Mindbenders ('It's Just a Little Bit Too Late') and 'You're No Good' – a number 3 UK hit for The Swinging Blue Jeans in the time before Terry Sylvester had joined them.

'Fifi the Flea' (L Ransford)
Yes, there used to be Flea Circuses, and Graham sings this melancholy song about a flea who tragically falls in love with a clown – 'dying of love' – with

sad, dramatic effect over a simple acoustic guitar strum, investing the ludicrous story with poignant dignity. Paul & Barry Ryan were the cutely pretty twin sons of 1950s Postrel Marion Ryan; slowing the carousel-swirl tempo, with added harpsichord, Graham coaches a cover for their 1967 *Two of a Kind* album (Decca LK 4878). The Everly Brothers do a stand-out version of 'Fifi the Flea', while in the US, a single by the Sidekicks takes this song to bubbling-under status.

'Stewball' (Herald, Rinzler, Yellin)

Although credited to the Greenbriar Boys, this traditional broadsheet-ballad had been recorded by Woody Guthrie, The Weavers – who took their reading of it from Leadbelly – and in the UK by Lonnie Donegan in 1956. It was also done as a 1967 single by 'tatty-'ead' comedian Jimmy Tarbuck, a Dovedale primary school contemporary of John Lennon; Tarbuck's rapid-fire scouse-wit routines and Beatles fringe made him part of the Northern upsurge, despite his later unfortunate support for Margaret Thatcher's Conservative policies. For a BBC TV appearance, Allan introduces 'Stewball' as 'one of our favourite numbers we always do in cabaret, this was recorded by a favourite group of ours called Peter, Paul & Mary'. A French-language version (recorded at two sessions 20 December 1965 and 4 January 1966) was included as part of the 1998 *The Complete Hollies* six-CD set.

'I've Got a Way of My Own' (L. Ransford)

Originally the B-side of 'If I Needed Someone', a precise 2:07-minutes of Allan's most Blues-wailing harmonica, Graham's driving assertions of the need for independence, and the unrivalled collective group-chorus harmonies. It was also recorded by The Electric Prunes. I ask Allan if he'd heard that one? 'No, I don't think I have. The Electric Prunes? What a great name. Was it a single?' No, it was a studio outtake included as a bonus track on their 2007 *Too Much To Dream* CD album.

'I Can't Let Go' (Taylor, Gorgoni)

The Hollies close the album in great style, with their recent hit single. Quintessential Hollies.

Related Releases
Beat Group (Imperial LP-9312 mono, LP-12312 stereo)

These songs form the core of The Hollies third American album, issued in May. And there are intriguing anomalies involved in the transatlantic music biz. A prime example for Beatles fans is the Larry Williams song 'Bad Boy', which was included on the Capitol album *Beatles VI* but remained unreleased in the UK until *A Collection of Beatles Oldies* in December 1966, necessitating British fans either paying over the odds for an American import album, or waiting to buy the full UK album in order to obtain just that one song! Same with The Hollies' 'A Taste of Honey'. Written by Ric Marlow with Bobby Scott (who also co-wrote 'He Ain't Heavy, He's My Brother') for the Broadway stage-presentation of Shelagh Delaney's gritty Manchester-based play, adapted into the 1961 Rita Tushingham movie, 'A Taste of Honey' had been a huge instrumental hit for Herb Alpert & The Tijuana Brass, and was side two, track five of The Beatles' first album. The Hollies performed the song on radio slots and had two attempts at recording it, the first – 1 March 1966, during the *Would You Believe?* Sessions, with slow-down tempo-change, and punctilious Dave Clark Five drum-breaks. Although not included on the album, it somehow ended up on its American counterpart. The second attempt, with the Bernie Calvert line-up, a burst of scat, horns and strings, recorded 12 and 16 August 1968, remained unissued until the 2003 *The Long Road Home* Box-set. The full *Beat Group* is:

'I Can't Let Go', 'That's How Strong My Love Is', 'Running Through the Night', 'Oriental Sadness (She'll Never Trust in Anybody No More)', 'A Taste of Honey', 'Mr Moonlight', 'Don't You Even Care', 'Hard, Hard Year', 'Take Your Time', 'Fifi the Flea', 'I Take What I Want'

'I Can't Let Go' (Taylor, Gorgoni) b/w 'Look Through Any Window' (Gouldman) (Capitol (D)T-6152)
To further complicate things, the Canadian edition was retitled after the hit singles, and issued 6 June:

'That's How Strong My Love Is', 'Stewball', 'Take Your Time', 'Running Through the Night', 'Fifi The Flea', 'Look Through Any Window', 'A Taste of Honey', 'Hard, Hard Year', 'I Take What I Want', 'Oriental Sadness (She'll Never Trust in Anybody No More)', 'I Can't Let Go'

'Bus Stop' (Gouldman) b/w 'Don't Run and Hide' (Ransford)
Personnel:
Allan Clarke: vocals, harmonica
Graham Nash: vocals, rhythm guitar
Tony Hicks: vocals, lead guitar, banjo
Bobby Elliott: drums
Bernie Calvert: bass guitar
Produced by Ron Richards at EMI Studios.
Released: 17 June 1966, Parlophone R5469

With an unbroken string of stand-out 45-rpms, The Hollies had become masters of the singles medium, hits that have become as comfortable as old friends. Without the heavy subversive darknesses of The Stones or The Who, they were either writing or remodelling other's material with a killer instinct for melody and rhythm, using idiosyncratic alchemy to turn confectionery-cute pop into carefully constructed vignettes of endearing charm and energy. Twenty-three-year-old Bernard 'Bernie' Calvert joined The Hollies as new bass player – formerly a member of The Dolphins with Tony Hicks and Bobby Elliott. Born 16 September 1942 in Brierfield, Nelson, Lancs, 5' 11", he's was a former apprentice-engineer who liked Count Basie, and made his TV debut on *Five O'Clock Club* (2 September), and radio debut on the *Joe Loss Pop Show*. He debuted with the group live at the Morecambe Central Pier, and joined in time to contribute to this Graham Gouldman song on 18 May 1966, during his first day as a member. 'We went straight in and did 'Bus Stop' in exactly one hour and forty minutes', recalls Bobby Elliott. 'Not only was it the fastest single we ever recorded, in my opinion, it was one of our best.' The song tells an endearing love story, making full use of Gouldman's sharp, perceptive eye, taking everyday detail and weaving a narrative about it. Strangers share an umbrella on a rainy day as they wait for the bus, only for it to blossom into romance. There were tie-in group promotional photos of The Hollies in city-gent bowler hats, and carrying brollies, standing at a bus stop. Then they perform it on BBC radio *Saturday Club* as part of the promotion, alongside 'Shake' and 'Hard Hard Year' – recorded 28 June 1966 and later collected onto the *Radio Fun* CD compilation. The single hit a UK *Record Retailer* number 5 – and number three on the *New Musical Express* chart below The Kinks' 'Sunny Afternoon', just as the LP *Would You Believe* reached UK number 16. In September, 'Bus Stop' hit US number five (Imperial 66186), The Hollies finally achieving their long-awaited and well-deserved major American breakthrough.

US journalist Lillian Roxon rationalised that 'The Hollies' big tragedy in America right from the start was a lack of image. They didn't come on as meanies, or cuties, or groovies, or heavies. They didn't go in for gimmickry and stunts. They just sang well, and as everyone knows, that's not always enough for the sort of giant promotional campaign needed to establish an English group in the United States.' (In her *Rock Encyclopedia*, 1971, Grosset & Dunlop.) Yet persistence had finally paid off; although that also presents problems. 'What tended to happen was we always used to go over when we'd got a hit in the charts, rather than going over there and spending time doing tours and getting ourselves established as an act,' Allan admits. 'We just used to go over on the strength of a hit record.' Nevertheless, a hit record it was, and 'Bus Stop' also reached number one in Sweden, number two in Australia, number three in Holland, and number nine in Germany. After September cabaret dates at the Stockton 'Fiesta' (4th), the Nottingham 'Sherwood Rooms' (19th), the Bridlington 'Royal Hall' (20th) and Weston-super-Mare 'Winter Gardens' (27th), they toured as the opening act for a US Herman's Hermits tour through autumn 1966. A fellow Mancunian band, Herman had leapfrogged The Hollies both by reaching the UK number one slot first – ten months ahead of 'I'm Alive' – and by scoring a major American hit with their debut single 'I'm

Into Something Good' in September 1964. Touring with Herman attracted The Hollies, a useful backwash of loyal fans.

Eric Haydock plays on the L Ransford B-side 'Don't Run and Hide', reinforced by session-player John Paul Jones, and a nagging *Rubber Soul* guitar riff, matched to a slight harmonica phrase. Also done – perhaps even better by The Everly Brothers – the ambiguously paranoid lyric urges 'stay with me' in the face of other people's lies, because to run would be to condemn yourself: 'don't run and hide now, 'cause you're only hurting yourself.' The harmonies reach a piercing crescendo, with Graham taking solo vocal lines.

Bus Stop (October 1966, Imperial LP-9330) Chart place US: 75

The Hollies fourth US album and the first to chart, compiled to take advantage of the hit single, as Allan complains: 'our albums always sold off a hit single rather than selling off their own merit.' It reached number 75.

'Bus Stop', 'Candy Man', 'Baby That's All', 'I Am a Rock', 'Sweet Little Sixteen', 'We're Through', 'Don't Run and Hide', 'Oriental Sadness', 'Mickey's Monkey', 'Little Lover' (from *Stay With The Hollies,* with Don Rathbone playing drums), 'You Know He Did', 'Whatcha Gonna Do About It?'

'Stop Stop Stop' (Clarke, Hicks, Nash) b/w 'It's You' (Clarke, Hicks, Nash) (7 October 1966, Parlophone R5508)

Written by the group and driven by Tony Hicks' irresistibly distinctive six-string banjo riff processed through a tape-delay effect, it reaches number 2 with ease, and charted around the world – number one in Canada and number seven on the American *Billboard* Hot Hundred (Imperial 66214), Number 4 in Germany and Holland, number 5 in Denmark, and number 9 in Australia. As international stars, by now, The Hollies had sophisticated into a slick hit-making outfit, and this is the perfect little pop single expertly targeted at record-buyers. The banjo riff – which Tony had in his mind for weeks previously – is largely used as a novelty element, but its treated balalaika-sound could equally be interpreted as part of that experimental Yardbirds movement that was opening up the possibilities of rock. The narrative lyric, according to Graham Nash, inflates the tale of the group's first visit to New York's *Round Table* up-market strip club, as a guest of American 'Roulette Records' impresario Morris 'Mo' Levy, although I'm certain Manchester had its own share of such dubious nightlife attractions! With the slightly risqué storyline emphasised by Bobby Elliott's burlesque cymbal-smashes, and echoes of The Coasters Leiber & Stoller song 'Little Egypt' – 'strutting wearing nothing but a button and bow' – the song ascends into the moment where the protagonist rushes the stage 'knocking over tables, spilling all the drinks', only to be thrown out into the street. The immaculate punchline reveals that this 'happens every week'! The song is fresh enough to be covered by The Boys for their Punk-era *Alternative Chartbusters* LP in February 1978 (NEMS NEL6015).

The B-side opens with a masterful drum-fusillade and harmonica into driving three-voice harmonies. There's a more involved relationship lyric, 'I'm a simple man at heart', the cause of their impending break-up is not him ... it's her!

After a row over top-billing, from 15 October 1966, The Hollies headline a nineteen-date package tour with the disgruntled Small Faces, plus Paul & Barry Ryan, Paul Jones and The Nashville Teens. When they appear on US television, Mike Douglas presents them with a gold disc for 'Stop Stop Stop'. Then they complete the year by being placed fourth in the *NME* British Vocal Group section of the annual poll, and ninth in the World Vocal Group list.

For Certain Because

Personnel:
Allan Clarke: vocals, harmonica
Graham Nash: vocals, rhythm guitar
Tony Hicks: vocals, lead guitar, banjo
Bobby Elliott: drums
Bernie Calvert: bass guitar except 'Don't Even Think About Changing', piano
Eric Haydock: bass guitar on 'Don't Even Think About Changing'
plus Mike Vickers: orchestral arrangements for 'High Classed', 'What Went Wrong',
'Crusader'
Produced at EMI Studios by Ron Richards, 20 June-17 October 1966, with 'Don't
Even Think About Changing', 17 November 1965.
Released: 2 December 1966, Parlophone PMC/PMS 7011
Running time: 32:24
Highest chart position: UK: 2

According to Bobby Elliott, the album title was three words plucked from the
novelty nursery song 'Teddy Bears' Picnic', chosen in retaliation for a joke stage
announcement from Allan and Graham about their young drummer's repertoire.
   Where 21st century acts routinely take years to record and tour an album,
this was The Hollies' second long-player of 1966. While The Beatles were
liaising with George Martin for the same label, the Clark-Nash-Hicks axis
went on with increasing confidence, working across a punishing schedule to
create a run of hits only rivalled by The Beatles themselves. Largely recorded
between 20 June and 17 October, building a close relationship with producer
Ron Richards at the now-familiar Abbey Road Studios, the album was issued
in a gatefold sleeve and was welcomed by an *NME* review feature as 'an
imaginative, entertaining and at times disturbing fusion of talent. It is also the
best album they have cut.' The cover-photo documents changes, with a newly-
bearded Graham, 'The Holly Who Has Found His Face', who enthuses 'Pop
music is moving forward at an incredible speed. It's not just progressing – it's
running full tilt into tomorrow' (to Keith Altham, *NME* 28 October 1966). It's
also their first album with new bass player Bernie Calvert. As well as being
the first Hollies album made up of all-original material, the songs are credited
under their own names. The 'L Ransford' alias had been vital in building the
group identity as a distinctive creative self-contained musical unit. Having
achieved that objective, the 'L Ransford' tag could be shrugged off, enabling
them to move on. Gary Leeds, The Walker Brothers drummer who flat-shared
with Graham off Marble Arch, wrote the sleeve notes. The album reached UK
number two.

'What's Wrong With the Way I Live' (Clarke, Nash, Hicks)

Tony comments, 'it's important for the kids to feel a part of what is being
written. A great deal of this so-called 'Freak Out' music and progressive-pop

is way above their heads ... this is about real people, living a real life.' Yet there's curious instrumentation here, with Tony riffing banjo-style on a sixties-themed declaration of the rights of the individual to autonomy against the predominantly conformist social restrictions of the time. 'People should live their lives, leaving me to mine', then, taking a step ahead of the rest, 'it's about freedom, peace and love'.

'Pay You Back With Interest' (Clarke, Nash, Hicks)
A building keyboard riff leads into tempo-inventive power vocals, complete with chiming bells, electric piano and Indian drums. This is a major step forward for The Hollies, in that it's one of their first songs to be subject to a cover version battle. Issued as their final US hit single for Imperial (66240), it peaks at number 28 on the *Billboard* chart. It was instantly seized upon by other artists, as Dana Gillespie effectively records a 'Pay You Back With Interest' (March 1967, Pye 7N 17280), which runs from soft opening through a girl-group harmony build, closing with horns. In a hotly contested sales battle, it loses out to sibling duo Paul & Barry Ryan, on their *Two of a Kind* album. There was a further cover by a UK band called the Corsairs (April 1967, CBS 202624).

'Tell Me to My Face' (Clarke, Nash, Hicks)
There's a count-in, 'three, four', then Graham sings on an unusual excursion into Latin rhythms, with Bobby on kettle-drum, and a lyric concerning an unsigned letter. Simple and uncluttered, the song was covered by Keith (James Barry Keefer) as a follow-up to his major hit '98.6', his version reaching the US Number 37 in May 1967, and logging a single week at the UK number 50. The melody was 'sampled' by Alice Cooper for his song 'Billion Dollar Babies', while 'Tell Me to My Face' was later covered by Dan Fogelberg & Tim Weisberg on their 1978 album *Twin Sons From Different Mothers.*

'Clown' (Clarke, Nash, Hicks)
Graham's slow 'Tears of a Clown', the jangling 'serious artist behind the mask' with his painted-on smile turned upside-down. With just a melodic nod in the direction of the Everly Brothers 'Ferris Wheel', it's an impressive and powerful track, delivered with innovatory confidence and fairground circus effects. 'The rule of the clown is simple, and the show must go on as always.' 'Clown' has dense guitar drizzle and heavily-echoed vocals, which *NME* called 'almost an intrusion into his private thoughts'.

'Suspicious Look in Your Eyes' (Clarke, Nash, Hicks)
Hallmark harmonies and guitar-jangle, although it's Tony Hicks taking one of his rare lead vocals – his delivery effectively slurred, with 'bop-bop-bop' back-up voices. Tony tells *NME*, 'we went out to get a Byrds-type sound on this one

... it's no use doing a Yardbirds lyric – those things just spin your mind!' It's easy to interpret that as an attack on Graham's emerging esoteric tendencies. Tony retains a strong and loyal fan base.

'It's You' (Clarke, Nash, Hicks)
Already issued as the B-side of 'Stop Stop Stop', but well worth hearing again. He dumps the reason for their impending break-up squarely on her, 'you'll have to find a man who does just what you say,' Allan's hard-edged harmonica adds its own vehement accusation.

'High Classed' (Clarke, Nash, Hicks)
Treated as a kind of vaudeville show-tune, with a built-in mid-point dance routine exclaiming 'ah, sing those songs!' She eats caviar, he eats toast, but despite their social differences, they will love in secret. It's the kind of novelty item Davy Jones could perform with top hat and cane in a *Monkees* TV episode. Running to a tidy 2:24-minutes, three tracks – this, 'Crusader' and 'What Went Wrong' – benefit from orchestral arrangement by Mike Vickers of the Manfreds.

'Peculiar Situation' (Clarke, Nash, Hicks)
'We're lovers, but we don't make love' (they are friends without benefits), 'but when these things mean so much to us, well, that's alright'. Bernie Calvert plays piano, which was his original instrument, before switching to Fender Precision bass. There are piercing harmony voices and counter-harmony in the contagious chorus, with a spacey do-do-do-do mid-section in which individual voices chart their own entwining course. The track was considered strong enough to be issued as a German A-side single on the Odeon label b/w 'Pay You Back With Interest'.

'What Went Wrong' (Clarke, Nash, Hicks)
Recorded 17 October 1966 and running to an economical 2:07 minutes, with swaggering 'Tom Jones' horns and percussive opening, this song is pure Hollies. All successful bands have a special internal dynamic. And The Hollies is a unique coming together of talents. Graham is expansive, ambitious, driven. Tony has the inventive studio control, with one eye on business. Allan is quiet and reserved but fiercely opinionated when he feels strongly about an issue. The traits balance and complement each other, transmuting into gold.

'Crusader' (Clarke, Nash, Hicks)
Its mandolin delicacy betrays a hint of the 'Lady Jane' kind of Rolling Stones medieval minstrelsy. Allan plays guitar against reflective tambourine taps on a track that fades out to the sampled sound of tramping feet. 'We found a sound tape in the EMI library of Beefeaters marching and used it as a substitute for the drumming track' comments Graham. There are images of the dry moat

graceful in decay, in memories that go round in his head of the life he has lived. The echo effect was achieved 'while using the enormous Studio One, by placing the mike at one end and singing from the other! The sound bouncing around the walls is unbelievable', as Graham explains.

'Don't Even Think About Changing' (Clarke, Nash, Hicks)

A step back to basic, stripped-down beat-group sounds, with taut harmonica and handclap rhythms, recorded earlier than the rest of the album, 17 November 1965, with Eric Haydock still playing bass. Tony says, 'we heard The Who in their early days before they had become famous and cut this because we liked their ideas and wanted to experiment with similar things ourselves.' There might be particles of Pete Townshend in the opening guitar jabs, but this is Hollies all the way.

'Stop Stop Stop' (Clarke, Nash, Hicks)

The Hollies were not only more than equal to feeding regular fresh hits into the voracious pop machine, but advancing the agenda too on a gradual single by single basis. They close the album on a chart high.

Related Release

Stop! Stop! Stop! (December 1966, Imperial LP-9339 mono, LP-12339 stereo) Chart place US: 91

Although retaining the same tracklisting, the American album was retitled after the single and reached US number 91.

1967

'Devi Avere Fiducia In Me' (Specchia, Martini) b/w 'Non Prego Per Me' (Battisti & Mogol) (Italy only, Parlophone QMSP 16402)

Meanwhile, The Hollies open 1967 with a January appearance at the 'San Remo Festival' – taking time to party with Gene Pitney on his hired yacht and performing the driving 'Devi Avere Fiducia in Me' (written by Specchia & Martini) with typical Hollies instrumentation and Allan singing in uncertain Italian. Issued as an Italian single b/w 'Non Prego Per Me' (written by Battisti & Mogol), both songs were salvaged in previously-unreleased stereo versions onto the 2011 *The Hollies: The Clarke, Hicks & Nash Years April 1963-October 1968*.

'Kill Me Quick' (Clarke, Hicks, Nash) b/w 'We're Alive' (Clarke, Hicks, Nash) (Italy only, Parlophone QMSP 16410)

Two Clarke-Hicks-Nash songs recorded at a single 22 February 1967 session, with Mitch Mitchell standing in on drums for an ill Bobby Elliott. The A-side is an up-tempo rewrite of their demo 'Bring Back Your Love to Me', adapted for the soundtrack of the Francesco Maselli-directed comedy-caper movie *Fai In Fretta Ad Uccidermi ... Ho Freddo* (*Kill Me Quick, I'm Cold*), in which Giovanna (Monica Vitti) and Franco (Jean Sorel) play lovers who con people by presenting themselves as brother and sister. The film title does not occur in the lyric. From the same soundtrack, 'We're Alive' has a warmer fast-paced harmony sound, with Allan and Graham's voices in celebration of living, 'sailing through life without a care'. Only released in Italy, the tracks were eventually gathered onto the *Thirtieth Anniversary Collection*. Both sides are also included as bonus tracks, in both mono and remastered stereo (with backing vocals) versions on the expanded 2003 Rhino *Evolution* CD reissue.

'On a Carousel' (Clarke, Nash, Hicks) b/w 'All the World Is Love' (Clarke, Nash, Hicks) (10 February 1967, Parlophone R5562)

Filmed by Granada-TV for *World in Action* footage about the music industry, this track was extracted from the album sessions and recorded at Abbey Road the same day The Beatles were recording 'Penny Lane'. It became another in a glittering run of superb pop hits. A catchy twangy rubber-band guitar sound introduces the unique storyline; Graham sings the opening lines betraying traces of Northern accent, then the voices work together like instruments to conjure a fairground atmosphere in which the girl hooks ducks out of the water, then he's moving from horse to horse on the old-fashioned fairground carousel as the guy strives to reach his love-object. There were two major UK charts at the time: in the *Record Mirror* chart, the single enters at number 34 (16 February) – number 24 on the rival *New Musical Express* chart. It climbs to a high of number 4 (16 March) – number 5 on *NME*, below 'Release Me' by Engelbert Humperdinck and that same 'Penny Lane' b/w 'Strawberry

Fields Forever' – The Beatles most highly-rated single, but the first of their run of hits not to reach number 1! The Hollies' fourteenth UK chart single, 'On a Carousel' reached number eight in Germany and Sweden, number ten in Australia and Denmark, while during May, it reached the US number 11 (Imperial 66231). Flip it over, and with eerie echoey play-in, strong bass lines and tricky drum patterns, the B-side is a trip into proto-psychedelia that would have made a collectable cult A-side for any number of *Nuggets* bands. Jangling-metallic guitars are set against woozy vocals, 'I have left my mind somewhere' sings Graham as the tempo falters, then picks up, before rising into new realms of strangeness.

The Hollies were constantly touring, from March 11 (at the Mansfield Granada) until 2 April (the Liverpool Empire), they headlined a 21-date package with The Spencer Davis Group and The Tremeloes. David Booker, who played with the Richard Kent Style on the same bill, recalls that Paul Jones, as 'Special Guest Star', closed his set by taking his shoes off – the better to perform Robert Parker's 'Barefootin''.

  Bobby Elliott suffered acute peritonitis caused by a burst appendix during a German tour, collapsing after a show: 'the guys were listening to The Beatles' latest single. I faded out to the strains of 'Strawberry Fields Forever'.' He was hospitalised in Hamburg for several weeks, with Tony Mansfield – formerly of Billy J Kramer & The Dakotas – deputising until Bobby rejoined for the 17 March date. They flew out to Singapore on 8 April to play New Zealand and Australia before a concert in Honolulu opened twenty-five days of American dates from the first until the end of May. By June, they were in Yugoslavia, and from 10 August, they commenced a ten-day Scandinavian tour.

'Carrie Anne' (Clarke, Nash, Hicks) b/w 'Signs That Will Never Change' (Clarke, Nash, Hicks) (26 May 1967, Parlophone R5602)

Another Clarke-Hicks-Nash song, which took over two years to write, and completed during TV studio rehearsals and recorded in just two takes on 1 May 1967. The cute schooldays lyrics are designed to snare airtime, with a steel drum instrumental break both novel and play-again listenable. Tony Hicks takes a verse, Graham takes a verse, Allan sings the rest. Allan writes the middle-eight, 'you're so like a woman to me'. What's your game now, can anybody play? Emphatically yes! How could it fail? It soars to a UK number 3. Then, following an American label switch, it hits a *Billboard* number 9 (Epic 10180), number 5 in Denmark and Australia, number 6 in Holland, and number 8 in Germany. The pastoral B-side, recorded 2 July 1967, makes this a value-for-money package. Seasons change, tadpoles become frogs, nature is ever-renewing; with Allan's voice well to the fore in an effectively simple arrangement, Tony and Graham add their voices to the chorus before shifting into a near false-ending instrumental fade. It would later be gathered onto their 1978 *The Other Side of the Hollies* compilation.

Evolution

Personnel:
Allan Clarke: vocals, harmonica
Graham Nash: vocals, rhythm guitar
Tony Hicks: vocals, lead guitar
Bernie Calvert: bass guitar, harpsichord on 'Ye Olde Toffee Shoppe'
Bobby Elliott: drums on 'When Your Lights Turned On', 'Have You Ever Loved
Somebody', 'Lullaby to Tim'
plus Dougie Wright, Mitch Mitchell, Clem Cattini: session drums
Elton John (as Reg Dwight): session piano on 'Water on the Brain', Hammond
organ on 'You Need Love'
Produced at EMI Studios by Ron Richards, 11 January-17 March 1967.
Released: 22 July 1967, Parlophone PMC 7022
Running time: 32:17
Highest chart position: UK: 13, US: 43

If the sixties were pop's greatest confection, 1967 was the cherry at its very
apex. The Beatles and The Rolling Stones straddled the year like gods, The
Kinks and The Who positioned just below them. Then Manfred Mann and
The Hollies were proven, seasoned beat-boomer producers of deliciously
reliable hit singles, but still growing, still developing. In America, The Byrds,
Lovin' Spoonful and The Mamas & The Papas were established, with the
enticing lure of a newer wave of Jefferson Airplane, Grateful Dead, Love and
The Doors making seismic waves. As The Searchers, Herman's Hermits and
even the Yardbirds declined, there were Pink Floyd, Traffic and Procol Harum
pointing out newer directions. A new generation with a new explanation.
People in motion.

There had been two original Hollies albums issued during 1966 – *Would
You Believe?* running to 29:26-minutes, and *For Certain Because* at 32:24. As
the pop scene reconfigures around them, convulsing into the newer, more
gaudy shapes of nuclear-warfare in a vinyl groove, there were two more albums
during 1967 – *Evolution* running to 32:17-minutes and *Butterfly* at 33:14,
a total of twenty-four new group compositions created at a hectic pace. At
first reluctant to embrace the sweet-smelling beguilement of Hip, these two
albums capitulate in no uncertain terms. The naturally abstemious Allan had
mused to *NME* that 'The Hollies are about as psychedelic as a pint of beer wi'
t' lads!', despite Graham's willing seduction – with Nash as the pot-smoking/
acid-dropping 'cat' to the other Hollies as 'five pints a night lads'. Graham
had already wandered into a Jimi Hendrix session at the Olympic studio, to
end up adding backing vocals and foot-stomp percussion to 'If Six Was Nine'
and 'You Got Me Floatin''. Then on 25 June – just 24 days after the release of
Sergeant Pepper's Lonely Hearts Club Band – Paul McCartney invited Graham
to the Abbey Road recording of the BBC-TV *Our World* global satellite livecast
performance of 'All You Need Is Love'. Singing alongside Graham and wife

Rosie, with the Four Kings Of EMI – as Monkee Micky Dolenz dubbed The Beatles – was the rock-aristocracy of Mick Jagger with Keith Richard and Marianne Faithful, plus Eric Clapton, Jane Asher and Pattie Boyd, Keith Moon and Mike 'McGear' McCartney. It was a huge Flower-Power Happening, a zeitgeist invocation to the transcendental spirit of Love-Love-Love.

Graham also monopolised attention at the *Evolution* Press launch by appearing in a full-length psychedelic yellow-patterned nightshirt with thong sandals. Alan Smith comments, 'though I can heartily recommend the album, I'm afraid the nightshirt drew most of the attention and most of the comment!' (*NME* 22 July 1967). The album was recorded over an intensive six Abbey Road days spread between 11 January to 17 March – although they were interrupted in February by Bobby Elliott's illness – with session players Clem Cattini (who had played on Joe Meek's transatlantic number one hit 'Telstar'), Dougie Wright and Hendrix drummer Mitch Mitchell standing in. Issued in a psychedelicised art cover concocted by Simon & Marijke, The Fool, using William Morris and Art Nouveau effects, *Evolution* was welcomed by *NME* reviewer Allen Evans with a special track-by-track breakdown as 'an ear and eye-opening production' (3 June 1967). It reached UK number 13 and US number 43. No one went away feeling short-changed. With American distribution switched from Imperial Records to Epic, Imperial exercises its sell-off period with additional releases so that 'product' from the two labels overlap. 'Pay You Back With Interest' on Imperial reached the US number 28, while 'Carrie Anne' hit number nine for Epic. Imperial compilation LP *The Hollies Greatest Hits* also reached US number 11.

'Then the Heartaches Begin' (Clarke, Nash, Hicks)
Sticking within the 2:41 minute limit, the fast-strum acoustic suddenly erupts into a florid gush of Tony's fuzz-tone guitar like a burst faucet, and 'a harmonica or organ which sounds like a bagpipe' (Allen Evans), as a signifier that these are new pathways for The Hollies, rising to meet the accelerating pulse; yet never once do they neglect the need for strong melody-line and compulsive harmonies.

'Stop Right There' (Clarke, Nash, Hicks)
A sweetly descending acoustic guitar figure leads into Graham's breathlessly strong lead voice, blending into dual-tracked self-harmonies and soaring scribbles of supernatural Romany violin, 'tell me what you're doing to my mind in there'. While urgently pleading for her to 'stop', the low, intimately whispered harmonies carry definite traces of West Coast exotica in its patchouli-scented breeze.

'Water on the Brain' (Clarke, Nash, Hicks)
The swaying Arabic-style rhythms and the mid-point tuba solo can't distract from the fact that this is an attractively novel song directly in The Hollies style,

about drip-drip-dripping rainwater from a broken drain keeping poor Allan awake. Recorded over two hugely productive sessions on 8 and 17 March, which also result in 'Heading for a Fall', an unknown Elton John plays piano on this one.

'Lullaby to Tim' (Clarke, Nash, Hicks)

Phasing was the magic bullet audio ingredient for 1967, limning the chorus of 'Lucy in the Sky With Diamonds' and adding a trippy swish to The Small Faces' 'Itchycoo Park'. It is achieved by running two identical tapes together, but slightly out of synch, or in-and-out-of-synch to create a fuzzy distortion. Electricity can be fun! But perhaps the decision to phase every part of Graham's vocal on this charming, surreal slide down psychedelic rainbows is a tad excessive? It 'makes you think the record player has gone wrong' grumbles Allen Evans. And which Tim is the song intended to lullaby – Tim Hardin, Tim Buckley, Tim Rose? The obvious candidate would be LSD-guru Timothy Leary, who wrote the influential book *The Politics of Ecstasy*, also hymned by The Moody Blues on their 1968 album track 'Legend of a Mind'.

'Have You Ever Loved Somebody?' (Clarke, Nash, Hicks)

On 29 September 1966, Paul & Barry Ryan enjoyed a single week at number 49 on the *Record Retailer* chart with their cover of this song. A fortnight later (13 October), The Searchers go one better by taking their superior fuzz-tone version up to number 48. It would have done better were it not for the high-rotation pirate radio-play granted the Ryans. For The Searchers, it was to be their final chart entry after an impressive run of influential singles. 'I started writing that song as I was going into Abbey Road', Allan told me. 'I thought The Searchers did a very good version of it.' The Hollies original could easily have been a bigger hit single than either of them, with immaculate harmonies driven by compulsive bass, drums and fuzz-guitar additions. As it is, it's a forceful reminder of just how powerful the regular Hollies template could be.

'You Need Love' (Clarke, Nash, Hicks)

A lovely twinkling Tony Hicks guitar figure leads into pure ultra-precise three-way Hollies harmonies on an anthemic thrash, with 'a choral effect, the vocalists shouting at times and sounding a little hysterical' (*NME*). The high harmonies are focused to a cutting knife-edge laser intensity that they'd never recapture after Graham's defection. Elton John plays Hammond organ on this one, and Dougie Wright is on drums.

'Rain on the Window' (Clarke, Nash, Hicks)

Despite their expanding ambitions, they no longer allowed indulgent space for improvisation, just a precisely scored instrumental break for horns. Nothing here exceeds singles-length; this, the longest track, clocks in at an economical

3:16. Although it seems to chronicle a planned seduction, the lyrics retain the innocence of the 'Bus Stop' encounter beneath the shared umbrella.

'Heading for a Fall' (Clarke, Nash, Hicks)

There's an oddly intriguing play-in drone, matched to a revolving music-box mid-point instrumental break, but this is never less than pure Hollies, with Allan's strong offbeat lead voice to the fore. His friends tell him that he's blind, but he's hypnotised by her beauty; her arms magnetise him even though he fears he's wasting his time. If the psychedelic clothes adopted for the cover photo seem like an unnatural fit for The Hollies, on this evidence, their musical confidence has only grown stronger.

'Ye Olde Toffee Shoppe' (Clarke, Nash, Hicks)

A twee harpsichord-effect and toy-shop instrumentation conjure the nostalgia of childhood, with noses pressed up against the shop window-pane, charming memories of cold stone streets brightened by gob-stoppers in my pocket, lollies to suck that last all day, and sugar that looks like sand. 'It develops into a pleasing gavotte' notes Allen Evans. Was there ever a real Ye Olde Toffee Shoppe? If there wasn't, perhaps inspired by The Hollies song, there are now – check them out on Google!

'When Your Lights Turned On' (Clarke, Nash, Hicks)

Attractively catchy straight-pop, and the first track to be recorded for the album; a 'leave your light burning in the window as a message' lyric delivered over fast, tight harmonies and delicious guitar figures. Traditional Hollies, perhaps, but fine-tuned and leaning into newer things. Bobby Elliott plays his Ludwig drumkit on this, as well as 'Have You Ever Loved Somebody?' and 'Lullaby to Tim', before his incapacitation.

'Leave Me' (Clarke, Nash, Hicks)

The album's penultimate track opens with a descending instrumental figure before expanding out into classic close harmonies with elongated 'pleeeeease' phrasing, and no affectations other than an organ break. She can slander his name all over the place; he no longer cares, just as long as she packs her things and gets out of his sight. Recorded on 3 March 1967 and running to 2:14, it needs no more.

'The Games We Play' (Clarke, Nash, Hicks)

A delightful return to slyly lascivious chart-friendly Hollies pop, with exceptionally well-honed songwriting skills applied to a teasing mischievously naughty lyric about their parentally-approved relationship; 'all the family get along with' her, and her mother thinks he's such a pleasant boy, but they don't know what they get up to when the two of them are alone! How long can they keep getting away with it? Will they eventually have to pay the price? 'Sometimes The Hollies lyrics really strike home at everyday teen life. Don't they? Or do they?' asks *NME*. The Hollies toured what was then Yugoslavia, where they appeared in Zagreb beneath a huge 'Hollies Love Peace' banner, and distributed flowers to the audience. They wore black armbands in sympathy with the ongoing Mick Jagger-Keith Richard drugs trial. Later, they appeared on the BBC radio's *Top Gear* (13 October 1967) to perform one song from *Evolution* – 'The Games We Play', plus 'Charlie and Fred' and 'Away Away Away' from *Butterfly* ... which were all be collected onto the *Radio Fun* compilation CD.

Related Releases

Evolution (US release. Epic LN 24315 mono, BN 26315 stereo)
The US edition: 'Carrie Anne', 'Stop Right There', 'Rain on the Window', 'Then the Heartaches Begin', 'Ye Olde Toffee Shoppe', 'You Need Love', 'Heading for a Fall', 'The Games We Play', 'Lullaby to Tim', 'Have You Ever Loved Somebody?'

'Bird Has Flown' (McDougall and Burns) b/w **'Breaking Down'** (Frame, McDougall, Struthers, Burns**) by The Societie** (Deram DM 162)
During the 1950s, the Oldsters would sagely advise young singers that 'this Rock 'n' Roll fad won't last. If you want a show-biz career, you must learn a few dance steps, tell a few gags, and get crossover appeal to the mom and dad audience.' Well, that didn't work out too well. In the 1960s, the logic was: 'your hit-making appeal won't last. If you want a career in music, you must learn to write and produce hits for other people.' Hence this echoey one-off 1967 Brit-Psych single which carries the legend 'produced by Allan Clarke for Hollies Recording Co Ltd', featuring David's McDougall and Struthers; the group later evolved into the cult Andwella. Allan went on to produce 'Meet Down the Middle' in July 1973, an echoey rocker for Liverpool group Colonel Bagshot (Polydor 2058 381).

'Annabella' (Nash, Duncan, James) b/w **'You Don't Understand Me'** (Maus) **by John Walker** (Philips BF 1593)
As a creative outlet for song ideas that wouldn't work within The Hollies spectrum, Graham Nash began co-writing with Kirk Duncan and Nicky James, penning this debut single for former Walker Brothers singer John Maus, which climbed to number 24 during July 1967. The dramatic string-laden arrangement is by Reg Guest. Duncan and James were former members of a band called The Moggs, who had functioned as backup musicians during the Walker Brothers tour.

The same Nash-Duncan-James team wrote 'Yellow Rainbow', a charming, whimsical slice of pop-psych recorded by The Piccadilly Line at the Bond

Street Studios in Autumn 1967, and issued as CBS 3595 in July 1968. Piccadilly Line was essentially the duo of Rod Edwards and Roger Hand, who produced the highly collectable LP *The Huge World of Emily Small* (CBS 63129), and although a non-album A-side single, 'Yellow Rainbow' was later included as a bonus track on the album's 2006 CD reissue (Lightning Tree Light Flash CD 004).

Meanwhile, The Mirage were a Hertfordshire-based sixties band who issued Hollies-specialty 'It's in Her Kiss' at Graham's suggestion as a 1965 single (CBS 201772), and then the L Ransford song 'Go Away', with Graham and Allan getting joint producer credits as a November 1965 single (CBS 202-007). Kirk Duncan later became a member of Mirage before joining Jawbone. He also played keyboards on Allan Clarke's solo albums *Headroom*, *Allan Clarke* and *I've Got Time*.

As well as being instrumental in signing Elton John to Dick James Music, Nicky James was recruited to the Moody Blues label Threshold as a solo artist. He also later co-wrote with Allan Clarke.

Butterfly

Personnel:
Allan Clarke: vocals, harmonica
Graham Nash: vocals, rhythm guitar, harmonium on 'Dear Eloise'
Tony Hicks: vocals, lead guitar, electric sitar on 'Maker'
Bobby Elliott: drums
Bernie Calvert: bass guitar, keyboards
plus Johnny Scott: strings and brass arrangements
Produced at EMI Studios by Ron Richards, 1 August-6 October 1967.
Released: 23 November 1967, Parlophone PMC 7039
Running time: 33:14
No chart placing.

The Hollies began recording the LP at the start of August, through to 6 October at Abbey Road Studios, with typically precise production tidying-up from Ron Richards. 1967 was the year of some of the greatest, most iconic albums in the history of Rock, and both that year's Hollies sets were caught up in the surging lysergic post-*Sgt Pepper* Summer of Love euphoria, elements that expand not only minds but the scope and ambitions of the music. Initially wary of the more trendy aspects of the new hip, this album, issued November 1967, not only dabbles in lysergic territory, but fully embraces it.

Interspersed during the recordings, theyed play Swedish dates, including the Folkets Park, Vänersborg (23 August), where Allan was favourably impressed by the audience, who listened politely to the performance, then applaud enthusiastically after each song – in contrast to the wall of screams they play to in the UK. He explained to journalist Alan Smith: 'there was a time when we loved screaming. Now we get a tremendous kick out of trying new sounds on stage, or achieving the depth we're trying for on our records.' (*NME*, 7 October 1967.) Although the group – other than Graham – had a somewhat ambivalent attitude to Britpsych, it's Allan who contributed the giddy 'I'm so high' astral projection mind excursion that is 'Elevated Observations', and Tony Hicks is the motivating force behind 'Pegasus'. When all these elements come together, they could be breathtaking, with the wonderfully strange 'Dear Eloise' spun-off to become a US singles hit. In *Record Collector* magazine's *100 Greatest Psychedelic Records* (Diamond Publ, 2005), David Wells says *Butterfly* 'remains by far their most adventurous studio album, described by one pundit as 'a Northern England counterpart to (The Zombies) *Odyssey and Oracle*.' And for The Hollies, it was a career peak and a breakpoint.

'Dear Eloise' (Clarke, Nash, Hicks)

Recorded 26 September, at the same session as 'Elevated Observations', the track – and the album – is introduced by Graham on harmonium. The song then slides into vocal distortion, a Bobby Elliott one-two-three count-in, and an epistolary lyric in the form of a letter. It breaks into urgent group harmonies before winding back down, bookending into a closing Graham-with-harmonium fade. Written predominantly by Allan in 'about twenty minutes' while waiting to go into a meeting at EMI's head office, this superb track is rightly regarded as one of The Hollies' finest moments.

'Away Away Away' (Clarke, Nash, Hicks)

Lured in by Pied Piper dancing woodwind and Johnny Scott baroque string twiddles, this escapist fantasy of dragging your feet in the edge of the sea, swirls as light as clouds in sunshine. 'We are walking hand-in-hand, throwing a shell across the sand.' Written mainly by Graham in a more playful mood, both stereo and mono mixes are similar, although the orchestral overdubs are a little more prominent in the mono mix version.

'Maker' (Clarke, Nash, Hicks)

Plunging fully into wonderfully preposterous psychedelic phantasia, kitted out with rippling sitar and tabla percussion, 'days of yellow saffron, nights with purple skies', giant moths flitter hither thither and yon as the moon hides beneath the sea. The vague pantheist spiritual overtones of the 'maker' seem to suggest this as Graham's experience of tripping, while the swaying melody stays unmistakably Hollies. The sitar that Tony plays is, according to an oft-repeated tale, one left in the studio by George Harrison. Far out! There are inconsistencies within the different editions. The original UK mono mix has a longer intro and outro, outlasting the stereo version by nearly thirty seconds, while the US mix omits the sitar intro but leaves the longer ending from the mono version – but in stereo.

'Pegasus' (Clarke, Nash, Hicks)

Tony Hicks takes his first full vocal on what is largely his own composition, a thrilling mélange of celestial harmonies and reverse-tapes; his unforced voice invests the track with an air of childlike wonder as he invites the listener on a flight into fantasy to far-away lands on the wings of the mythological flying horse. Follow me follow, see what you see; it's a charming journey that closes in a breathy horse's whinny. With attention focused on the Lennon-McCartney sibling-rivalry behind the Allan-Graham axis, it's often overlooked that Tony is more than just The Hollies' George Harrison. Studio engineer Ken Townsend recalls, 'Tony Hicks was musically the strongest Hollie and, without doubt, he led the band in the studio.' When people speak with awe about classic sixties guitarists, they mention Eric Clapton, Jeff Beck, Peter Green, Jimmy Page but seldom Tony Hicks. Yet, although underestimated, his solos were always concise and economical, never flashy or self-indulgent, and always the perfect fill for the track. He was also the third angle of the L Ransford triangle. And as other voices have come and gone, he and Bobby Elliott have provided The Hollies' unifying core continuity. For Bobby, 'I can be criticised by (jazz drummer) Kenny Clare, who I think is the greatest drummer in England,

and appreciate it, but I don't like being criticised by someone who's not an authority and doesn't know what he's talking about.'

'Would You Believe?' (Clarke, Nash, Hicks)
Nothing to do with the earlier album of the same name; this is a stately stand-out Allan showcase, slow-paced with soulful depth emphasised by the sympathetic orchestral scoring. They seldom got better than this. David Wells commends its 'surging backward strings and church bells collision' in his *Record Collector: 100 Greatest Psychedelic Records*. Allan would re-record this ode to his wife, Jennifer, on his 1973 solo album *Headroom*.

'Wishyouawish' (Clarke, Nash, Hicks)
Recorded 5 September 1967, this is one of Graham's bouncier oddities, with 'Mellow Yellow' horns, a sunshine Lovin' Spoonful vibe, and a strange 'closed' vocal effect achieved by Graham singing with a bin over his head – although Tony, who barely considered this song strong enough to release, was less than enthusiastic. The mono mix features birdsong which the stereo mix doesn't, but by way of compensation, the stereo mix features more sound effects throughout the song – such as pouring water, which the mono mix omits. Why the clean, no effects version made it onto the *Dear Eloise/King Midas in Reverse* edition is not clear. The Hollies perform the song on a *Saturday Club* appearance.

'Postcard' (Clarke, Nash, Hicks)
With the sound of gulls and tide lapping on the beach, this is a 'wish you were here' message written by Graham during the trip to Marrakesh, during which he also wrote 'Marrakesh Express', 'Lady of the Island', 'Southern Cross' and 'Sleep Song'. The version included on the *Dear Eloise/King Midas in Reverse* edition loses the gulls and the tide, but speeds it up, as though someone at Epic had decided it was too slow!

'Charlie and Fred' (Clarke, Nash, Hicks)
Steptoe and Son was a popular BBC-TV sit-com about two down-at-heel Rag-&-Bone men. This song, written by Graham and Allan, tells the poignant story of Charlie the Ragman and his horse – with gorgeous acapella harmonies at the tragic end, and a rhyme that suggests but cleverly avoids the last line, 'Charlie is dead'! Again, the American *Dear Eloise/King Midas in Reverse* LP is short-changed by using a different stereo mix that excludes the whistling and clip-clop sound effects.

'Try It' (Clarke, Nash, Hicks)
Travelling the astral plane to a place that has no time, with audibly different mono and stereo mixes but the same trippy reverse-tape invitation.

Amazingly, this far-out trippy slice of psychedelia was actually written by Allan. What is it we are being asked to try? Answers on a tab of blotting paper, please. Supposedly, Allan was heavily into Astral Projection at the time. It's cosmic, with a stoned 'it's beautiful' refrain and head-ripping effects but it is a catchy tune as well. Because, even at their most freaky, The Hollies never omit the catchy tune. The mono mix has effects coming in at different times as well as a rough intro-fade, putting it on the offbeat. The stereo mix is better, while a rare early alternate version was issued as the Australian 'Jennifer Eccles' B-side, featuring the identical backing track with different vocals and no sound effects.

'Elevated Observations?' (Clarke, Nash, Hicks)
Selected as the US B-side of the single 'Do the Best You Can', this is another giddy psychedelic mind-excursion, strangely enough, again, written by Allan ('that was my idea, based on my interest in astral projection'), although Graham helped him complete it with the trendy 'ego is dead' refrain. From the top of the hill, he's high enough to touch the sky, with whirring wind effects and an accelerating vocal line to add strangeness. The German version of the LP (Hansa 77133-IT) features a rare 'double' version of the track running to 4:58; as it finishes, it starts again, but the repeat play doesn't speed up, and there are no wind effects.

'Step Inside' (Clarke, Nash, Hicks)
Anticipating the album sessions, there was an early never-released run-through of this song – the only true Clarke-Hicks-Nash composition on the album, recorded on 3 March 1967 with drummer Clem Cattini. 'Step Inside' is a warm, affectionate piece of working-class Manchester, catching something of the Graham Gouldman common touch, and bursting with harmonies from start to finish. 'You don't need an invitation, if you feel the inclination, you just come on speculation.'

'Butterfly' (Clarke, Nash, Hicks)
With neo-classical shimmers of twiddly orchestration, Graham's swansong makes a suitably touching closing track. An exercise in solo composition and voice, a departure from just about anything The Hollies had yet recorded, he draws on the psychedelic imagery of candy-floss snow and lemonade lake to create a genuinely effective pastoral idyll. Performed live at the Lewisham Odeon (4 May 1968), Graham introduces it as 'a little fairy story from the album'. During their 1968 American tour, The Hollies used the stereo orchestral session backing tape in order to perform it live. The stereo and mono mixes feature different attempts at adding reverb over the song's last line – 'me and my true love will never grow old,' while the track, like the sentiment, contains a timeless truth.

Yet the album failed to impress record-buyers, overwhelmed by other freakier competition. Commercially it sank to the bottom of its very own lemonade lake, and after this moment, The Hollies would never be quite the same again. There were still great anthemic hits to come, including some of their most recognised and celebrated tracks. But the momentum of their growth and evolution as a group over the years since '(Ain't That) Just Like Me', and their growing confidence in the studio and as songwriters reached a peak on these two 1967 albums. That process would not continue. Instead, there would be other directions to explore, other pathways to follow.

Related Releases
Dear Eloise/King Midas in Reverse (US release. 27 November 1967, Epic Records LN 24344)
The renamed US edition, with: 'Dear Eloise', 'Wishyouawish', 'Charlie and Fred', 'Butterfly', 'Leave Me', 'Postcard', 'King Midas in Reverse', 'Would You Believe?', 'Away Away Away', 'Maker', 'Step Inside'.

'King Midas in Reverse' (Clarke, Nash, Hicks) b/w 'Everything Is Sunshine' (Clarke, Nash. Hicks) (22 September 1967, Parlophone R5637)
This should have been The Hollies most gilded achievement, their crowning moment. It's an awesome record to stand with the very best of the era's greatest singles. Like 'Pegasus', it draws on Greek mythology, the legend of Phrygian King Midas, cursed that everything he touches turns to gold. It was chiefly written by Graham Nash; 'I remember sitting down with Graham to work on it, but not to the extent that he did', recalls Allan, 'it was his idea with my ideas inside it. Graham was the one who said, let's have an orchestra and get Johnny Scott in to do the score.' The song reverses the Midas curse so that everything he touches turns to dust. It was recorded on 3 August 1967, when the backing track was laid down and vocals added. The drum fills effect was achieved by speeding the tape to record them so that on playback, they appear deeper in pitch, sounding more like timpani. The Hollies performed 'King Midas in Reverse' on the BBC radio *Top Gear* show, introduced by Brian Matthew, on which it can be heard overdubbed as it would have been done live in the studio without the tape varispeed effect. Johnny Scott's towering baroque orchestration was overlaid later, adding to the lavish production but never overshadowing the strength of song or vocals.

Record labels frequently add the inappropriate saccharine of strings in the mistaken belief that it softens raw edges and as a bribe to make the record more radio-friendly – such as Donovan's 'Catch the Wind' or Tim Hardin's 'Hang Onto a Dream'. Among the few examples of integral orchestration, George Martin's scoring for The Beatles 'A Day in a Life' ... and this Hollies record. 'The level of intelligence and ambition evinced by 'King Midas in

Reverse' made it nothing less than a benchmark release', says David Wells,
yet, released in defiance of producer Ron Richards' advice, it reached the UK
number 18 in October and US number 51. Generally regarded as a chart-failure
at the time, a stigma that precipitated Graham's departure from the group,
to hop aboard the Marrakesh Express for more exotic climes; it must be with
some sense of vindication that it is now rightly considered The Hollies' artistic
zenith, and a British psychedelic classic. 'Yes, I always loved that track, y'know',
Graham tells me. 'And yes, it was an interesting point because so far, we had
all moved our energies towards that point, and we saw that that record was
an important record – not to over-blow things. We knew that it was something
different for us. And I think it's remained a favourite – certainly, of mine, since
the day we cut it.' The track was later remastered and collected onto *The
Hollies at Abbey Road 1966-1970* (1998, EMI 4934502). The Clarke/Hicks/Nash
B-side – recorded over two sessions 3 August and 5 September 1967, adds
cotton-candy spun harpsichord on a summery-bright fly-away everything is
sunshine 'when you hold my hand' lyric.

'Dear Eloise' (Clarke, Nash, Hicks) b/w 'When Your Lights Turned On' (Clarke, Nash, Hicks) (Epic 5-10251)

Issued as a US December 1967 single, backed by the *Evolution* track, to tie in
with their American tour, by January, it was listed as 'bubbling under' and then
reached number 50. It's during this tour that Graham Nash met David Crosby
in Los Angeles and made waves. The single did better in Germany and Holland,
where it reached number 8.

1968

'Wings' (Clarke, Nash)

Although recorded during January 1968, this song was held over and released as part of the eco-charity LP *No-One's Gonna Change Our World* (December 1969, Regal Starline SRS5013) for the World Wildlife Fund, compiled by comedian Spike Milligan with other contributions from The Beatles ('Across the Universe'), Bee Gees ('Marley Purt Drive') and Spike himself ('Ning Nang Nong' and 'Cuddly Old Koala'). There's a slow delicacy and Graham's highest falsetto to this Allan-Graham song – 'why do they want us to walk, when we can fly', which Graham later attributes to the influence of Buffalo Springfield's Neil Young song 'Expecting To Fly'. Extending into 2 April 1968, new sessions commenced towards the next Hollies album, trying out Graham's 'Marrakesh Express', most of which was not used, or left unfinished, although the instrumental backing track for 'Marrakesh Express' exists.

'Jennifer Eccles' (Clarke, Nash) b/w 'Open Up Your Eyes' (Clarke, Hicks, Nash) (22 March 1968, Parlophone R5680)

'I haven't yet heard a bad record by The Hollies, and this maintains the group's standards' enthused the *NME* singles reviewer. To follow the perceived failure of the ambitious 'King Midas in Reverse', a great deal was at stake. They needed a hit. So they wrote a hit. Leaving nothing to chance, the Clarke-Nash team deliver another of The Hollies Perfect Pop confections. There are schoolyard rhymes, a bubblegum la-la-la chorus, and cute wolf-whistle guitar effect (which Steve Miller would later use on his 'The Joker'). Tony Hicks plays it live, but it is supplied by Rod King's pedal steel in the studio, to create what *NME* calls 'a very commercial number that's heavily laden with gimmicks'. Jennifer was the name of Allan's wife, while Graham's wife was Rose née Eccles.

The return to straight pop promptly rewards The Hollies with a top ten hit, at UK number seven (number five on *NME* 27 April 1968), number four in Sweden, number eight in Germany and top twenty in Holland and Australia. The Clarke/Hicks/Nash B-side is smiley sunshine pop with Tony's banjo-effect instrumental break, and maybe a sly glance back at Jennifer with 'schoolgirl in pigtails with freckly nose, trying to remember her Latin prose'. The 2:47 track is eventually collected onto the *Rarities* album, which comments that 'it highlights two of the band's 1967-1968 lyrical preoccupations, world peace and schoolgirls'. In May, 'Jennifer Eccles' made the US number 40 (Epic 10298), with a different B-side, 'Try It', lifted from *Butterfly*. The Hollies appeared on the BBC radio *David Symonds Show* (25 March 1968), promoting 'Jennifer Eccles' while also performing 'Wings' and 'Step Inside' – the three tracks later collected onto the *Radio Fun* compilation. During May, The Hollies toured (assisted by Road Managers Rod Shields and electrical engineer Derek Whyment) with Paul Jones and The Mike Vickers Orchestra. The Scaffold were also on the bill, and Graham later added guest vocals to their 'Lily the Pink', which references 'Jennifer Eccles had terrible freckles'. Issued in November 1968, Scaffold's novelty hit was number 1 throughout the month of December.

The Hollies Greatest (20 August 1968, Parlophone PMC/ PCS 7057) Highest chart position: UK: 1

After the hectic two-albums-a-year productivity of 1966 and 1967, 1968 saw something of a confusing change of pace. Following legal proceedings that proved serious financial mismanagement, Michael Cohen was ousted as Hollies manager by promoter Robin 'Robbo' Britten. Around the same period – January 1968 – Ron Richards had gone into partnership with George Martin, Peter Sullivan and John Burgess to form their own breakaway, AIR (Associated Independent Records), a London production team created to more accurately reflect the significance of their input. A 24 May concert at London's Lewisham Odeon was recorded by EMI for a live LP that never happened, although a sequence of tracks (including 'Stop Stop Stop', 'Look Through Any Window' and 'The Times They Are A-Changin'') were eventually included as part of the excellent 2011 6CD box-set *The Hollies: Clarke, Hicks and Nash Years*. In July, The Hollies management announced that Graham Nash and Bernie Calvert were both planning solo albums, while rumours were already circulating that Graham was due to quit. By August, The Hollies were playing a UK cabaret season, promptly ditching the rainbow raiments they'd worn for the *Evolution* and *Butterfly* promo photo-sessions in favour of matching suits, and including songs such as 'Puff (the Magic Dragon)' and Roger Miller's 'Dang Me'.

To fill the gap, this compilation was issued in August, gathering all the singles recorded during what must now be termed the 'Graham Nash' period. For Hollieastes, only the stereo version of 'Yes I Will' differs from the 1965 single, with a different introduction and a distinctively different Tony Hicks guitar break, in a version lifted from a previously unreleased 1964 session – the result of an EMI administrative error not picked up until after the album's release. It spends twenty-seven weeks on the album chart, and by October, it topped the UK chart for seven straight weeks, The Hollies' only number 1 album. Ironically, in the year's end *NME* poll, The Hollies are placed second only to The Beatles in the Best British Vocal Group list.

The full tracklisting is: 'I Can't Let Go', 'Bus Stop', 'We're Through', 'Carrie Anne', 'Here I Go Again', 'King Midas in Reverse', 'Yes I Will' (alternate version recorded 15 December 1964), 'I'm Alive', 'Just One Look' (with The Hollies now hot in America, Imperial belatedly reissue 'Just One Look' just one more time in October 1967, a wise decision as it reached US number 44, outscoring four of the next five Epic releases), 'On a Carousel', 'Stay', 'Look Through Any Window', 'Stop, Stop, Stop', 'Jennifer Eccles'

'Listen to Me' (Tony Hazzard) b/w **'Do the Best You Can'** (Clarke, Nash, Hicks) (27 September 1968, Parlophone R5733)
Driven by a morse-code guitar figure; although it only makes UK number 11, it climbs to number 7 on the *NME* chart (26 October 1968), number 4 in Denmark, number 7 in Holland and number 13 in Germany. Writer Tony Hazzard tells me, 'It was the last song they recorded with Graham Nash. 'Listen to Me' was originally called 'You Didn't Care About Love', but the publisher thought the repeated phrase should be the title. I already knew there was a Buddy Holly song of the same name. I was with them at EMI Studios (later Abbey Road) when they were doing it. I was there with them and played them another song that Graham liked. He was the most enthusiastic and expressed the hope that we might have a relationship like they'd had with Graham Gouldman. But it didn't happen. Graham left and that was that. I used to be friendly with Tony Hicks and he offered to play his guitar part on my own album version of 'Listen to Me'. We met a few years ago when they were in Cornwall, now a virtually new band. The new chaps I'd never met were really friendly. I never met Bobby Elliot.'

Nicky Hopkins played piano at the session, while the B-side – one of the last Clarke-Nash-Hicks compositions to appear on a Hollies record, was flipped as the US A-side. The 2:46 long 'Do The Best You Can' reached number 93 on its solitary top hundred appearance, although it did better in the Netherlands, where it climbed to number five. Driven by banjo and Allan's harmonica break, Graham took a solo vocal spot before the aspirational three-way harmony chorus. Performed live in Split in 1968 – now Croatia, then still part of Yugoslavia – Allan told the audience, 'this one has a lot of messages in it, so listen to the words'.

1969 – Terry Sylvester replaces Graham Nash
Hollies Sing Dylan

Personnel:
Allan Clarke: vocals, harmonica
Terry Sylvester: vocals, rhythm guitar
Tony Hicks: vocals, lead guitar, banjo
Bobby Elliott: drums, percussion
Bernie Calvert: bass guitar, piano, organ
plus Lew Warburton: string arrangements, except 'Blowin' in the Wind'
Mike Vickers: string arrangement and conductor on 'Blowin' in the Wind'
Produced at EMI Studios by Ron Richards, 14 August 1968-4 March 1969.
All songs written by Bob Dylan unless stated
Released: May 1969, Parlophone PMC 7078
Running time: 36:07
Highest chart position: UK: 3

This is the album that tore The Hollies apart. Was it worth the pain? Tony Hicks' proposal to record a Bob Dylan tribute LP finally provoked Graham Nash to announce he was quitting the group, although – as he admits in his *Wild Tales* autobiography – he couldn't bring himself to tell Allan face-to-face. The high-flying artist versus prosaic Beat-group dichotomy was already clearly defined. 'The reason I left The Hollies was simply that I was smoking a lot of dope, and they weren't. It was as simple as that,' he jokes. But this ill-advised album of what Graham considered jauntily trivialised Dylan songs, was the final decider. 'Our pushing ahead with the (Dylan) project helped Graham to make his decision to split', writes Bobby Elliott on the sleeve notes.

Graham's final appearance with The Hollies was at an 8 December 'Save Rave' charity concert at the London Palladium. After the January 1969 auditions, Allan confided to *Melody Maker*, 'we were supposed to have gone through about nine-hundred applicants, but it was only about thirty really' (9 March 1974). Singer/guitarist Terry Sylvester was drafted in as replacement, which he says was 'the happiest day in my life'. He was signed by Hollies manager Robin Britten and was newly outfitted on a spree with Tony. Born in the Allerton area of Liverpool, he'd formed The Escorts and recorded 'Dizzy Miss Lizzy' with them in 1964, then went on to join The Swingin' Blue Jeans in February 1966, replacing Ralph Ellis, though sometime after the group's brief span of hits. Their 'Hippy Hippy Shake' had been in the same January 1964 UK top ten as The Hollies 'Stay'. Terry did play on The Swingin' Blue Jeans' later single 'Rumors, Gossip, Words Untrue' b/w 'Now That Summer's Gone' (1966, HMV POP 1564), running a knife across the guitar strings to achieve a slide effect.

Announced to the press on 16 January 1969, Terry debuted with February sessions for the 'Sorry Suzanne' single, and played his first gigs as a Hollies member at Cardiff University and Swansea (12 and 13 February), while Abbey Road sessions for the Bob Dylan project commenced 14 August 1968 to 4 March 1969. They selected a curious mix of known familiar titles, leavened with a few lesser-known 'Basement Tapes' songs, well-intentioned, but none of them imaginatively reworked in a positive way. And yes, commercially, it did work – it reached a UK album-chart number 3 – although artistically, as Graham argued, it was not enough just to tribute Dylan; the best way to acknowledge influence is by emulating it, by taking it further, as 'King Midas in Reverse' exploits the lyrical-poetic freedoms that Dylan had instigated. The Epic US release was retitled *Words and Music by Bob Dylan*, but retained an identical tracklisting. When a 2005 CD reissue added two bonus track versions of 'Blowin' in the Wind' – a Graham Nash studio take (14 and 15 August 1968 issued as a German B-side) and a live performance – plus a live 'The Times They Are A-Changin'' also with Graham (24 May 1968 at the Lewisham Odeon), critic Patrick Humphries called it 'a period piece' that erred 'towards the jaunty rather than reverential' (*Vox* magazine). *Q* called the album 'famously ill-advised'.

'When the Ship Comes In'

Written in August 1963 and included on Dylan's *The Times They Are A-Changin'* album in 1964, it became the lead track on Peter, Paul & Mary's fourth studio album *A Song Will Rise,* in 1965. Allan's sharp, clear lead vocals stand out over an almost novelty up-tempo cantering instrumentation, with Tony on banjo, Bernie Calvert on piano, and vaudeville percussion effects. There would be further interpretations of the song, slow and reflective by Arlo Guthrie, and a swirling version by The Pogues.

'I'll Be Your Baby Tonight'

'We picked this one for the catchy phrasing', Tony Hicks told a *NME* review feature. Allan's harmonica leads into an easy slow-paced take on Dylan's romantic *Nashville Skyline* song of lush seduction, with tight shrill harmony chorus voices. But as a word of warning, Engelbert Humperdinck also recorded the song. 'The Hollies simply drown the song in syrup. Hideous.' said Bob Edmands (*NME*, 23 September 1978).

'I Want You'

Dylan's catchy 1966 hit single is given an inconsequential swing. The original was number 16 on 11 August, the same week The Hollies 'Bus Stop' slipped from number 19 to number 26. It makes a pleasant but hardly vital addition to The Hollies catalogue, with guitar replicating Al Kooper's intoxicating organ riff. 'Allan, singing in a cracked voice, tries, very tongue-in-cheek, to sound like Dylan' says the *NME*, which, if that's really Allan's intention, is surely to miss the point entirely?

'This Wheel's on Fire' (Dylan, Danko)

Written by Dylan with Rick Danko of The Band, already familiar from the charting Brian Auger-Julie Driscoll version, and later done by The Byrds, this is one of the album's better interpretations with a driving chorus repetition of the title, building into a rousing climax. 'The thing to listen out for on this one,' suggests Tony, 'are Bernie's fine organ playing and Bobby doing his nut on the drums. There's a great sustained effort near the end, which is very fast and very difficult.'

'I Shall Be Released'

An acoustic setting of Dylan's yearning, visionary song originally issued by The Band on their *Music From Big Pink* (1968) debut, with Allan's strong vocal catching its gospel-flavoured spirituality, broken by a rippling midpoint guitar solo, and Tony's sitar-effect in the instrumental fade. Dylan's lyrics are seldom straightforward, with most academic opinion interpreting this as a use of prison incarceration as a metaphor for redemption. Inevitably there was a spread of other versions, including one by The Tremeloes.

'Blowin' in the Wind'

When Peter, Paul & Mary took this song into global consciousness, it constituted Dylan's major breakthrough as a writer, becoming his enduring 'Imagine' anthem, and was the ignition point for the entire Folk-Protest boom. Covered by everyone from movie-diva Marlene Dietrich to Stevie Wonder's Motown treatment, what can The Hollies possibly add? They'd already featured it as part of their live set, including their December date at the London Palladium. Allan's solo pleading opening leads into easy-paced swing-along harmonies, sweetened by horn and string arrangements by Manfred Mann's Mike Vickers. It's pleasing enough but hardly essential. Nevertheless, when issued as a single, it reached number nine in Holland.

'Quit Your Low Down Ways'

Spattered with Biblical references, Dylan adapts the song from 'Milkcow Blues' as part of the early pirated acetates eventually issued as *The Bootleg Series Vol.9: The Witmark Demos: 1962-1964*. As Tony explained, 'Bob Dylan wrote some great songs, but they sounded unfinished.' Bobby Elliott describes their approach as 'we treated his recordings as demos and arranged them in our own distinctive way'. This track is a fairly radical example of that approach, with Dylan's raw yodelling demo varnished by their fast gospel-dynamism, a contrast from primitive country blues into flawless blemish-free Pop.

'Just Like a Woman'

The song feeds in with Bernie's church organ, embellished with a horn-arrangement by Lou Warburton, who also does 'My Back Pages' and 'Mighty Quinn'. There's an appealing edge to the harmonies – 'with her fog, her amphetamine and her pearls' – that adds little to Mike D'Abo's debut hit version as Manfred Mann vocalist, although The Hollies do incorporate the verse that The Manfreds omit. Dylan songs have been scrutinised for fragments of meaning, with suggestions that this narrative concerns doomed Warhol-Superstar Edie Sedgwick or just possibly Joan Baez.

'The Times They Are A-Changin''
Bob Dylan's first charting UK single, reaching number nine on 10 April 1965, CBS records advertising him clumsily as 'The New Cult Leader'. The Hollies interpret it in a fairly straightforward way, capturing none of the dramatic impatience to tear down the old order in the face of new social urgencies. But 'listen to that ending' Tony raves to *NME*, 'that's Bernie freaking out on the organ. What a climax! Yes, I like that one.' A live version recorded at the Lewisham Odeon in South London was later included on the *Rarities* album, where the sleeve-notes call it 'short on subtlety but high on power. And Allan Clarke's Dylanesque drawl makes for an interesting comparison with Graham Nash's unashamedly Mancunian vocal delivery.' The Byrds had already performed their jingle-jangle magic on the song on their debut album.

'All I Really Want To Do'
Dylan tosses out a thesaurus-ransacking splurge of internal rhyme on a playful throwaway item from *Another Side of Bob Dylan* (1964). The Hollies add the kind of steel drum break that might have been leftover from 'Carrie Anne' and a shift from three-four time to four-four. For the UK charts, this was The Byrds' follow-up to number 1 'Mr Tambourine Man', although they were beaten in the USA by a Cher cover. For The Hollies, this is another missed opportunity.

'My Back Pages'
Good and bad, critics define these terms quite clear, no doubt, somehow. And there's a spellbindingly peerless Byrds version on their *Younger Than Yesterday* album. Allan uses ideas as their maps, even when following a lead set more emphatically by others, his clear diction matched to the Hicks and Terry Sylvester harmonies makes for pleasant listening. It's 3:02 minutes, to which Lou Warburton donates dancing strings to the instrumental break. It seems churlish to complain that it could be more.

'Mighty Quinn'
Already a chart-topper for Manfred Mann, this is a song taken from Dylan's then still-bootleg 'Basement Tapes'. And at its basement level, The Hollies harmony-brand was by now a distinctive entity in its own right, capable of being grafted onto a wide range of mood and material, yet curiously they set the controls for a low-key easy-listening cabaret swing. Tony does his banjo-tuning, smooth horns ooze around the chorus, while Allan seems to be offering

a song-and-dance option. 'To me, it conjures the American brass band' suggests Tony, 'playing as the young men go off to war. It's a real foot-tapper, but quite sad in its own way.' Fun was had by all concerned.

Related Releases
Crosby, Stills And Nash (Atlantic 916-059)
Also issued on 29 May 1969, the debut album by Graham's new band became a number 6 *Billboard* success that subsequently qualified as quadruple-platinum. It leads off with the song The Hollies had rejected when Graham brought it into the studio, 'Marrakesh Express', the American charting single (number 28). As a perceptive journalist points out, 'Nash knew which side of the barricades he was on; The Hollies didn't even realise there were any barricades' (*Record Collector* number 168, August 1993). Meanwhile, in October 1969, The Hollies guest on UK TVs *The Bobbie Gentry Show*, singing several uncharacteristic country-flavoured songs.

'Suite: Judy Blue Eyes' (Stills), 'Marrakesh Express' (Nash), 'Guinevere' (Crosby), 'You Don't Have To Cry' (Stills), 'Pre-Road Downs' (Nash), 'Wooden Ships' (Crosby, Stills, Kantner), 'Lady of the Island' (Nash), 'Helplessly Hoping' (Stills), 'Long Time Gone' (Crosby), '49 Bye-Byes' (Stills)

The second set – *Déjà Vu* (March 1970, Atlantic 3190-002) – had Neil Young added to the line-up. Brian Southall's 2015 book *The Hollies Story* (Red Planet) is a largely utilitarian retelling of the group's biography, but he draws a very perceptive point about the newly reconstituted Hollies embarking on yet another European jaunt of Belgium, Switzerland, France, Denmark, Finland and Norway, while Graham played to an audience of 450,000 at Three Days That Defined a Generation, and CSN&Y played their second concert as a four-piece at the Woodstock Festival on 18 August 1969. The contrast provides the perfect illustration of their divergent paths, and clear justification for Graham's decision. *Déjà Vu* includes Graham's 'Our House' and 'Teach Your Children', and went on to sell eight million copies. By the time of the live double set *Four Way Street* (April 1971), they'd become the biggest band in America, with impeccably hip credentials. Graham does a moving solo acoustic 'King Midas in Reverse' as a bonus track on the June 1992 expanded CD reissue. Their continuing solo, duo, trio and group albums demand a separate book to recount the full history. They figure only incidentally in this ongoing story, until Graham decides to drop back into The Hollies again!

'Sorry Suzanne' (Macaulay, Stephens) b/w 'Not That Way At All' (Allan Clarke)
Personnel:
Allan Clarke: vocals, harmonica
Terry Sylvester: vocals, guitar

Tony Hicks: vocals, lead guitar
Bobby Elliott: drums
Bernie Calvert: bass guitar, keyboards
Produced at EMI Studios by Ron Richards, 27-28 January 1969.
Released: 28 February 1969, Parlophone R 5765
Running time: 3:34

Written by a pro songwriting team, 'a dull demo by Tony Macaulay and Geoff Stephens was transformed by our arranging skills into another Hollies chart-topper' (according to Bobby Elliott). Produced by Ron Richards, this has everything you expect from a Hollies single, and nothing that you don't – appealingly regretful harmonies, tidy guitar solo – although there's a definite impression that this is a group marking time with a 'business as usual' placeholder hit. Yet this is the record that saved The Hollies. 'When Graham finally broke the news that he was leaving The Hollies, I thought it was the end for us,' recalls Allan, 'I was totally unproductive for weeks'. He considered his future options until Terry arrived and 'he fitted in perfectly. If anything, the group's harmony is softer now.' With Terry singing the top line alongside Allan and Tony, that's undeniably true; If softness is what you require from The Hollies. Which is not necessarily so. Wasn't it the energy of that raw shrillness that had made the earlier hits so distinctive? Maybe the change forced upon the group was an opportunity to mature the sound? To reach more adult audiences who no longer wanted in-your-ears confrontation? To evolve it away from teen orientation to a newer more sophisticated level?

So The Hollies continued as durable consummate professionals, with an enduring mastery of tuneful harmony-rock and even bigger career-defining successes. They performed 'Sorry Suzanne' on TVs *Dee Time* chat-show, fronted by amiable former Radio Caroline DJ Simon Dee, and yet again on *Top of the Pops*, wearing clean white suits with dark ties, Bobby Elliott in his trademark fedora hat (the same outfits they wore for the *Hollies Sing Dylan* album photo taken by Bob Richards). In April, the single hits UK number 3, issued on 5 April in the US As Epic 5-10454, it stalls at Billboard number 56 (May 31 1969) but hits number 4 in Holland and Sweden, number 7 in Germany and number 12 in Australia. The B-side, recorded the same day (28 January), is a wistful look back at childhood memories, with a rocking horse and a thousand tin soldiers at your command. Written by Allan, it starts off with cleverly-constructed acoustic interplay, with some strange effects feeding into the instrumental break. With such strong original material, the album of covers seems even more unnecessary. The lyric poses the apt question, where we go, no-one knows...

Hollies Sing Hollies

Personnel:
Allan Clarke: vocals, harmonica
Terry Sylvester: vocals, guitar
Tony Hicks: vocals, lead guitar
Bobby Elliott: drums
Bernie Calvert: bass guitar, keyboards
Produced at EMI Studios by Ron Richards, 23 June-10 October 1969
Released: November 1969, Parlophone PCS 7092
Running time: 38:19. No chart placing.

Their ninth UK studio album was released just six months after the 'Bob Dylan' covers set. It didn't chart, despite fulsome praise from a *New Musical Express* feature. 'The moods are many and its listenability is high. And it's an album that, for me, sums up what creative but commercial Pop music is all about.' The line-up has stabilized as Allan Clarke (vocals, harmonica), Tony Hicks (lead guitar and vocals), Terry Sylvester (guitar and vocals), Bernie Calvert (bass and keyboards) and Bobby Elliott (drums). Although all of the tracks are group originals, the various combination of writer credits showed the group's democratic base. As sessions continued for the LP during two Abbey Road Studio Two stints on 25 June and 7 August, they also recorded 'He Ain't Heavy, He's My Brother', with Elton John playing the piano.

'Why Didn't You Believe?' (Sylvester, Clarke)
A vehement Allan with attitude over slow-paced walking drums: 'I'm sick and tired of this old world, there's so many religions to believe in.' It up-switches into frantic double-quick *Jesus Christ Superstar* gospel-chant with high fuzz-guitar, before reverting to slow but accelerating pace. A first writing contribution from Terry, written with Allan after they'd taken their duty-free fags through the barrier at Ostend Airport, this is a track that indicates there's still room for experimenting within The Hollies.

'Don't Give Up Easily' (Hicks)
For Tony, it's a fast-strum Beatles-style melody with keening figures and classic Hollies harmonies. *NME* described it as being in a 'chug-a-chug Tex-Mex style but with a swooping, chiming Moog in the background that soars to eerie but sensitive heights'. Yes, it's a tangy 2:21 minutes that could effortlessly have been plucked from any point in the band's long and eventful history, yet it still delivers for 'a foolish fool like me'.

'Look at Life' (Sylvester, Clarke)
Tony sings an Allan and Terry song that flaunts a kind of un-Hollies summer samba sway that blows like a warm breeze, the bobbing bass matched to

shuffling rhythms, subtle Tijuana horns and sweet Johnny Scott shivering strings. Tony has admitted lacking confidence in his own solo vocal abilities, but here he catches the reflective 'take a look around you ... doesn't it astound you' mood more than adequately.

'Please Sign Your Letters' (Sylvester, Hicks, Clarke)

There's a nagging suspicion that while experimentation and innovation are vital in refreshing a band's repertoire, there's a loss of cohesion apparent across these tracks. A low bass line introduces this tongue-in-cheek country shot, only part-spoof. There's a vaguely Everly Brothers edge to Allan's poignant appeal, as Tony picks banjo. Toe-tapping and finger-snapping, it's one of those songs where the chord progressions just happen because they're simply ... right.

'My Life Is Over With You' (Clarke, Hicks)

A Dylanesque phrasing from Allan, with softly unobtrusive strings and horns, a memorable hook that digs deep, and tempered with all the reassuringly familiar Hollies traits coming together into new constellations. A powerful track. In an *NME* feature celebrating the album, Allan admits the lyric is about Graham, 'you can take it (the song) straight or as a romantic thing towards a girl. But let's be honest, man – I'd lost a great and lifelong friend, and I was obviously writing about the experience.'

'Please Let Me Please' (Clarke, Hicks)

A lengthy chiming electric guitar play-in, with a phased right-to-left stereo swoop at the 31-second mark – which is twice revisited later – urged on by an Alan Tew-arranged horn break and vocals mixed low, this is naggingly catchy pop with a deliciously repetitive 'please let me please ya, Louise' hook. Contagiously proving that, despite the internal changes, there's kicking life in The Hollies yet.

'Do You Believe In Love?' (Sylvester, Clarke, Hicks)

Slap-drum introduction and bouncy guitar riff, while the three-way harmony recalls the raw edge of the early beat-group period. Do we believe in love? Of course, we do; there ain't no doubt about it. Everybody's gotta jump up and shout about it. A pleasantly positive message, even though there's nothing new here, and nothing we haven't heard before. And is that even necessary? Can't we just enjoy?

'Soldier's Dilemma' (Clarke)

'Please answer my question...': urgent acoustic strum sets a more serious intention, a soft anti-war refutation of the draft. 'Why should I die for something in which I don't believe?' There's an attractive country-picking guitar break until the vocals return to protest that Allan finds the whole government thing a bore. As a peacenik stance taken at a time of intensifying anti-Vietnam demonstrations, this is a track that Graham Nash would surely approve of.

'Marigold: Gloria Swansong' (Sylvester, Clarke)

If the album itself is patchy and inconsistent, this 5:29-minute segue provides its vindication, and could easily have held its own on *Evolution* or *Butterfly*. It starts with Dylan chords – or maybe it's 'Norwegian Wood' – with a beautifully haunting storyline about finding a note pressed between the leaves of a book and feeling the need to respond. An epistolary idea in the way that 'Dear Eloise' was. There's a mid-point switch into rippling semi-classical orchestration for the 'Swansong' sequence, closing with the touching line 'winter did not mean despair'. For one of Terry's first writing contributions to The Hollies, this is a major track.

'You Love 'Cos You Like It' (Sylvester, Clarke)

There's an easy-dancing woodwind circling around this celebration of feel-good mutual loving. Allan had once pointed out that, following Terry joining the line-up, 'if anything, the group's harmony is softer now,' which is true. From the softy-plucking intro, this is light fly-away shiny pop. But if that also means the hard bite of urgency is smoothed over, that's not necessarily to the collective sound's advantage.

'Reflections of a Time Long Past' (Calvert)

A Hollies instrumental? Why not. The Who drummer Keith Moon had contributed his instrumental composition 'Cobwebs And Strange' to their *A Quick One* (1966) album. The Beatles had dispensed with lyric vocals for 'Flying' on the *Magical Mystery Tour* soundtrack. So Bernie's writing contribution is a wistful piano-led melody, with sweeping strings, the soundtrack for an imaginary movie, or maybe a TV cigar commercial. Bobby freely acknowledges the arranging skills of Mike Vickers 'for scoring strings and cor anglais.'

'Goodbye Tomorrow' (Clarke)

The first Hollies album not to be issued in mono, The first Hollies album to be issued in EMI's new 'musicassette' format. Issued the same year as The Rolling Stones' *Let It Bleed* and The Beatles' *Abbey Road*. The album closes with metallic slow-paced guitar, a near-suicidal lyric and Allan taking a flattened note of plaintive endings, dreams falling apart at the seams, losings; only the busy guitar passages enliven the devastating sadness. Turning aside sympathy, he protests, 'I just want to be alone, my friend, will you please just go away.'

Related Releases
He Ain't Heavy, He's My Brother (Epic BN 26538)
Highest US chart position: 32

The American version, issued in December 1969, was re-titled after the hit, with different cover art and altered tracklisting:
'Why Didn't You Believe?', 'Don't Give Up Easily', 'Look at Life', 'Please Sign Your Letters', 'My Life Is Over With You', 'Please Let Me Please', 'Do You Believe in Love?', 'He Ain't Heavy, He's My Brother', 'You Love 'Cos You Like It', 'Reflections of a Time Long Past', 'Goodbye Tomorrow'.

'He Ain't Heavy, He's My Brother' (Russell, Scott) b/w 'Cos You Like To Love Me' (Hicks) (1 September 1969, Parlophone R 5806)

The song that turns The Hollies story around has an inspirational origin story of its own. Dying of lymphoma, movie-lyricist Bob Russell was introduced to piano-playing Jazz-veteran Bobby Scott (who wrote the melody for early Hollies speciality 'A Taste Of Honey') by Johnny Mercer in a California nightclub. The pair met only three times, and collaborated on just this one song, but it became a timeless classic. There are various theories to explain the source of the title, going back to religious and Socialist interpretations, but it's generally seen as an achingly sincere life-affirming message of family interdependence, facing loss and health issues, and beyond that, to the mutual support of people for people. Recorded first as a lush MoR theme by Kelly Gordon on his album *Defunked*, it was brought to The Hollies' attention – after it had been turned down by Joe Cocker – by Russell's son-in-law who happened to be living in London at the time, and it's their version that takes off to become the global best-seller.

Tony Hicks recalls how 'when we were short of songs I used to root around publishers in Denmark Street. One afternoon, I'd been there ages (at Cyril Shane Music) and wanted to get going, but this bloke said, 'Well, there's one more song. It's probably not for you.' He played me the demo by the writers (Bobby Scott and Bob Russell). It sounded like a 45rpm record played at 33rpm, the singer was slurring, like he was drunk. But it had something about it. There were frowns when I took it to the band, but we speeded it up and added an orchestra. The only things left recognisable were the lyrics' (to *The Guardian*, 24 February 2006). Introduced by the keening of Allan's melancholy Hohner chromatic harmonica, leading into his most moving vocal delivery, and delicious group harmonies – no guitars, but Johnny Scott orchestration and The Mike Samme Singers adding a choral blast, it hits UK number three on 1 November 1970 – beneath The Archies 'Sugar Sugar' – after which sales of 'He Ain't Heavy, He's My Brother' top a million as, issued 1 December 1969 in the US, it hits number 7 there (Epic 10532). It becomes number one in Sweden and Australia, and number 9 in Germany. Even stranger, reissued in 1988 (as EMI EM74), the single climbs all the way to a UK number 1. Flip it over, and the Tony Hicks song ''Cos You Like To Love Me' is more conventional pop-friendly

Hollies fare in the attractive way we've come to recognise. Added as a bonus track to the 1996 remastered CD edition, its teen-romance theme harks back to the flirty 'The Games We Play'.

'Dick Barton Theme (The Devil's Gallop)' (Charles Williams) b/w **'Breakdown Blues'** (Calvert, Quaye, Jackson, Dwight) by **The Bread and Beer Band** (February 1969, Decca F12891)
In a curious side-project, Bernie Calvert gets a writer credit – alongside guitarist Caleb Quaye, drummer Lennox Jackson and Reg Dwight (Elton John) – on the B-side of this hard-to-find one-off single. The group, formed by young Elton John, also recorded a full instrumental album with producer Chris Thomas at the EMI Abbey Road studio, with Bernie Calvert playing bass throughout, made up largely of covers such as 'Quick Joey Small', 'If I Were a Carpenter' and a bizarre 'Zorba the Greek'. Why anyone thought that would be a commercial proposition is a conundrum in itself! Planned for June 1969 issue, the release was cancelled, although bootleg editions continue to circulate. Bobby Elliott describes 'Breakdown Blues' as a jam session recorded during a studio technical intermission.

Into the 1970s

'I Can't Tell The Bottom From the Top' (Fletcher, Flett) b/w 'Mad Professor Blyth' (Clarke) (April 1970, Parlophone R 5837)

The power of love has turned his life upside down. Although taken very much in the 'He Ain't Heavy' mood, this Guy Fletcher and Doug Flett song is equally powerful in its own right and is featured on his own *Guy Fletcher* solo LP (1971, Philips 6303-013). Recorded during 10 March at Abbey Road, there's a distinctive Elton John piano play-in – he was still called Reg Dwight at the time and was paid session fee only. There's a strong Bernie Calvert bass underpinning – Bernie also takes the piano lead for live performance, while Allan hits just the correct note of achingly intense poignancy, enhanced by Johnny Scott's string arrangement. 'I Can't Tell The Bottom From The Top' hits UK number seven, 16 May 1970. In June, it peaks at US number 82, then number six in Denmark and number ten in Holland. It was revived on the controversial LP *My Beauty* (Creation Records) recorded by Kevin Rowland of Dexy's Midnight Runners. The novelty B-side, written by Allan, who also plays rhythm guitar, opens with descending bass leading into Tony's banjo, telling how the kids all laugh at the eccentric inventor, until he disappears by dematerialising himself into the fourth dimension! The track remained uncollected onto album until the August 1978 anthology *The Other Side Of The Hollies* (Parlophone PMC 7176).

'Gasoline Alley Bred' (Macauley, Cook, Greenaway) b/w 'Dandelion Wine' (Hicks) (18 September 1970, Parlophone R 5862)

During August, in a strange return to the group's hometown, The Hollies played cabaret dates at the Manchester 'Golden Garter' club. Then, written by the Cook-Greenaway team with Tony Macaulay, this song takes its title from a long-running syndicated comic-strip created by Frank King, which explains why 'Gasoline Alley' is also the title of a song on Rod Stewart's first solo album. With charming chiming guitars, Allan and Terry trade vocals, telling the story-song of a young couple who set out to make it big, but after years of struggle are faced with the prospect of never making it, and have to swallow their pride and return to the homestead, back to reality. Fate isn't on their side. Alan Parsons stood in as engineer for an absent Peter Brown, and its strong American flavour suggests an attempt to further penetrate the US market. The record reached UK number 14 in October and number 6 in Australia. Tony uses their record as a demo from which he works out his own arrangement.

There's an appropriately drunken sway and lazy sunshine harmonica on the Tony Hicks-penned B-side, with a sh-sh-shoe and a d-d-do stammered rhyme. There's a good-timey Lovin' Spoonful 'Daydream' feel to it, or maybe an easy-going shimmer of the Kinks 'Sunny Afternoon' as, now that they're through, he stays stoned all the time, but if only she'd return to him, he'd drink his Dandelion Wine from her sh-sh-shoe.

Confessions of the Mind

Personnel:
Allan Clarke: vocals, guitar, harmonica
Terry Sylvester: vocals, guitar
Tony Hicks: vocals, lead guitar
Bobby Elliott: drums
Bernie Calvert: bass guitar, keyboards
plus Johnny Scott: arranger and conductor on 'Man Without A Heart', 'Confessions Of A Mind', 'Frightened City', 'Too Young To Be Married'
Produced at EMI Studios by Ron Richards, 15 September 1969-4 May 1970
Released: November 1970, Parlophone PCS 7116
Running time: 39:13
Highest chart position: UK: 30

With stark black cover-art, only the title and band name in white lettering, these eleven new original songs from various combinations of group members were recorded with Ron Richards between 15 September 1969 and over the decade-rim into 4 May 1970. Crossing the event horizon from the Swinging Sixties into the less clearly defined seventies proved an awkward transition for many bands. Suddenly, The Beatles were no longer there. Brian Jones was dead. Jimi Hendrix and Al Wilson of Canned Heat died during September 1970, Janis Joplin shortly afterwards. Donovan's string of hits stopped. Manfred Mann split. The Hollies simply continue, with returning confidence and renewed self-assurance. Although to *NME*, 'the production was more immaculate than ever, but The Hollies were running out of memorable songs' (23 September 1978). The core musicians were Allan Clarke (vocals, guitar), Tony Hicks (bass, vocals), Terry Sylvester (guitar, vocals), Bernie Calvert (keyboards) and Bobby Elliott (drums). Alan Parsons joined the studio crew as tape operator and sound engineer. The album reaches UK number 30.

'Survival of the Fittest' (Nash, Clarke, Hicks)
The title – which doesn't occur in the lyric – was suggested by Bobby Elliott, for this final three-writer collaboration which makes for a strong album lead-in. It opens with piano notes, ghosted by guitar, into strong strident percussive power-pop, with toe-tapping tambourine intrigue about an actress who plays her role but 'she's so empty inside'; there's a Beatlesque downturn on the 'public acclaim's not the same, such a shame' line. Speculation about her real-life identity must remain undisclosed.

'Man Without a Heart' (Clarke, Sylvester)
From a slightly echoed 'la-la-la' launch, Allan's deep voice shows previously unsuspected range as he offers words of advice to a lonely man in a room; the track is broken by twirling cavorting strings arranged by conductor Johnny Scott, who performs the same function for the title-track, for 'Frightened Lady'

79

and 'Too Young To Be Married'. At 2:27-minutes, the song seems to close almost too soon, yet, issued as a single in Holland, it reaches a respectable number 25.

'Little Girl' (Hicks)
Allan takes the first lines a capella. A child is caught up in the crossfire between break-up feuding parents when even her teddy bear can't provide comfort. The sentimental, mawkish aspects are offset by hard-edged harmonica and duelling guitars. Where Graham once took the upper register voice giving a wild quicksilver edge, the grit in the Vaseline, Terry and Tony glide seamlessly in around Allan's lead with no trace of rawness.

'Isn't It Nice?' (Clarke, Sylvester)
In lush and lavish fairy-tale imagery, Cinderella has slipped down the rainbow, but for her, the clock 'will never strike twelve.' Allan sings unfeigned lead. Terry sings cut-glass high harmony and plays rhythm guitar. Nice, undeniably, although that could be to damn the song with faint praise. Writing solo, in combination with Allan, or with Allan and Tony, Terry was becoming a cornerstone of The Hollies, who would only become more vital as things developed along unexpected pathways.

'Perfect Lady Housewife' (Clarke, Sylvester)
A lazy loping bluesy rhythm, before a tempo-change into tight harmonies. The lyrics nudge into social satire, about a woman who is supernaturally house-proud to a kind of satiric pre-gender-equality *Stepford Wives* degree. The track's importance is retrospectively skewed by the fact that Elton John plays session keyboard. By now, he had issued a failed debut album – *Empty Sky* (June 1969) – with a strong 'Skyline Pigeon' single, but major recognition still lay out of reach.

'Confessions of a Mind' (Hicks)
Life on the road has its corporeal temptations, despite the best intentions of committed fidelity. His woman is true, she deserves to be loved, but while she's away, he gets the itch to play. These are his guilty confessions. Structured from segued sequences of entrancing acoustic guitar, tempo-change and pirouetting strings, it builds into electric squalls before returning to quiet reflection. The missing link between 'Good Vibrations' and 'Bohemian Rhapsody'.

'Lady Please' (Hicks)
This is the album that shows Tony's writing at its best, as if we needed reminding. There's a chirpy organ as Allan protests 'I'm not a man of many words' through Tony's lyrics. A passionate song, with pop sensibility, in the consummation of a long-anticipated love, if you lie with me, you won't sleep.

They performed this song on the *Julie Felix Show* on 26 April 1970, wearing their white suits.

'Frightened Lady' (Hicks)

Folky guitar, then tight drums propel some dramatic, sharp guitar soloing, with vocal swapping. There are dark images of a world of confusion, from Jerusalem to old Japan, yet students are marching in every land, we will never ever go to war no more. Well, maybe. The B-side of the German single 'Too Young To Be Married', the mild protest message ends on an optimistic woodwind instrumental passage.

'Too Young To Be Married' (Hicks)

Pop-picking can be a random process. Lifted as a single in Australia, this song reaches number 2 down-under. There's an agile acoustic guitar to illustrate the story of unplanned pregnancy leading to a dissatisfying marriage, building to a powerfully-scored peak. 'The words are about a couple who have to get married – 'I think it's a good story' explains Tony from the elegant confines of his newly-purchased St John's Wood home. It's 'a musical commentary on life in the 1960s,' adds Bobby. A *Top of the Pops* version taped 3 March 1971 is collected onto *Radio Fun* (EMI 440 7702).

'Separated' (Clarke)

Expect the unexpected. Clattering pattering toms, channelling an inner Incredible String Band vibe with background howls and screeches as Allan's solo voice takes the lead, yet it gets drawn into The Hollies continuum via a midpoint close-harmony burst. This would have fitted quite seamlessly onto *Butterfly*. A strange entry in the group's discography, but George Harrison would have approved.

'I Wanna Shout' (Clarke, Sylvester)

Terry takes the first verse over stripped-back Bobby Elliott drum-pattern, Allan takes the second verse, then echoed harmonies break in with an attractive quality of beat-group rawness; a burbling organ cuts in, proclaiming that they want to shout it out loud, but they can't let people know, for theirs is a forbidden love. Almost a summing up, a recapitulation of earlier band themes, a strange closer to a satisfying return-to-form album.

Related Releases

Moving Finger (US release. February 1971, US Epic E 30255)
Highest chart position: US: 183
There was a re-jigged tracklisting for a German issue titled *Move On*, while *Confessions of the Mind* was retitled *Moving Finger* for the American market, with appropriate cover-art designed by Ron Coro of twelve Don Hunstein

finger-gesture photographic images spelling out 'Moving Finger'. The credit reads 'A Hollies Production Produced By Ron Richards'. It reached number 183.

'Survival Of The Fittest' (Clarke, Hicks, Nash), 'Confessions Of A Mind' (Hicks), 'Lady Please' (Hicks), 'Little Girl' (Hicks), 'Too Young To Be Married' (Hicks), 'Man Without A Heart' (Clarke, Sylvester), 'Isn't It Nice?' (Clarke, Sylvester), 'Frightened Lady' (Hicks), 'Marigold: Gloria Swansong' (Clarke, Sylvester), 'Perfect Lady Housewife' (Clarke, Sylvester), 'Gasoline Alley Bred' (Cooke, Greenaway, Macaulay)

'Hey Willy' (Clarke, Cook, Greenaway) b/w 'Row The Boat Together' (Clarke) (14 May 1971, Parlophone R5905)

The Hollies played a high-profile sell-out Far East tour, including two Government-sponsored shows in Djakarta that pulled in audiences of 10,500 each, plus dates in Hong Kong and Singapore. In Australia, they played the 'Davis Cup' tennis stadium in Perth, where they were also loaned a big yacht and underwater swimming gear. Afterwards, their first session at the London AIR studios, on 16 March, produced 'Hey Willy', with its hard-rocking punchy guitar riff figures punctuated by consummate slam-down drums and handclaps. Written by Allan with the Cook-Greenaway team, the obvious taunting references about 'Willy is the singer with a Rock 'n' Roll band' are interpreted as an affectionate snipe at the departed Graham Nash – 'you don't care what they say about your hair, 'cos the fan mail's fine.' Meanwhile, there's a faint gospel tingle to the B-side, written by Allan alone, using the familiar idea of a 'brotherhood boat' as a racial integration metaphor, over snarly guitars. Inexplicably 'Hey Willy' peaks at no higher than UK number 18 on the *New Musical Express* chart, 12 June 1971.

Distant Light

Personnel:
Allan Clarke: vocals, guitar
Terry Sylvester: vocals, rhythm guitar
Tony Hicks: vocals, lead guitar
Bobby Elliott: drums
Bernie Calvert: bass guitar
plus Johnny Scott: arranger and conductor
Produced at AIR Studios by Ron Richards and The Hollies, 14 April-30 July 1971.
Released: 8 October 1971, Parlophone PAS 10005, US April 1972 Epic KE 30958
Running time: 44:14.
Highest chart position: US: 21, UK: did not chart

Distant Light was initially released without charting, but by September 1972 –
boosted by the success of an unexpected hit single lifted from it – this album
made the US number 21. The gatefold cover design, of a boy gazing into a
pastoral lake where there are surreal unconnected reflections, was by Storm
Thorgeson of Hipgnosis, using Colin Elgie art, the group-photo inner art
is simply credited to Hipgnosis. Within the grooves, The Hollies were now
well-focused professionals, writing not only in various combinations, but in
configurations with other successful songwriter teams. This was a practice that,
in later decades, would aid 'boyband' members to nudge their sad scribbles
into marketable shape. But Allan, with Tony Macaulay, or with Roger Cook
(Blue Mink front-man among his other achievements) was another matter
entirely, a genuine partnership of equal talents, bringing their abilities into
vigorous joint fusion. Meanwhile, Tony Hicks' writing was outstanding in his
new partnership with Kenny Lynch. As well as their five compositions here,
their song 'Faded Images' was recorded by Cilla Black for her *Images* album
(May 1971, Parlophone PCS7128).

As well as being a popular comedian and singer with his own pop hits, Kenny
had co-written 'Sha-La-La-La-Lee' for The Small Faces – and appeared on the cover
of Wings' *Band On The Run* album. *Distant Light* was credited as a joint Ron
Richards Hollies Production and was recorded at the AIR Studios in Oxford Circus.

'What a Life I've Led' (Hicks, Lynch)
There's a 'Let It Be' feel to the opening bars before Allan sings in a skewed
Western-movie accent as 'a bad man with a heart made of stone' looking back
over the events of his violent life without regret, riding into Dodge City with
horse and six-gun. *Melody Maker* poses the question 'why somebody from
the coal and moody bricks of Manchester should develop a singing accent that
would flatter maybe Tex Ritter', while supplying the restrictive answer 'that's
pop, and The Hollies are a pop group.' There's an audio clip from 23 August
1972 of The Hollies performing this song on the BBC *Pop Extra*, with organ
passage replacing the slide guitar intermission.

'Look What We've Got' (Hicks, Lynch)

A stately piano for a slow-paced wine-drinking ballad. It offers a different mood, but a lyrical return to the theme of 'Dandelion Wine', in that now she's gone, he drinks to kill the pain of regret. There's a bar-room sax break to paint in a sympathetic companion voice, 'look what we've got, there's nothing at all,' with the sax returning to wind down the melancholy track into the fade. Chosen as the US flip-side of 'Long Cool Woman'.

'Hold On' (Clarke)

She's not that kind of woman. So she says! Although it opens with eerily hesitant folk-blues guitar, it rapidly develops into a fast keyboard rocker with girl-group back-up vocals and smash-phased guitar in full glorious stereo separation. It falls back into an ambient interlude before surging into soulful organ. At 4:07-minutes, it's a densely textured track catching something of 'Long Cool Woman', when Allan howls 'Coo-oool!' He's right.

'Pull Down the Blind' (Sylvester)

Stark echoed vocals, powerful jousting guitar interplay, with subdued keyboard feeding in beneath. There's something of Donovan's 'Season Of The Witch' in its crawling insinuation, and something of John Lennon's 'Come Together' in the spellbinding instrumental cauldron at its core. He's drinking from an empty can of beer while wishing she was here. There's a sense that this is an album of separations, with less live interactions replaced by studio overdubs. Since *Hollies Sing Hollies*, Terry – as songwriter, guitarist and vocalist too – has been assuming increased visibility. But when it works, it hangs together immaculately.

'To Do With Love' (Hicks, Lynch)

3:29-minutes of organic folk-rock with cascades of fiddly acoustic guitar. Allan's strong lead voice urges that where new love is concerned, don't talk about the past, a kind of anonymity that erases past encounters and acquaintances is preferable. A pleasantly eccentric lyric, as voices wrap in around supportively. He's done with washing-up for Mother, and lighting pipes for Pa. He just wants a girl who likes the presents he buys her. This is such a smooth elision of complementary talents that it's difficult to accept that Allan is already planning a new solo tangent for his career.

'Promised Land' (Hicks, Lynch)

Not the Chuck Berry 'Promised Land' obviously, but a big choral opening, a mid-point tempo-switch, and hard guitar soloing from Tony. He asks, where is the Promised Land? It can't be found in Vietnam, so bring the soldiers home. Snatched from the TV news, continuing the social consciousness theme of his 'Frightened Lady', there's protest, violence and marches, so we've gotta make the world demand peace.

'Long Cool Woman in a Black Dress' (Clarke, Cook, Greenaway)

Although Ron Richards wasn't there when it was recorded, with engineer John Punter standing in at the control desk, this is arguably the most important song in the entire Hollies canon. The album did not chart, and it passed by virtually unnoticed, but when this track was later issued as a US single, it became their biggest-ever American hit, becoming the catalyst for reforming the line-up for what was to be The Hollies' entire subsequent lifetime. Without the 'Long Cool Woman's saving grace, there might have been nothing more. The story might have just frittered away to nothing.

Meanwhile, Roger Cook and Roger Greenaway were one of the sixties' most prolific and successful songwriting team, so it's ironic that – as the duo, David & Jonathon – the two Rogers' chart debut in their own right was made only with the help of a Beatles cover, 'Michelle'. Although Allan wrote 'Long Cool Woman' with Roger Cook alone, Roger Greenaway gets a contractual credit because they work as a team.

'You Know the Score' (Clarke, Sylvester)

Powerfully strange, with strong, distorted guitar-run propulsion … then, stop, and it gradually eerily fades back in again on the sound of blowing wind, before reverting back to its 'death and destruction' play-in energies. With Allan's strident throat-driven voice as the arrowhead of the three-way harmony, Tony and Terry so familiar with his breath-control that they tailor their voices to left and right accordingly. Then another pause, abruptly broken by Tony's dexterous guitar into the precise coda.

'Cable Car' (Sylvester)

Taken with lilting piano accompaniment, this is a cleverly wrought, sweepingly atmospheric ballad, 'did she go, or did she die?' Terry takes the lead voice in an initially sparse setting, into the long building instrumental fade carried on faint strings. Terry would later repossess the song and record it for his own solo debut album, with richer, more lavish walls of guitar, swelling West Coast voices and sighing steel guitar. Which version you prefer is simply a matter of choice.

'A Little Thing Like Love' (Clarke, Macaulay)

The accomplished professional songwriter behind 'Sorry Suzanne', Tony Macaulay (in partnership with John Macleod), had written a series of hits for Foundations, as well as Long John Baldry's breakthrough number 1 'Let The Heartaches Begin'. Now, from the Black Hills of Dakota to the plains, this is a likeable enough pop trifle sweetened by sawing strings courtesy of Johnny Scott's arrangement skills. She's going to leave him to find a better life; he doesn't intend to hold her back with his tears, his love, or with this slice of soft-core self-sacrificing moral blackmail.

'Long Dark Road' (Hicks, Lynch)

'My Sweet Lord' guitar, inspirational harmony and counter-harmonies, with organ played through a Leslie speaker. Regret. Loss. Desolation. It's over, but then again, it didn't have a chance to last. This is a theme for those facing recovery from lost love, or other addictions. By the time this track was issued as a November 1972 US single by Epic – when it reached a quite respectable number 26 – Allan was gone. Tony sings lead with the Mikael Rickfors line-up for promotional purposes.

Related Releases

My Real Name Is 'Arold by Allan Clarke (April 1972, RCA Victor SF 8283) Did not chart.

Perhaps the phenomenal success of Graham and his American friends with his 'three cats in the yard' had an unsettling effect? Because it was now that Allan suggested making a solo album as a Hollies side-project. 'The Hollies are run like a business', explained Tony, 'we all have an equal say at meetings and are ready to listen to another's point of view, and everyone can see where the money comes from, and where it goes.' It was at one of these round table meetings that Allan's suggestion was voted down by the other group members. 'Making a solo album is something I have to get out of my system', he insisted. So in August, he was left with little alternative but to quit The Hollies, and with manager Robert Weiss, signs to RCA for this solo LP. Self-produced, the backing work is shared between musicians of the stature of Herbie Flowers (bass), Tony Newman and Eric Dillon (drums).

Critic Chris Welch welcomed a 'most respectable debut album' and 'generally this is a more positive and successful album than oft emerged from The Hollies' (in *Melody Maker*). While Tony Stewart says, 'this is Allan Clarke striving to prove his talent as a solo performer, musician and songwriter. And he succeeds. Painstakingly he has removed himself from the Hollies images of block harmonies and pretty songs, and come up with a collection that incorporates guts, ability, sound musicianship and emotion' (*NME*). For Allan, it was simply 'me stripping myself bare of the past':

'Ruby' (Clarke, Glynn), 'Mary Skeffington' (Rafferty), 'Baby, It's Alright With Me' (Clarke), 'Moonshine Whiskey' (Clarke), 'Nature's Way Of Saying Goodbye' (Clarke), 'You're Losing Me' (Chater, Armand), Gary Brooker crops up on piano, and the track is lifted as a single b/w 'Coward By Name'., 'Let Us Prey' (Allan, Glynn), 'Patchwork Quilts' (Allan, Slater). The track has 'anguished vocals over emotive pedal steel from Ray Glynn that suggests dusty roads, blue denim and heavy black moustaches'. 'Walpurgis Night' (by Gerry Rafferty's former Stealer's Wheel partner Joe Egan). This 'song of singular power and menace, complete with freaky vocal track, and heavy drumming from Tony Newman, is outstanding', 'Bring On Your Smiles' (Clarke, Flowers)

Allan will follow the album with *Headroom* (July 1973, EMI EMA752) with Dee Murray (bass), Tony Newman (drums) and Graham's former writing partner Kirk Duncan adding keyboards for the May single 'Who' b/w 'I Looked Into Your Eyes'. Then *Allan Clarke* (August 1974, EMI 3041), produced by Roger Cook, with a March single made up of Roger Cook-Herbie Flowers' 'Sideshow' b/w 'Don't Let Me Down Again', which was supported by a series of live dates. It also features Randy Newman's 'I'll Be Home' and Bruce Springsteen's 'If I Were The Priest' with BJ Cole's steel guitar. The next album, *I've Got Time* (July 1976, EMI EMC 3130), was made up of songs penned by other writers, including Bruce Springsteen's 'Blinded By The Light' – recorded before the Manfred Mann's Earth Band version, plus songs by Janis Ian ('Light A Light'), Junior Campbell ('Hallelujah Freedom') and Melissa Manchester. Each album, in turn, was critically respected but failed to find a responsive audience. Allan would return to The Hollies but would also continue to maintain a parallel solo career.

Terry Sylvester by Terry Sylvester (1974, US Epic KE 33076)
No chart placing.

Allan was not the only member of The Hollies to put out tentative solo feelers; this promising eponymous album features Terry's interpretation of Stevie Wonder's 'I Believe' – also covered by Art Garfunkel – and Albert Hammond's 'For The Peace of All Mankind'. The album was revised and reissued in 1976 as *I Believe* (Polydor 2383-394) with a couple of the songs he'd written for The Hollies, 'Cable Car' and the B-side 'Indian Girl', adding glistening steel guitar to his solo version. He claimed 'I fought a million men' for his Native American girl. The press was less than enthusiastic about the album, with *Sounds* calling it 'the kind of pop sound you hear trilling away behind the booze or soft drink advertisments in the cinema,' while reserving praise for the track, 'I Believe' itself (17 July 1976). Meanwhile, Terry contributed to the Alan Parsons Project *Tales of Mystery and Imagination* (May 1976, Charisma CDS 4003), singing lead on the track 'To One In Paradise' and back-up vocals to 'The Cast Of Amontillado'. The album was a concept based around the Edgar Allan Poe horror mythos.

The Mikael Rickfors Years
Romany

Personnel:
Mikael Rickfors: vocals
Terry Sylvester: vocals, guitar
Tony Hicks: vocals, lead guitar
Bobby Elliott: drums
Bernie Calvert: bass guitar
Produced at EMI Studios by The Hollies, 13 April-30 August 1972
Released: November 1972, Polydor LP 2383144
Running time: 45:29. Highest chart positions: US: 84, UK: did not chart

What is the defining characteristic of a band that immediately identifies it's sound? For The Hollies, it was the three-part Allan Clarke-Graham Nash-Tony Hicks harmonies. After Graham's defection, it was still recognizably The Hollies. But once Allan departed? Swedish vocalist Mikael Rickfors, formerly with Bamboo – who'd played support to a recent Swedish Hollies tour – officially joined as new singer in January 1972. To find himself placed in an impossible situation. He wasn't with the outfit for long, but rose to the challenge and performed remarkably well. But was it still The Hollies? Did it still sound like The Hollies? Manfred Mann lost vocalist Paul Jones, but went on to have a further run of less hard-edged, more pop-friendly hits with Mike D'Abo. Pink Floyd lost charismatic Syd Barrett, but were still Pink Floyd. The Spencer Davis Group lost Steve and Muff Winwood, but despite making some fine records with replacements Pete York and Eddie Hardin, they never quite recaptured their chart glory days. This album started well, with high expectations, but swiftly lost momentum, so that, issued in November, 'Magic Woman Touch' – despite its obvious appeal – became the first-ever Hollies UK single not to chart.

Romany was a watershed album in other ways; even The Hollies themselves are divided over these 'missing years'. Tony Hicks has nominated *Romany* as one of his favourite albums, where Bobby Elliott dismisses the era completely as a 'bland period' for the band while Terry Sylvester rolls his eyes and talks about the problems of Mikael Rickfors singing in what was not his native language. 'Produced By The Hollies', this was also the band's first album without the watchful eye of Ron Richards – just Alan Parsons and Peter Bown (aka Peter Brown) engineering, and it was their first for a new label. After eight years and 21 Top Ten singles, they'd quit the EMI group to sign a new three-year contract with Polydor. Even the cover-art tracks the changes, the green summer scene beside the forest pool of *Distant Light* takes on starker winter hues.

'Won't We Feel Good (That Morning)' (Crane, Weiner, Gluck)
A driving opener with strong thrash guitar, and although the vocal lacks conviction as though Mikael's voice is mixed low to his disadvantage, the

cruising chorus harmonies and Tony's rippling guitar breaks lift the song. The lyric urges a new, more independent stance, 'don't take nothing low down, it's much better when you're making your own way.' A new resolve. A new beginning. Well … maybe.

'Touch' (Rickfors)

Blonde Nordic Mikael Rickfors is no Allan Clarke soundalike. Initially identified as a possible replacement by Tony, a choice confirmed by Ron Richards at 'The Baby' try-out session, without going through the usual group consultation process, his deep voice has a lower register than Allan's, one that catches an occasional Scott Walker resonance. This track has a slow acoustic strum, strong harmonies, quiet shadows and a richly textured instrumental break.

'Words Don't Come Easy' (Jennings)

A softer, slower mood, reflective, with room to write a poem, hung on frozen lips, going introspective places The Hollies had never ventured before. In a break from their previous working methodology, they'd begun to rehearse and familiarise themselves with new material for the album through April in the Cholesbury Village Hall set in the scenic Chiltern Hills, 'getting it together in the country,' before shuttling back to Abbey Road for the actual recording. When this commuting became a pain, at George Martin's helpful suggestion, they use a nearby Boy Scout hall, as work extends through to the final mixing on 21 May.

'Magic Woman Touch' (Jennings, Watt-Roy)

Writers Colin and Garth had first recorded this song as part of the second album by Harvest label band The Greatest Show On Earth, with padding congas and America-style soft-harmonies. Inevitably, there's a story, because Tony Hicks had encouraged Colin Jennings in his other band, Taggett, and produced both the debut single by the four-piece, 'Time' (March 1973, EMI 2009) – welcomed as a 'rare delight' by John Peel in his *Disc* column – as well as their subsequent eponymous album (1974, EMC 3015, USA. 1975 United Artists UA-LA407G). Here, Tony adds sitar, as The Hollies take the song at a slightly faster 2/4 pace, with a definite Crosby Stills & Nash edge to the 'cast your spell upon me one more time' vocal blend. Re-recorded 6 October, it was lifted as a March 1973 US single b/w 'Indian Girl', which reached an American number 60, but hit number 8 in Holland. An acoustic alternate Hollies version was issued as a bonus track on the 2007 remastered CD edition of *Romany*, along with other tracks that were later gathered onto the *Changin' Times* 5CD set.

'Lizzy and the Rainman' (Henley, O'Dell)

Originally recorded by Bobby Goldsboro on his 1972 *California Wine* album, this track was omitted from the US edition of *Romany*. Terry takes strong lead vocals on the textured Hollies telling of the tale, with strong ticking Bobby Elliott drums. Cher wanted to cover this narrative song with a Western setting about the promises made by the fancy man in the painted wagon and the doubting Lizzy Cooper who said he was a 'lying cheat,' but Tanya Tucker did it instead and had a Country number one with it in 1975. Sometimes the dream is more important than the truth.

'Down River' (Ackles)
This album has an impeccable choice in the songs it sources. Ackles is one of those underrated tortured-artist names dropped to impress. Also recorded by Spooky Tooth, the piano-led 'Down River' is from the first of three albums that Ackles recorded for the Elektra label, *David Ackles* (1968). He cut just one further album for the Columbia label in 1973. Closely following the Ackles blueprint, addressed conversationally to 'Rosie', the deep-voiced narrative gradually reveals the bitter-sweet nostalgic tale lost down the river of time. A powerful performance from Rickfors, if not so readily identifiable as The Hollies.

'Slow Down' (Crane, Weiner, Gluck)
Hard rocking and forceful, with organ interlacing around Tony's driving guitar figures. Not the same Larry Williams song that The Beatles once covered, but Mikael's voice tends to work better on the harder material, urging The Hollies into heavier territory than they've ventured for quite a while, posing intriguing possibilities of what might have been. Unlike the previous album, there's a sense that the band are pulling together here. And The Hollies can rock hard when they so choose. Just that they will choose to do so infrequently across the albums to come.

'Delaware Taggett and the Outlaw Boys' (Jennings)
The first track recorded for the album, jumpy guitars and spine-tingling harmonies give it a country swing. Bustling instrumentation, with lyric whispers and shadows as his Mama, warns him not to hang around that front gate too long in the impatient adolescent testosterone burn. Colin Jennings, who also wrote 'Magic Woman Touch', had recorded this song as part of the Tony Hicks-produced eponymous *Taggett* group album.

'Jesus Was a Crossmaker' (Sill)
From Oakland, the beautiful and tragic singer-songwriter Judee Sill had been discovered by Graham Nash and David Crosby, for whom she toured as opening act. Graham produced her original version of 'Jesus Was A Crossmaker' as her debut single and lead-track on her first album – which was also the first release from David Geffen's Asylum label. Allegedly written for former lover JD Souther who'd dropped her to hook up with Linda Ronstadt,

Linda later recorded her own version of the song – retitled 'A Bandit And A Heartbreaker' in 1985, issued as part of her 1999 box-set. For Judee, although critically well-received, when large-scale acceptance failed to materialise, following a second album and some sessions in preparation for a third, she died of a narcotics overdose on 23 November 1979. The Hollies take her composition stately slow with almost choir-like purity for the lyric about 'sweet silver angels over the sea.' It was released as a February 1973 German single, with b/w Terry Sylvester's 'I Had A Dream' (Hansa 12-728AT).

'Romany' (Jennings)
An acoustic showcase for Mikael who also adds ghostly harmonica, with only the chorus harmonies to remind the listener that yes, this is The Hollies. And please, no elaborate theories about the line 'Romany sank like stone', this is not about the fate of the album itself; it's a song about a ship sailing icy waters in the moonless night. And this is the sound of The Hollies reinventing themselves again. They'd done it after Graham quit. They'd picked themselves up and started anew. This album constitutes a second resurrection. And on tracks as strong as this, it works.

'Blue in the Morning' (Hicks, Lynch)
Tony takes the lead voice on his own composition, with close country-rock harmonies all the way and just a hint of Crosby, Stills & Nash. This is 3:14-minutes of toe-tapping fast guitar riffing weaving around Bobby Elliott's snappy drums. 'God help me, don't wanna be, don't wanna be a loser, no more.' Issued as the B-side of the Germany-only single 'Don't Leave The Child Alone' (1973, Hansa Records 12 541AT).

'Courage of Your Convictions' (Rush, Cullers)
Strong and hard guitar with riffing jousting collusion, if you know you're right, when the others are wrong, you just have to go with it. Drummer Randy Cullers of the writing team played some session overdubs for Elvis Presley; together, they were members of the band Jubal, who recorded this song on their eponymous 1972 Elektra label album, which also included 'Castles In The Sand' covered by Brenda Lee.

Related Releases
Romany US release (Epic KE 31992)
While the label-switch to Polydor covered European markets, it did not affect their American status with Epic, where the US edition was released with a slightly altered tracklisting. Reviewer Greg Stone favourably compares The Hollies new vocalist to Alex Chilton of The Boxtops, or David Clayton-Thomas of Blood Sweat & Tears (*Rolling Stone* magazine), and the album climbed to a highest position of number 84.

'Magic Woman Touch', 'Touch', 'Words Don't Come Easy', 'Won't We Feel Good', 'Down River', 'Slow Down', 'Delaware Taggett and the Outlaw Boys', 'Jesus Was a Crossmaker', 'Romany', 'Blue in the Morning', 'Courage of Your Convictions'

'The Baby' (Taylor) b/w 'Oh Granny' (Hicks, Lynch)

Personnel:
Mikael Rickfors: vocals
Terry Sylvester: vocals, guitar
Tony Hicks: vocals, lead guitar
Bobby Elliott: drums
Bernie Calvert: bass guitar
Released: February 1972, Polydor 2058-199

This was the rejigged line-up's first single together, wearing their new faces, in purple velvet bell-bottoms, platform shoes and shag haircuts, although with Ron Richards still sitting in the producer's chair. It was recorded on Wednesday, 29 December 1971 in the AIR studios above London's Oxford Circus, with Richard Hewson's orchestral embellishments added during the final mix on 10 January 1972. Meanwhile, as a deliberate spoiling operation Parlophone issue 'Long Cool Woman', so that there are two simultaneous 'New' Hollies singles.

'The Baby' – written by Chip Taylor with Rickfors vocals – is in many ways a fine single with Tony's 'electric dobro thing' tuning, a guest L.A. percussionist, discreet strings, and the lyric 'in the passion of the spring, came the baby'. It entered the *New Musical Express* chart at number 29 (4 March 1972), climbing to number 23, then to number 21. It got no higher. On the rival *Record Retailer* chart, it peaked at UK number 26. Still issued on their regular American label, Epic, it didn't chart there, although it hit number eight in Holland and goes top thirty in Germany. The B-side is a Tony Hicks-Kenny Lynch composition, sung predominantly by Terry, harmonising with Mikael. A later version with Allan Clarke vocals is included on the compilation album *The Hollies: Singles A's & B's 1970-1979* (April 1993, Music For Pleasure CD-MFP 5980).

Out On the Road

Personnel:
Mikael Rickfors: vocals
Terry Sylvester: vocals, guitar
Tony Hicks: vocals, lead guitar
Bobby Elliott: drums
Bernie Calvert: bass guitar
Released: April 1973, Hansa 871191IT
Did not chart

Despite the title, this is a full studio album, with the band delivering a much harder, edgier rocking set, full of up-tempo material, which sounds as if it was created as close to live as possible, and then sweetened with a few overdubs. The final mixing was done on 29 March, but following the poor sales performance of *Romany*, the label was wary, and it was only issued in Germany – with gatefold sleeve, where The Hollies had a strong and loyal fan-base. It was eventually issued as a CD by the French Magic label (September 2006, Magic 3930593) with bonus tracks 'The Baby', 'Oh Granny', 'Magic Woman Touch', 'Indian Girl', 'If It Wasn't For The Reason That I Love You' and previous B-side 'I Had A Dream'. It also collects the choppy harmonica-driven 'Mexico Gold', which is the first song a returning Allan Clarke cut with the group. The full album was eventually included as part of The Hollies 2015 5CD box-set *Changin' Times*.

'Out on the Road' (Lynch, Hicks)

Fronted by Mikael Rickfors, The Hollies were very much 'out on the road,' with an east coast to west coast trip across America as Richard Nixon beat George McGovern in the Presidential elections, then on to Australia and back for more dates across the USA.. This song is very much a tour song. Subsequently re-recorded with Allan Clarke vocals for the *Hollies* album (see entry for more details), Mikael opens with walking bass, then gifts a loose hard-edged Rock 'n' Roll feel to the band, bringing it both closer to a rawness it was thought The Hollies had long since outgrown while allying it with a more contemporary full-on mid-Atlantic stomp.

'A Better Place' (Lynch, Hicks)

Snarling growling guitar-led anthem with a catchy sing-along chorus, a country-style song construction about his Daddy being a wandering man while his Mom was good and true, with Tony bending the guitar notes into a startling hard solo, concluding with the uplifting idealistic sentiment 'we gotta teach people to love, we gotta teach children to sing.' Kenny Lynch recorded his own softer solo version as Atlantic K 10178 in May 1972 with Tony playing electric sitar and just possibly Terry and Bobby helping out in the mix.

'They Don't Realise I'm Down' (Rickfors, Sylvester)

A track found nowhere else than here, recorded 3 January with the band set up in a circle, facing one another. Mikael slows the tempo for the impassioned lead lifting into a high crescendo, with Tony and Terry adding chorus harmony voices and Tony giving a slight wah-wah bend to the guitar. Whether the message of heartache stress underlying a bravado that 'all the people looking round' can't see, is a reflection of Mikael's own uncertain status within the band is something only he knows.

'The Last Wind' (Rickfors)

The kind of simple, uncluttered acoustic harmony ballad that could have come from the Graham Nash song-bag, although the mid-point instrumental break quivers into some vaguely psychedelic territory. An effective change of mood for the album, and one that might have indicated profitable new routes to explore, had Rickfors hung around a little longer. But both he and the band had other plans.

'Mr Heartbreaker' (Sylvester)

A hesitant piano sway introduces Terry singing a song he'd co-written with Dean Ford. According to Terry, Dean had been invited to join The Hollies when Allan first quit, but he declined – having already written songs as strong as the number 1 'Reflections On My Life', Dean's career with Marmalade still had considerable mileage, yet this slow acoustic exercise in harmonies, with tasteful harmonica interjection, shows evidence of a creative chemistry. The lyric uses the metaphor of a stage-performer – the Mr Heartbreaker of the title – who knows 'the show must go on' yet asks 'why can't we take off our make-up?' Dean Ford's own weary solo version of the song, enveloped in strings and cooing girl backing voices, appears on his 1975 album *Dean Ford* (EMI EMC 3079).

'I Was Born a Man' (Lynch, Hicks)

With Tony taking unusually forceful lead voice on his own song, there are strong no-frills guitar figures as he sings with pointed confidence about his hard-luck childhood, working 'sixteen hours of every day'. Is this commemorating the stolen childhoods of the young millworkers of Manchester's industrial revolution, or is that to overthink it? This track saw an early UK release when it was later lifted to be the B-side of 'The Day That Curly Billy Shot Down Crazy Sam McGee'.

'Slow Down, Go Down' (Lynch, Hicks)

An almost Rolling Stones-like lick crashes into Terry's lead vocals on a fast rocker, albeit with dubious and hopefully tongue-in-cheek lyrics about 'give me a woman than I can trust, and I don't have to beat', rising into high middle-eight and churning no-nonsense guitar break and long instrumental fade. It's good to see The Hollies pulling out all the stops and simply playing good rock music.

'Don't Leave the Child Alone' (Rickfors)
Recorded at Abbey Road on 2 January 1973, with a strong, forward melodic thrust rubbing up against the stand-out ridges of Tony's nicely-distorted guitar. While the well-intended lyrics stumble a little clumsily, about 'a child bright shining as the sun' caught up in the web of the world's cruelties, none of that really matters when Mikael's solo voice melds into country-flavoured harmony passages. Issued as a German and Spanish single b/w 'Blue In The Morning' (Hansa/ Ariola 12-541AT), the story of misplaced migrant peoples is still as relevant.

'Nearer to You' (Lynch, Hicks)
The crisp guitar figure is elevated on a lilting vaguely-skanking rhythm, an attractively light tune and simple hitching-a-ride coming-home message, not a world-changer by any means, but on a strong album – if one that died on the vine, even this filler is not exactly lacking in merit. The piping instrumental break is intriguing – 'I whistle a highway song' and remains annoyingly uncredited.

'Pick Up the Pieces Again' (Sylvester)
Terry sings his own composition, co-written with Dean Ford, as he also sings it on his solo *I Believe* album. It's a gauzy dream of a song that's also lifted intact onto The Hollies' next official album. The impressionistic lyric, 'your eyes, paradise, what do they say, leaving, loving, stay one more day,' is made even more evocative by Tony's sitar-tuning. Although this track constitutes a declaration of Terry's own artistic independence, it remains strongly integrated into the band album.

'Transatlantic Westbound Jet' (Elliott, Sylvester)
Bluesy guitar phrases, then crawling slapback percussion, with Mikael's deep sultry voice well-suited to this hard-rocker about the rigours of being a touring musician, to 'travel the world and see nothin',' Tony's guitar flicks in and around harmonica and keyboards with a busy jazzy freedom that's rare for a Hollies record, over Bobby's solid's drums. It builds and gathers energies into high atmospheric harmony passages, taking them in directions that the band could have fruitfully followed. Before The Hollies were seduced away by the commercial lure of big emotive balladry, this album represents a stop-off at the last chance saloon of being taken seriously as a hard rock band. The full 4:41-minute track will later be re-shaped with Allan Clarke vocals.

'Long Cool Woman In A Black Dress' (Clarke, Cook, Greenaway) b/w **'Cable Car'** (Sylvester) (14 April 1972, Parlophone R 5939)

'Long Cool Woman In A Black Dress' (Clarke, Cook, Greenaway) b/w **'Look What We've Got'** (Hicks, Lynch) (US, Epic 10871)

In America, The Hollies had been riding a Rock 'n' Rollercoaster, a big hit followed by a relative failure, followed by another big hit. Then, while the entire *Romany* saga was being played out, their American label chose to maximize their options by lifting another track from the *Distant Light* album – as was their right. It picks up radio plays and begins inexorably climbing the chart to eventually hit US *Billboard* number two – their highest-ever charting single, with a million-plus sales (on the rival *Cashbox* chart, it makes number one for a single week). Re-promoted by EMI in the UK, it climbed to number 32, while it was number three in Australia, number ten in Sweden, and number 15 in Germany.

As Allan later recalls, 'I put myself about with other writers, and I wrote with Roger Cook. The song that I wrote with Roger Cook was 'Long Tall Woman', which was classed as an album track … we wrote it in half an hour, and I think we finished a bottle of brandy within that half-an-hour while we did it. And I thought 'this'll be a good LP track'. I was recording with The Hollies at that particular time, so I took it to the studio and played it to the boys and they said 'yeah, great, it'll go on the album'.' Recorded 16-30 July 1971 in the London AIR studios, the track is unusual in that Allan plays lead guitar and there are no harmony-voices. Then 'it went onto the album. And about a month afterwards, I got a phone call from America and this chap said he wanted to do the publishing, and I said 'why?', and he said 'because we think it's going to be number 1 in America.' It was reissued in September 1975 b/w 'Carrie Anne' as EMI 2353.

'Long Dark Road' (Hicks, Lynch) b/w **'Promised Land'** (Hicks, Lynch) (November 1972, Epic 10920)

Also lifted from *Distant Light* as a single in Germany and the Netherlands, it climbs to US number 26. The Hollies are on tour in Augusta, Georgia, when they hear it has entered the Top 50.

Right: The Hollies – their Famous Five adventure was underway.

Left: The Hollies in 1970 – wearing their new faces.

Below: Staying power. The twenty-first century Hollies.

Left: The raw, beat-boom Hollies, their promise to *Stay* will be fulfilled. (*Parlophone*)

Right: Taste and class for The Hollies second long-player. (*Parlophone*)

Left: Because they do things differently, this is the American edition. (*Imperial*)

Right: Originally issued in mono only, with monochrome colour to match, *Hollies* from 1965. (*Parlophone*)

Left: Juggling tracks into a new configuration for the American market, *Hear! Here!* from 1966. (*Imperial*)

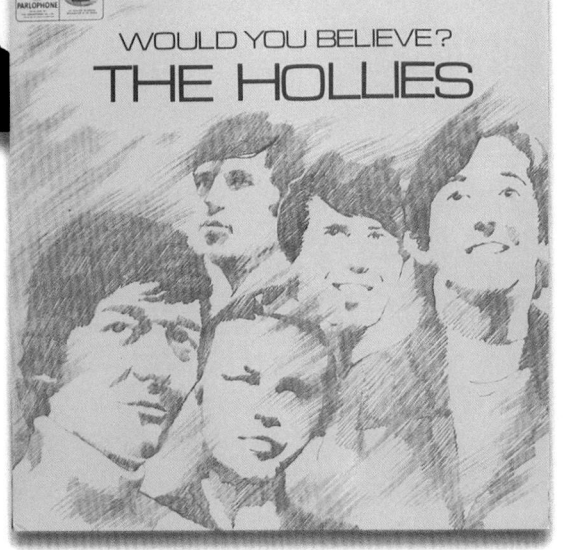

Right: Jennifer Sebley inks the impressive cover-artwork for The Hollies fourth long-player. (*Parlophone*)

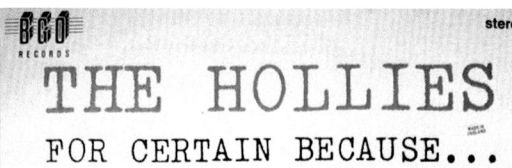

Left: *For Certain Because*, but the album title is derived from 'The Teddy-Bears Picnic'. (*Parlophone*)

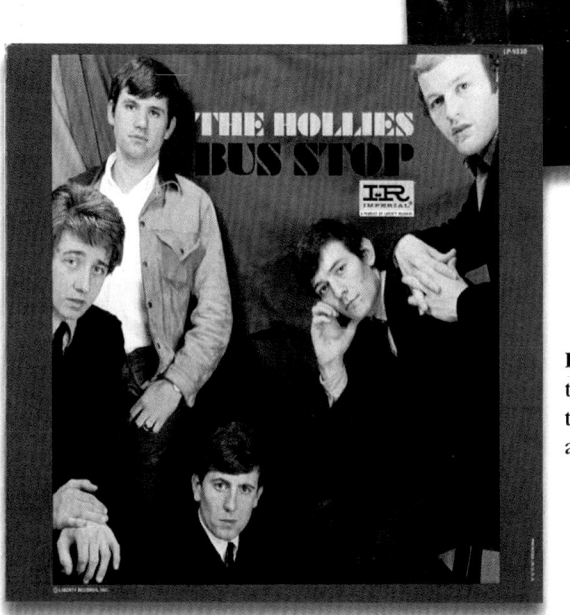

Right: They called bands beat groups in 1966, hence the title of this American collection of Hollies tracks. (*Imperial*)

Left: Taking advantage of the success of the single, the fourth American Hollies album is *Bus Stop*. (*Imperial*)

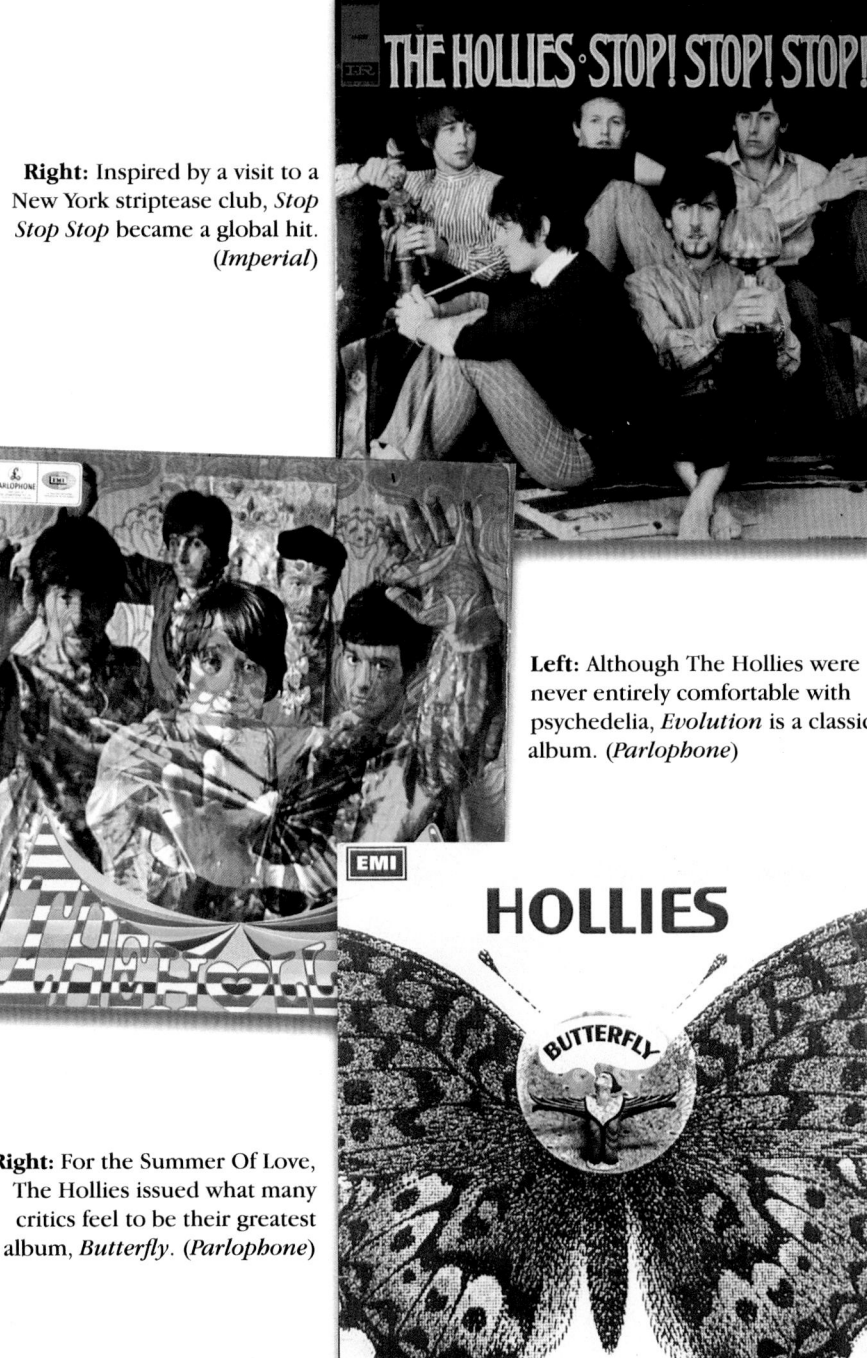

Right: Inspired by a visit to a New York striptease club, *Stop Stop Stop* became a global hit. (*Imperial*)

Left: Although The Hollies were never entirely comfortable with psychedelia, *Evolution* is a classic album. (*Parlophone*)

Right: For the Summer Of Love, The Hollies issued what many critics feel to be their greatest album, *Butterfly*. (*Parlophone*)

Left: Playing 'Look Through Any Window'. It was was The Hollies' ninth single, the follow-up to their first number one, hit 'I'm Alive'.

Right: The Graham Gouldman song also provided their breakthrough American top forty hit, peaking at number 32.

Left: The slick frontline of Graham Nash, Allan Clarke and Tony Hicks, with sharp Bobby Elliott on drums and Eric Haydock on bass.

Right: Tony plays banjo, with Graham on acoustic guitar for The Hollies' cover of the Peter Paul & Mary song 'Very Last Day'.

Left: Hey, 'Carrie Anne' – it was Graham Nash on the original single, but he had left The Hollies by the time they performed the song on this 1969 TV show.

Right: Terry Sylvester had been a member of The Escorts and The Swingin' Blue Jeans, but he said that 'the day he joined the Hollies was the happiest day in my life'.

Left: The wonderfully strange 'Dear Eloise' was culled from the *Butterfly* album to become an American single in its own right and lead to an album with a different title in the US. (*Imperial*)

Right: By 1969, the times they were a-changin, and this was to be the album that tore The Hollies apart. (*Parlophone*)

Left: A title-change for the American edition of *Hollies Sing Dylan* – although the track-listing remained the same. (*Epic*)

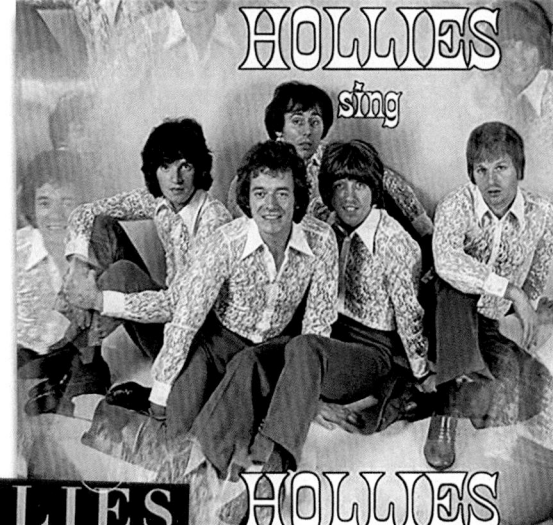

Right: Despite an ambitious collection of all-original songs, *Hollies Sing Hollies* failed to chart. (*Parlophone*)

THE HOLLIES

HE AIN'T HEAVY, HE'S MY

Left: Fortunately, with a title-switch taking advantage of their massive hit 'He Ain't Heavy, He's My Brother', the American edition climbed to number 32. (*Epic*)

Right: The Hollies first album of the 1970s met with mixed fortunes. There was an Australia-only single that hit number two down-under, while the album itself stalled at a UK number 30.

Hollies

Confessions of The Mind

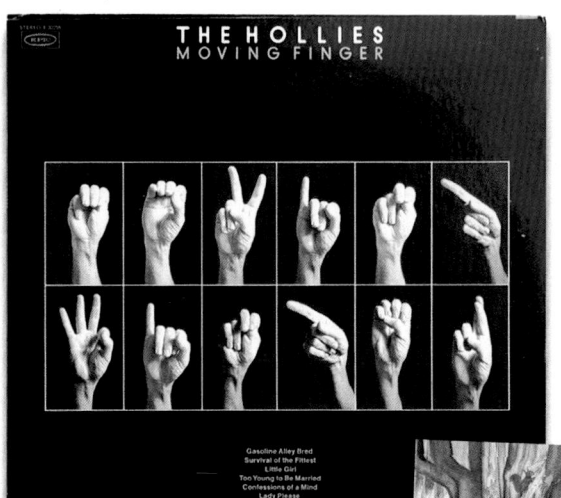

Left: *Confessions Of The Mind* was retitled for its American release, with an amended track listing. (*Epic*)

Right: *Distant Light* was initially released without charting, but – boosted by the success of its unexpected hit single, 'Long Cool Woman in a Black Dress', made number 21 in the US. (*Epic*)

Left: *Romany* was The Hollies first album with Mikael Rickfors on vocals and was their debut for Polydor. (*Polydor*)

Right: Issued in Germany, *Out On The Road* is a unique Hollies album, much prized by collectors. (*Hansa*)

Left: Allan Clarke returned, and the album was emphatically titled *Hollies*, in case there were lingering doubts. (*Polydor*)

Right: *Another Night*, a strong collection for The Hollies' fifteenth official studio album. (*Polydor*)

Left: 'The road is long, with many a winding turn'. The song that turned The Hollies story around, here being performed in 1969.

Right: Arguably the most important song in the entire Hollies canon, 'Long Cool Woman In A Black Dress' took them to an American number two.

Left: The Hollies perform 'Long Cool Woman In A Black Dress' on *Midnight Special*.

Right: The Hollies' 'He Ain't Heavy, He's My Brother' from another *Midnight Special* – but with Mikael Rickfors on vocals.

Left: Tony Hicks has been The Hollies continuity-figure through all the changes, here from a performance of 'The Air That I Breathe' on *Top Of The Pops*.

Right: The Hollies returned to *Top Of The Pops* when the reissued 'He Ain't Heavy, He's My Brother' hit number one in 1988.

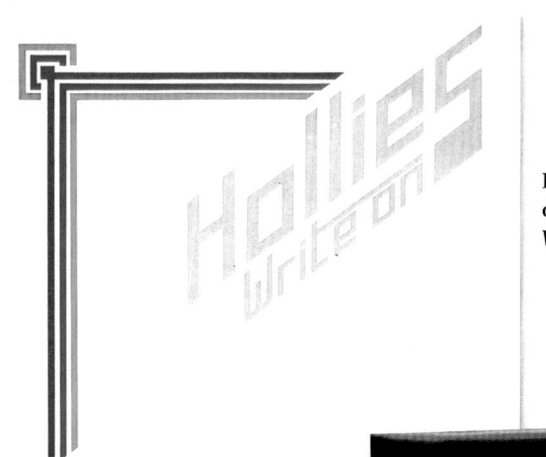

Left: By 1976 the hits might have dried up, but The Hollies simply *Write On.* (*Polydor*)

Right: *Russian Roulette* was the first Hollies album not to get an American release. (*Polydor*)

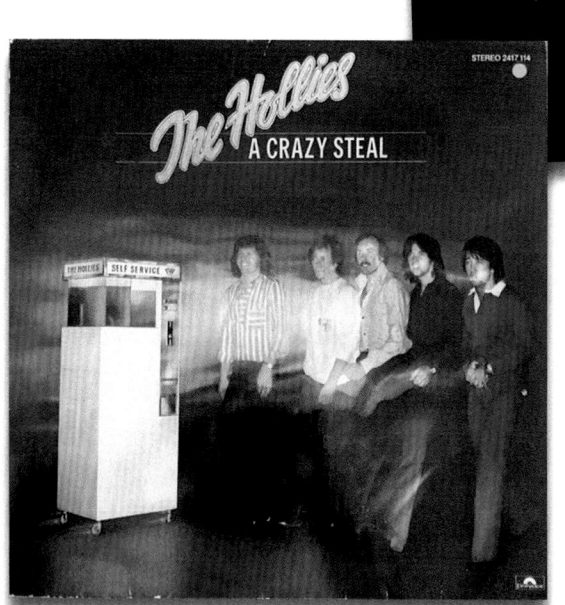

HOLLIES

STEREO 2417 114

The Hollies A CRAZY STEAL

Russian Roulette

Left: *A Crazy Steal* from 1978 features The Hollies' fine version of the Emmylou Harris song 'Boulder To Birmingham'. (*Polydor*)

Right: An inverted reading of the digital numbers that form this album title appears to spell Hollies. (*Polydor*)

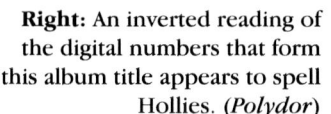

FIVE THREE ONE - DOUBLE SEVEN O FOUR

Left: 'The day the music died', but a high-profile tribute album from The Hollies. (*Polydor*)

Right: The cover-photo emphatically shows Graham Nash, Allan Clarke, Tony Hicks and Bobby Elliott, who reformed for this one-off album for Atlantic. (*Atlantic*)

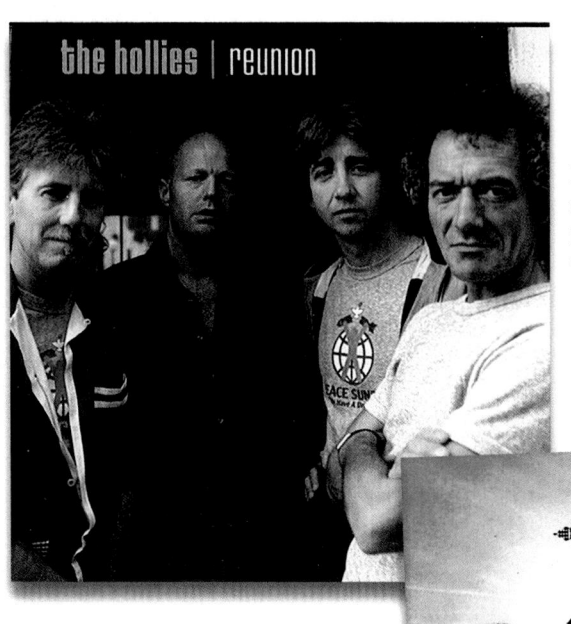

Left: A live Reunion album recorded during the American promotional tour, with the Clarke-Hicks-Nash-Elliott line-up. (*Snapper Music*)

Right: By 2006, only Tony Hicks and Bobby Elliott remained from the 1960s line-up, but they had *Staying Power*. (*EMI*)

Left: The Hollies not only survive, but continue and prosper, *Then, Now, Always*. (*EMI*)

Allan Clarke Returns

Hollies

Personnel:
Allan Clarke: lead vocals
Terry Sylvester: vocals, rhythm guitar
Tony Hicks: vocals, lead guitar
Bobby Elliott: drums, percussion
Bernie Calvert: bass guitar, keyboards
plus Jim Jewell: saxophone on 'It's A Shame, It's A Game' (tenor), 'Transatlantic Westbound Jet' (soprano)
Duffy Power: harmonica on 'Down On The Run'
Chris Gunning: orchestral arranger on 'Don't Let Me Down', 'The Air That I Breathe', 'Love Makes The World Go Round'
Produced at EMI Studios by Ron Richards and The Hollies, 7 August-17 December 1973
Released: March 1974, Polydor 2383-262
Running time: 41:42
Highest chart placing: UK: 38, US: 28

Emphatically 'Hollies', in case there were lingering doubts, because Allan had apparently decided his real name was not 'Arold after all. As 'Long Cool Woman In A Black Dress' unexpectedly took off in the States, the Rickfors-fronted Hollies undertook series of major US dates – although it's Terry who sang lead when they performed the hit. Nevertheless, the tour's perceived commercial failure inevitably lead to Allan Clarke and his familiar voice officially rejoining in July after his two solo LPs – although he retained an option for future solo projects. 'I needed to go back to The Hollies just as much as they needed me,' Allan told the *NME*, 'I can swallow my pride as well as anybody else.' The line-up was now Allan Clarke (vocals), Tony Hicks (guitar, harmony vocals), Terry Sylvester (rhythm guitar, harmony vocals), Bernie Calvert (bass, keyboards), and Bobby Elliott (drums, percussion), with added input from Pete Wingfield (keyboards) and production tweaks by Ron Richards, Alan Parsons and Mike Jarrett.

Reviewed in *NME* as 'unmemorable, if characteristically professional,' this LP reached UK number 38, and in June, it made the US number 28. With its Hipgnosis mug-shot cover, it will be their last original album to chart in either market.

In the meantime, Rickfors returned to Sweden, where he inaugurated a successful solo career, commencing with the LP *Mikael Rickfors* (1975) and *The Wheel* (1976). Several albums later, his best-selling *Vinegar* (1988) was followed by new work as part of Swedish supergroup Grymlings, while his compositions were being covered by Carlos Santana, Percy Sledge, Jim Capaldi and Carla Olson.

'It's a Shame, It's a Game' (Hicks, Jennings)

Handclaps and dance-horns, tongues in multiple cheeks with Allan looking wild in white, a spoof on style? (although he claims 'I really felt hip wearing my stripes, Baby'.) There are answering response-vocals that hark back to the Coasters, a swaggering sax solo, and Allan declaims denials into the fade – 'there's so many rumours about me, and about you, I don't know what to do.' As the opening track on their reunion album, the 'shake hands and make up again' lyric strikes a certain appropriate note.

'Rubber Lucy' (Clarke)

Nudge-nudge wink-wink. Bobby Elliott's thumping drums, noodling slivers of guitar, 4:12-minutes of witty teasing lyrics ... 'as the queen bee, I'll make your honey, I'll even populate your hive'; a Blues innuendo that can probably be traced all the way back to Slim Harpo ('I'm a King Bee'). The floozy jibes could be considered politically incorrect in the way that The Rolling Stones ('Stray Cat Blues') or The Faces ('Stay With Me') dabble provocatively into that disreputable groupie milieu, but for Allan Clarke, it's delivered in a disarmingly warm caring way. More *Carry On* movie than it is confrontational.

'Pick Up The Pieces Again' (Sylvester)

A dreamy west-coast ambience, with Terry's vocals and Tony's sitar-tuning, this track is a direct lift from the Germany-only *Out On the Road* album (see entry), and is later collected onto the French anthology *Terry Sylvester: The Complete Works 1969-1982* (Magic AUD362009014).

'Transatlantic Westbound Jet' (Elliott, Sylvester)

Written by Bobby with Terry during the American tour, there's a cymbal-shimmer to represent jet-stream. Deep-down funk pulse, Allan's phased treated vocals, soulful organ and Floydian fade courtesy of Alan Parsons. This is another re-recording of an *Out On The Road* track, with Allan reshaping the original Mikael Rickfors vocal about 'travel through the nation, in search of stimulation.' And there's a distinct difference between the two versions: the original is harder and stripped-back to solid rock instrumentation, whereas the second version has a more smoothly-finished cauldron of sound, urging 'boogaloo, well walk on through, my prescription's good for you,' while it's debatable which prescription offers the better remedy for the Rockin' Pneumonia And The Boogie-Woogie Flu. This is one of the few examples that offer a convincing argument for Mikael Rickfors coming out shining. It was collected onto the 1998 *The Hollies At Abbey Road: 1973 To 1989* (EMI 496 4342).

'Out On the Road' (Hicks, Lynch)

Busy 'wailing my guitar' swagger about having sold his soul to the devil or the King of Rock 'n' Roll, all the things he should have done while he was out touring and living the rock lifestyle. It's a re-recording of the Germany-only track, replacing the attractive original walking bass, and with hoarse new Allan vocals. At the time he was writing this song, Tony was living in the St John's Wood Loudoun Road address that would later be domicile for Liam Gallagher of Manchester's next Britrock wave.

'The Air That I Breathe' (Hammond, Hazlewood)

Sometimes music can touch the very soul. Sometimes it can voice the impossible promise of eternal love. The Hollies seldom bettered this peak moment at any time during their long and eventful career arc. If The Hollies only ever made one record, this would engrave their page in the Book of Love (see the entry on the single for full details).

'Falling Calling' (Clarke, Sylvester)

Paul & Linda McCartney call around during the recording session, from the adjacent studio where they're working on Wings tracks. The pair get to hear the clattering, dislocated percussion that sets this song's tone of doubt; he didn't believe in the Bible, he didn't believe the good book, he got into bad ways and ended up in a prison cell. When he's served his five thousand days, he'll come out a better man wearing a new face. A dark, moody confessional that reached number 31 in Holland, where it was issued as a single.

'Down on the Run' (Hicks, Jennings)

Easing back into smooth, feel-good harmonies, despite an edgy lyric about a Marlon Brando biker's weekend 'chicken run'. The Hollies don't make for convincing Hells Angels; they never did. 'Sweating in my leathers' indeed! Nice tune, though, despite what *Melody Maker* calls a 'clumsy change'. This is another product of Tony's fruitful writing association with Colin, who would reach the chart in his own right as part of the novelty Star Turn On 45 Pints – number 12 in April 1988 with 'Pump Up The Bitter'! And the harmonica is not from Allan, but a guest appearance by veteran rocker Duffy Power.

'Don't Let Me Down' (Clarke)

Recorded in Studio Two, Allan lays down guide vocal, Tony and Terry feed in acoustic guitars, Bernie and Bobby underscore bass and drum patterns. It's a slow love pledge with Allan at his most vulnerable as he awaits her arrival – 'giving us an insight into his life at the time' according to Bobby. Allan's tenor voice goes from almost conversational interior dialogue to strained elongated-vowel pleading. The subtle guitar, French horns and bowed double basses, with Chris Gunning's string embellishments catch a breath of the air that I breathe, which, according to an unsympathetic *Melody Maker* review, 'just about escapes drowning in its own syrup.'

'Love Makes the World Go Around' (Clarke, Sylvester)

In spite of relativistic Einsteinian physics, neither gravity nor orbital spin apply, it seems the world just can't revolve without love. There's a low bass line to define an affectionate soda-pop jukebox fifties-style smoothness, in The Hollies style, with some lyric input from artist John Bowstead, older brother of Allan Clarke's wife Jenni. The song is taken from an experimental 1970 stage production called *Oh Flux* which he devised with Allan and Terry; the song was dismissed as 'Radio Two schmaltz' by *Melody Maker*, and the track was subsequently omitted from the American edition.

'The Day That Curly Billy Shot Down Crazy Sam McGee' (Clarke)

Allan tells Peter Doggett that this was 'an attempt to recapture 'Long Cool Woman''. It was the first track he recorded with The Hollies after the estrangement (with 'Mexico Gold'), and 'the logical step after 'Long Cool Woman'.' Bobby Elliott agrees that 'this was Allan's 'welcome back' track. We thought it was a good idea to carry on where we'd left off' (*Record Collector* magazine). Some claim to detect a hint of Creedence Clearwater Revival in the slap echo of Bobby's snare-drum and Tony's vari-speed multitracked guitars; others feel there's something inside every male psyche that enjoys that western-movie trigger-happy swagger. Allan wears a cowboy hat for the solo *I've Got Time* cover photo, and lives out the two-fisted trigger-happy frontier lore on this hit single.

Related Releases
Hollies US listing (as Epic KE 32574):

'Falling Calling', 'It's a Shame, It's a Game', 'Don't Let Me Down', 'Out on the Road', 'The Air That I Breathe', 'Rubber Lucy', 'Transatlantic Westbound Jet', 'Pick Up the Pieces Again', 'Down on the Run', 'The Day That Curly Billy Shot Down Crazy Sam McGee'

'The Day That Curly Billy Shot Down Crazy Sam McGee' (Clarke) b/w 'Born a Man' (Lynch, Hicks)

Personnel:
Allan Clarke: lead vocals
Terry Sylvester: vocals, rhythm guitar
Tony Hicks: vocals, lead guitar
Bobby Elliott: drums, percussion
Bernie Calvert: bass guitar, keyboards
Released: 1 October 1973, Polydor 2058-403

With Western gunfighter swagger aplenty, Allan's composition has one slitted-eye on the heavy guitar and echoed vocals construction of 'Long Cool Woman', but adds a strong melodic storyline, with Hollies harmony-passages too. 'We went into the studio and when the session was over, we listened to the song. It sounded fantastic, and from that evolved the idea of an album' Allan told *Melody Maker*. With Ron Richards there, and Alan Parsons as sound engineer on hand when it came to editing thirty seconds off the master tape to achieve an acceptable 4:30-minutes, the single hit UK number 24 in a *Record Retailer* chart (27 October) topped by David Cassidy, and number 25 on *NME* (10 November) with former-colleague Elton John's 'Goodbye Yellow Brick Road' in the same Top Ten. Yet it makes number 1 in Holland! Premiered on 'Top of the Pops', introduced by Noel Edmonds – 27 September 1973, it features an open-jacket bare-chested Allan playing guitar while delivering power vocals with effortless confidence. Meanwhile, from the Tony Hicks-Kenny Lynch pen, born in the land of the free, the hard-scrabble self-pitying B-side effectively tells the tale of his deprived childhood. Another track lifted from the *Out On The Road* album.

The Hollies Greatest Hits (October 1973, Epic KE 32061). Highest US chart position: 157

They might not have been 'heavy' in the Heavy Rock sense, but they sure had class. There have been a lot of hits compilations. This one tells the story from a slightly American perspective, it reached US number 157 during November. There's also a Canadian edition (Columbia BOT-10076).

'Bus Stop', 'Carrie Anne', 'Stop, Stop, Stop', 'Look Through Any Window', 'Dear Eloise', 'Long Cool Woman in a Black Dress', 'He Ain't Heavy, He's My Brother', 'Just One Look', 'King Midas in Reverse', 'Pay You Back With Interest', 'Long Dark Road', 'On a Carousel'

'The Air That I Breathe' (Hammond, Hazlewood) b/w 'No More Riders' (Sylvester, Gordon) (January 1974, Polydor 2058435)

Written by the team of Albert Hammond and Mike Hazlewood, The Hollies record 'The Air That I Breathe' after hearing the Phil Everly version of the song, which, considering the group's earlier Everly connections, seems entirely appropriate. 'Ron Richards' secretary, Shirley, heard it, and she drew our attention to it', Allan told me. 'She said we should do it. And she was right. It became our last really big record.' Aching with sincerity, Allan delivers one of his finest vocal performances, on a love song of classic purity etched with Tony's hauntingly high electric guitar lines, played through a Hammond organ's Leslie speaker. The rhythm track was recorded with Ludwig drums using a deeper, damped Super Sensitive 402 snare drum, which Alan Parsons' microphone placement transmutes into tympani. Vocals were laid down the following day. The final guitar and tom-tom overdub was added on 22 November 1973, in Abbey Road Studio Three, with strings scored by Chris Gunning. It hit the UK number two on 23 March 1974 – ludicrously kept off the top spot by 'Billy, Don't Be A Hero' by Paper Lace! Then, continuing their US chart rollercoaster, 'The Air That I Breathe' (US Epic 5-11100) reaches number 6 in August, another million-seller, number 2 in Germany and Australia.

The B-side was a product of Terry Sylvester's writing partnership with David Gordon, which would result in a number of songs on Terry's solo album. Later collected as a bonus track on the *Hollies* expanded edition, the 2:50-minute 'No More Riders' extends the elegiac Western theme with snarling guitar and golden eagles circling in the windless skies above Native American braves on the warpath. Terry's voice delivers with silky efficiency.

When they talk about classic rock, 'The Air That I Breathe' is what they mean, although it would be the last of twenty-seven major Hollies hits – they'd not chart significantly again, barring reissues. With an air of confused hurt, Allan explains that 'we carried on working. We kept trying different things. But that was our last really big record.' But what a high to go out on! When it was used to subtitle yet another Greatest Hits compilation, *Vox* said that 'anywhere The Hollies went, they did so with consummate professionalism' (May 1993). When Graham Nash said he'd never have left The Hollies if he'd known they were going to make records like this, he was only half-joking. A reissue in December 1988 (EMI EM80) reached number 60.

Another Night

Personnel:
Allan Clarke: lead vocals, guitar, harmonica
Terry Sylvester: vocals, guitar
Tony Hicks: vocals, lead guitar, banjo, mandolin, bass, keyboards
Bobby Elliott: drums
Bernie Calvert: bass guitar, keyboards
plus Pete Wingfield: keyboards
Produced at EMI Studios by Ron Richards, 19 March-4 October 1974
Released: February 1975, Polydor 2442-128
Running time: 40:21
Highest chart position: US: 123, UK: did not chart

The Hollies' fifteenth official studio album was also the second for the returning Allan Clarke, with Ron Richards safely back in the producer's chair. Music archivist Peter Doggett says that 'like all their subsequent albums in the seventies, it bore comparison with the work of the top American studio bands, rather than the singles groups who had been their chief rivals in the sixties. But the trademark harmonies remain as a statement of faith in their past.' It was also the strongest collection of group originals since *Hollies Sing Hollies,* with Allan and Tony writing in partnership with Terry. The only non-original – the Bruce Springsteen-penned 'Sandy' – was lifted as a single, and although it failed to chart in the UK, it hit the US number 85. Allan Clarke recorded other Springsteen songs for his subsequent solo albums. Bruce Eder of the online *AllMusic Review* considered that 'latter-day Hollies may not be first on too many people's lists of priority acquisitions, but if someone is going to start listening to the post-'Long Cool Woman' band, this is the place to begin.' By April, this LP reached the US number 123.

'Another Night' (Clarke, Hicks, Sylvester)
A slinky swamp-rock feel that captures the weary loneliness of life on the road: 'the DJ plays a song from the past I remember'. The Hollies back catalogue offers plenty of those to choose from! Alan Parsons took time to step out from engineering to play the synthesizer part on a Moog borrowed from Paul McCartney! During a stop-over in L.A. The Hollies perform this song on CBS-TVs *The Dinah Shore Show* broadcast 22 May 1975. A star of the 1940s Big Band era, Dinah was romantically linked to Burt Reynolds during this phase of her highly-rated chat show.

'Fourth of July, Asbury Park (Sandy)' (Springsteen)
The gentle melodic sway and three-voice frontline harmonies evoke the full poignancy of the finely-turned lyric, edited down from the full six-minute original and embraced by subtle Chris Gunning orchestration. The Hollies

were always ahead of the game when it came to talent-spotting new singer-songwriter names, as their previous covers have proved. And it's worth bearing in mind that Bruce Springsteen was still a new artist only appreciated by the cognoscenti and self-appointed hiperati. Allan was even to get a singles bite at the epic 'Born To Run' (October 1975, b/w 'Why Don't You Call') and later recorded 'Blinded By The Light' for his solo set *I've Got Time* (July 1976). A live Hollies version of 'Sandy' was added as a bonus track on the CD edition of *Another Night*.

'Lonely Hobo Lullaby' (Clarke, Sylvester)

There's a knock-knock-knocking on heaven's door feel to this sad paean to wandering boot-heels rootlessness, with the harmonica catching a restless urge to travel any horizon that I choose. In a bizarre series of coincidences, this song was picked up by Percy Sledge for his 2004 album *Shining Through The Rain*, which also features a number of Mikael Rickfors compositions, including the title song.

'Second Hand Hang-Ups' (Clarke, Hicks, Sylvester)

Magical sighing strings with an intoxicated lilt, bending into harmony lines that sweetly elongate as the song gathers momentum. Lyrically, while they've been apart, he's been hearing 'Chinese Whispers' about her from mutual friends while protesting 'I'm not disillusioned, I'm a member of the union, membership paid, done my dues.' It builds into an impressively layered orchestral culmination and became the B-side of several editions of the single 'Sandy (Fourth Of July, Asbury Park)'.

'Time Machine Jive' (Clarke, Hicks, Sylvester)

Hard riffing guitars, echoed vocals, rocking boogie piano, naggingly repetitively chanted chorus – 'LOOK OUT!', look out your window tonight. 'You gotta reach out and try to grab my glitter suit' Allan sings, 'snatch your handful of stars, take a trip in my seven-league boots,' with a passing reference to 'my *Star Trek* music'. What it actually means is anyone's guess, although the three-way writer credits provide a good example of The Hollies as an H.G. Wellsian Time Machine in its own right, shifting unscathed through years and decades.

'I'm Down' (Clarke, Hicks, Sylvester)

Reality is calling, in paced sighs, structured layers of guitar and harmony, with orchestration scored by Tony Hymas, who also plays piano. The lyric concerns mixed-up family intrigue in which, he's 'not ungrateful' to the folks who brought him up. Described by Bobby Elliott as 'a sombre masterpiece,' it's a million light-years from The Beatles' same-name screamer: 'the ballad was brilliant in its own way. Maybe those heart-rending songs were a device created by our frontman to try and release the heartache he was experiencing at the time.' A live version was added as a bonus track on the CD edition of *Another Night*.

'Look Out Johnny (There's a Monkey on Your Back)' (Clarke, Hicks, Sylvester)

A taut big-city east-side narco-glimmer, a cruising wheeler-dealer midnight chorus, plus stinging guitar solo distortion, with the monkey on your back as junkie-slang for addiction. Everybody's got something to hide, except Johnny and his monkey. This is the closest The Hollies are likely to get to crash-bash street-hard and nasty. With Bernie ill during the recording sessions, Tony plays bass on this – and on 'Lucy'.

'Give Me Time' (Clarke, Sylvester)

This song starts with Allan's harmonica borrowing just a hint of the Last Post bugle riff, feeding into Tony's bottleneck Gibson and what Bobby Elliott calls his 'music of the mountains' strumming. A thoughtfully slow and considered track, he needs time to think it over; he's not ready to go steady. The Hollies perform this song – along with 'I'm Down' and 'Sandy' on an episode of *The Eddy Go Round Show* – hosted by Eddy Becker, filmed 4 March in the Hilversum TV-Studio and broadcast by the Netherlands NCRV 6 March 1975. Duane Eddy and Frank Ifield also star, with Abba performing 'Honey Honey' and current single 'I Do, I Do, I Do, I Do.'

'You Gave Me Life (With That Look in Your Eyes)' (Clarke, Sylvester)

With tick-tock flanging across your ears from speaker to speaker, and Danelectro sitar stirred over a choppy rhythmic mélange, she's on the street-corner feeding another guy the same line that got him hooked. Allan's voice is set to the strident 'Long Cool Woman' mode. Tony's descending guitar riff and distorted soloing jostles Bobby's phased drum-pulse. This is 3:43-minutes of head-on confrontation, with lots of odd elements that shouldn't work yet come together deliciously.

'Lucy' (Clarke, Hicks, Sylvester)

Tender and tragic, he just got his partner's terminal diagnosis in a phone call from the doctor. Should he lie to her? How is he going to tell the children that Mama's 'going away'? He pledges that if she stays, he'll strive to make what remains of their future together more beautiful, living day to day. For there are no diamonds left in this Lucy's sky. The mawkish aspects of the big country-flavoured ballad are tempered by simple strummed accompaniment, with a restrained use of strings. We Close the album with a big emotional tear-jerker.

Related Releases

'Son of a Rotten Gambler' (Taylor) b/w 'Layin' on the Music' (Clarke, Sylvester) (May 1974, Polydor 2058 476)

Chip Taylor called in at the studio to audition this song live for The Hollies. Chip, who had written previous singles 'I Can't Let Go' and 'The Baby', wrote this with more than a passing nod at Don Gibson's 'Sea Of Heartbreak'. Already a country hit for Anne Murray, it became The Hollies' third slice of Americana, taken at a country-slow pace with Allan's voice emotionally cracking into half-spoken line-endings. Sweetened by tasteful strings, it rises into hallmark Hollies mid-section harmonies. Issued in May, the single slipped below the radar – Bobby Elliott called it 'a disaster,' although it went top thirty in Holland and Germany. The Clarke-Sylvester flip has itchy feet, with hoedown funk and a whoop in the instrumental break. But perhaps boogaloo is not quite the right pose for The Hollies.

Both sides are collected as bonus tracks onto the CD edition of *Another Night*, alongside live versions of 'Another Night' and 'I'm Down' plus 'Come Down To The Shore' (a 3:50-minute song by Colin Horton Jennings) – with crawling drums and harmonica, a skanking rhythm with an easy loping Caribbean feel.

The Hollies played a lucrative week's cabaret at the Batley Variety Club and perform 'Rotten Gambler' as guests on comedian Les Dawson's Yorkshire TV show *Sez Les*, then they played a Manchester Free Trade Hall concert with additional musicians from the local Hallé Orchestra.

'I'm Down' (Clarke, Hicks, Sylvester) b/w 'Hello Lady Goodbye' (Clarke, Hicks, Sylvester) (8 November 1974, Polydor 2058 533)

Seriously considered as the album's lead single, until the advent of 'Son Of A Rotten Gambler', its eventual release failed to chart, although it made the top thirty in Germany, Holland and Australia. It also becomes a US single b/w 'Look Out Johnny (There's A Monkey On Your Back)' as Epic 8-50144.

'Sandy (Fourth of July, Asbury Park)' (Springsteen) b/w 'Second Hand Hang-Ups' (Clarke, Hicks, Sylvester) (16 May 1975, Polydor 2058-595)

Two tracks lifted from the album, and previously mentioned. It proved a success in Holland, where it peaked at number eight, and in Germany, where it hit number 22.

'Another Night' (Clarke, Hicks, Sylvester) b/w 'Time Machine Jive' (Clarke, Hicks, Sylvester) (May 1975, Epic 8-50110)

The album title track, issued as a 2 May 1975 single in Canada and the US only, reaches an American number 71 in July. Meanwhile, although it's a song from the album, the B-side version of 'Time Machine Jive' is taken at a faster pace.

Write On

Personnel:
Allan Clarke: lead vocals
Terry Sylvester: vocals, guitar
Tony Hicks: vocals, lead guitar
Bobby Elliott: drums, percussion
Bernie Calvert: bass guitar, keyboards
plus Pete Wingfield: piano, organ, ARP synthesizer
Hans-Peter Arnesen: piano, clavinet
Rod Argent: piano, synthesizer on 'Star'
Tony Hymas: string arrangements
Produced at EMI Studios by The Hollies, 9 June-18 September 1975
Released: January 1976, Polydor 2442-141
Running time: 34:32
No chart placings

The Hollies finally split from producer Ron Richards, and they self-produced this album at Abbey Road, as 'A Hollies Production'. 'It seemed that when he left, we stopped having hits' mused Allan. 'Maybe we had too many hit singles for our own good?' countered Bobby Elliott, 'and the singles didn't always equate with the albums? We had poppy singles, but we were trying to do a deeper sort of album' (to Peter Doggett of *Record Collector* magazine). To be fair, it does seem that no matter what they attempted, the critics insisted on referring back to their 'golden age of hit singles'. Although Noel Edmonds made *Write On* his Radio One album of the Week, playing a different track each day.

The regular band line-up is augmented by Pete Wingfield on keyboards, plus Hans-Peter Arnesen (piano and clavinet), and Tony Hymas (string arrangements). The album was completed with the final master cut at Abbey Road on 8 October 1975. All the tracks are written by Allan, Tony and Terry Sylvester, with one exception:

'Star' (Clarke, Hicks, Sylvester)
The vocalist protests his 'star' status and plays the sweet hitchhiker, a track from his latest LP on his Cadillac in-car sound system, but she doesn't recognise him. She turns out to be a movie star, too, on her way to a premier. Rod Argent plays piano and zooming Moog synthesizer over a jaunty shuffle. Unfortunately, when issued as an April single, b/w 'Love Is The Thing' (Polydor 2058-719), record-buyers fail to recognise its star quality too.

'Write On' (Clarke, Hicks, Sylvester)
An inspirational message from Allan and Tony, with time and fame wearing heavy on their shoulders, it's difficult not to read an autobiographical content

to their knowing familiarity with the frustrations of a musical fast, 'don't feel sad because the radio ain't playing 'em', just believe in Rock 'n' Roll, and shine on. The lines 'sing your Rock 'n' Roll with a touch of soul, ballads with feeling, send your audience reeling' seem like the album's manifesto. A powerful affirmation of the power of music.

'Sweet Country Calling' (Clarke, Hicks, Sylvester)
Honky-Tonk piano, with both Rod Argent and Pete Wingfield in the mix, and Allan adopting his Nashville voice, to escape the city and head home because 'I want to hear the bluegrass.' Tony plays twangy guitar, sweet as morning dew or, according to the *NME*, with 'deep-buttoned upholstery'. Hopping the Rock Island Line freight train is an obvious reference back to the Skiffle that started it all for The Hollies, while 'last time I saw her she was waving me goodbye' could just be quoting the Chuck Berry song they'd covered on *Stay With The Hollies*.

'Love Is the Thing' (Clarke, Hicks, Sylvester)
Recorded at the Emison Studios in Queensway, 14 July 1975, involving treated piano and flowing tides of voices, slow-paced and tender with romantic memories, this is a heartfelt paean to the saving grace of Love that raises simplicity to an art-form. Bobby Elliott is less impressed, as in his autobiography he wrote 'to me, it seemed as though we were attempting to ape 'I'm Not In Love', the classic 10cc song. The result was a pointless, pretentious wash.' Of course, Graham Gouldman, who wrote 'Bus Stop', was by then a member of 10cc.

'I Won't Move Over' (Clarke, Hicks, Sylvester)
He refuses to believe the stories that are circulating. He refuses to believe it's over. Sharply keening guitar from Tony, but Rod Argent's Moog is a little intrusive. Recorded on 1 September, the final orchestral overdubs were added on 18 September 1975 at Abbey Road. At first, Allan was dubious about using electric keyboards, but the advantages of Pete Wingfield's ARP synth in replicating orchestral effects for touring purposes made obvious sense, and were soon to make greater inroads into The Hollies' sound.

'Narida' (Clarke, Hicks, Sylvester)
3:59-minutes of shuffling Latin rhythms from Allan and Terry, complete with Santana-style guitar. With a full Mardi Gras in her hoochie-coochie sway, hard-headed Na-Na-Na-Na-Narida is the Queen of the backstreet avenue girls, and no one's gonna beat her. This was recorded Tuesday 2 September 1975 during the album's second session on the new Abbey Road 24-track recorder, with Peter Bown sitting at the controls vacated by Ron Richards.

'Stranger' (Clarke, Hicks, Sylvester)

From Tony and Allan, with Austrian keyboard-player Hans-Peter Arnesen on hand to add clavinet to a tough, tight Bowery-boys G-Men Harlem street-story, as dark as it is moody, rife with intrigue. A down, down, down dirty strutting rhythm that rhymes stranger with danger. Chosen as the B-side of German number 31 hit single 'Write On', it gets about as close as white boys from Manchester will ever get to US street life.

'Crocodile Woman (She Bites)' (Clarke, Hicks, Sylvester)

With a Clarke-Sylvester-Hicks credit, the sharp jumpy toe-tapping rhythms hit the then-contemporary Rock 'n' Roll revival style, with Tony's distorted guitar playing against boogie piano. The lyric draws on the voodoo 'she uses charm like a witch casting bad spells,' with the warning that she's a sly girl, a good timer social climber, but beware! This track is collected onto the 1998 *The Hollies At Abbey Road: 1973 To 1989* (EMI 496 4342).

'My Island' (Clarke, Hicks, Sylvester)

A soft and warm tropical samba shuffle with synth, he's done his time, now he wants to go home. Bobby Elliott recalls how, when they'd first recorded 'Just One Look' in the same studio, he'd had a single microphone suspended over the drumkit, now 'I couldn't move for mics – there was one placed on every drum' of his silver Ludwig kit. There's a live version of 'My Island' on *Hollies Live Hits* (March 1977, Polydor 2383-428), which also includes on-stage renditions of 'Star', plus 'Another Night' and 'I'm Down'.

'There's Always Goodbye' (Richards)

The album's only non-original composition is a tender romantic song with a soft-edged country sway. Also recorded by Frankie Valli and Anne Murray, as well as writer Randy Richards own version – recorded as 'There's Always A Goodbye' on his 1976 *If You've Ever Loved* album (Little Angel Records LAR1111). The Hollies lead in with disconcertingly eerie guitar sounds before Allan oozes into the regretful lyric about the doomed fragility of love – 'you smile softly as you leave my bed,' then merging into the full group harmony voices. There's a false ending, reintroduced by clear piano notes, and powerful title repetitions into the close, ending the album on a high.

Related Releases

Write On (France, Magic Records 5244142)

There was no US edition, but there was an expanded 1999 CD edition that includes bonus tracks 'Boulder To Birmingham', 'Star' and 'My Island' live. There's also an unedited version of Allan Clarke's composition 'Samuel' – pronounced 'Sam-you-well' – with Spanish acoustic guitar offset by curling bent-notes, 'light a candle' where muddy waters run clean (included on *The*

Hollies At Abbey Road 1973-1989), plus Allan's solo version of 'Born To Run'. He'd initially urged The Hollies to record the Bruce Springsteen song, but after a perfunctory run-though, when they declined, he did it himself.

'Boulder to Birmingham' (Harris, Danoff) b/w 'Crocodile Woman (She Bites)' (Clarke, Hicks, Sylvester) (February 1976, Polydor 2058-694)

Graham Nash's one-time significant other, Joni Mitchell, once perceptively pointed out that 'something's lost, but something's gained in living every day,' and who can tell if the loss outweighs the gain? The Hollies forsake their sixties pop hooks in favour of the more mature template established by 'He Ain't Heavy' or 'The Air That I Breathe', in a quest for another big power ballad. Written by Emmylou Harris and Bill Danoff (of the Starland Vocal Band), as a tribute to the late Gram Parsons, Allan adapts the poignant lyric and delivers it with faultless sincerity. In the elusive hunt for credibility and commerce, the Emmylou connection must have made the song an attractive proposition. So its chart failure must have been perplexing, although the single was well-received in New Zealand. And yes, the B-side, lifted from *Write On*, bites.

'Star' b/w 'Love Is the Thing' (April 1976, Polydor 2058-719)

Two fine tracks lifted from the *Write On* album, which trouble the chart compilers not one jot.

Russian Roulette

Personnel:
Allan Clarke: lead vocals
Terry Sylvester: vocals, guitar
Tony Hicks: vocals, lead guitar
Bobby Elliott: drums, percussion
Bernie Calvert: bass guitar, keyboards
Produced at Basing Street Studios by The Hollies, 14 July-2 September 1976.
Running time: 35:47
Released: December 1976, (Polydor 2383 42)
No chart placings.

Self-produced, with no heavy orchestrations this time around, recorded
between 14 July and 2 September at the Notting Hill Basing Street Studios, this
was The Hollies' second album of the year – although neither of them nor the
four singles lifted from them, managed to chart. If 'King Midas in Reverse' had
been deemed a failure when it peaked no higher than number 18, they'd have
been delighted for any of these singles to chart that high! Even *NME* was forced
to concede that 'those gilded harmonies never lose their shine or their edge,'
but this album did not even get an American release. They were all original
Clarke-Hicks-Sylvester songs.

'Wiggle That Wotsit' (Clarke, Hicks, Sylvester)
Just to prove The Hollies have not lost their sense of humour, this jokey
throwaway disco shot was issued as an October 1976 single b/w 'Corrine'
(Polydor 2058-799), and did fine in some markets, number 11 in New Zealand,
and number 23 in Holland. A fun dance-craze pastiche, it involves a punchy
horn section that includes jazzers Henry Lowther on trumpet, John Mumford
on trombone and Bobby Elliott's schoolfriend Jimmy Jewell on alto and tenor
sax (he'd played with the Gallagher & Lyle duo on their hit *Breakaway* album
earlier in 1976). Yet Bernie Calvert was embarrassed by this track; it made
him cringe! The B-side, cut at the same July sessions, but left off the album,
is a rather unconvincing stab at skanking, with Hollies vocals over a reggae
backing. It was eventually collected onto the six-disc *Head Out of Dreams,
August 1973-May 1988* compilation.

'Forty-Eight Hour Parole' (Clarke, Hicks, Sylvester)
Heavier rocking Hollies with dual chiming guitars and jabbing keyboards. Just
a touch of 'Long Cool Woman' in the hard-edged echoed vocals – 'I wasn't
born, I was carved out of stone,' but streamlined with harmonies. Tony's
snarling guitar solo threatens to 'set the town on fire.' The track was to hang
around long enough to become the B-side of a May 1977 'Hello To Romance'
single.

111

'Thanks for the Memories' (Clarke, Hicks, Sylvester)
Comedian Bob Hope had once dueted with Shirley Ross on a song called 'Thanks For The Memory'. This is not that song. Instead, ghosted electric keyboards, soft smoky horn and light congas conjure a sound that captures the mood of the cover images of exotic cocktails. We are already three tracks into the album, and we've seen three very different faces of the band. Track-by-track there will be more forays down novel trails showing either an openness to new times, or just maybe, a loss of self-confident focus.

'My Love' (Clarke, Hicks, Sylvester)
A return to tight familiar harmonies, as though this track is some lost 1965 B-side. 'Please don't take my advances too lightly', Allan pleads with eloquent courtesy, in a catchy up-tempo glide with sweet guitar-work from the mid-point break. A simple uncomplicated declaration of affections, don't 'throw it all away.' When The Hollies start doing pure pop, it's as good as done.

'Lady of the Night' (Clarke, Hicks, Sylvester)
Sizzling electric keyboard, long soaring Jim Jewell alto sax solo, on a Clarke-Sylvester-Hicks ode to the stalking streetwalker who has Allan's mind racing. She's got him confused, but tantalised; next time, he's sending out a warning to other guys, she's gonna get you! A sultry 3:34-minute strut with jazz-tone guitar, the full last minute given over to rolling and tumbling rhythms in a steaming instrumental bouillabaisse of simmering funk.

'Russian Roulette' (Clarke, Hicks, Sylvester)
The title track has dramatic stop-start poised guitar riffs interspersed with squonking keyboards and the sound of tumbling dice, all spinning on a blizzarding percussion. He's a compulsive gambler on a downward spiral – or maybe that's just the metaphor? – because a lyric can speak truths through an assumed persona. Allan wears his shades to visit a lowlife dive in New Orleans where whisky kills the pain because it's 'cheap at twice the price.' He finds a hundred dollar bill lying at his feet. So he'll 'give it one more spin' on the roulette wheel, then 'that's me, I'm through.' Although quitting seems an unlikely prospect.

'Draggin' My Heels' (Clarke, Hicks, Sylvester)
Funky within an inch of the dancefloor, oozing silk vocals on pattering congas from Australian jazz-percussionist Chris Karan and jazz-slanted Pete Wingfield keyboards, Latin maracas, zinging synth-lines, it all invites – and gets – a twelve-inch Club remix. 'If I had the chance to go back again, I wouldn't do the same, I learned by mistakes.' No one drags their heels when The Hollies get down and strut their stuff.

'Louise' (Clarke, Hicks, Sylvester)
Bopping at the hop guitar, boogie piano, Jim Jewell's outstanding sax-work and a touch of title echo on the frightenin' lightning. Among the mid-seventies mélange of fads and fancies was a part tongue-in-cheek part-nostalgic glance back at greasy blue-jean early Rock 'n' Roll. This fine jiving song with sleek Clarke-Hicks-Sylvester harmonies works well and rocks hard, they sound like they're having fun. But throughout the album's style-diversity, it's the vocals that unite it all into very obviously the 'Hollies' identity.

'Be With You' (Clarke, Hicks, Sylvester)
'Blue Jay Way' organ fades in, to a slow romantic harmony showcase illustrating what Clarke, then Clarke-Sylvester, then Clarke-Hicks-Sylvester each contribute to the complete 'mark 2' Hollies sound – just as 'Stewball' once did for the Clarke-Hicks-Nash line-up back in 1966. A swaying 'Across the Universe' chorus repetition of twenty-two 'I's hits an awesome level of intensity.

'Daddy Don't Mind' (Clarke, Hicks, Sylvester)
Daddy don't mind what Daddy don't see. The characters Sass E Frass and Joe D Glow cruise in the Chevy, soft-top down, he thinks he's James Dean in the mirror. But they never make it to the movie when seduction intervenes. A kind of steamy swampy Southern feel, punctuated by Wally Smith's trombone break. Issued as a September 1976 single b/w 'C'Mon' (Polydor 2058-779), it peaks at number 21 in Holland. The B-side, recorded at the same Basing Street sessions but excluded from the album, is a sweet harmony sway with the kind of immaculate harmonies they can knee-jerk as easily as breathing.

Related Releases
Hollies Live Hits (March 1977, Polydor 2383 428) UK: 4
This celebration of their repertoire was recorded on a Studer 16-track deck operated by engineer Peter Hitchcock across five nights from 24 to 28 February 1976 at the Christchurch Town Hall, New Zealand and was first issued only in Australasia and Europe. Although there was no American release, when it was eventually released in the UK, TV-advertised and promoted by three concerts in Bradford and Edinburgh, then one at the Royal Albert Hall, it took The Hollies back up to number 4 on the album chart. Although the tracklisting is leavened with recent songs, its chart appeal is obviously weighted by re-runs of the 'classic' hits.

'I Can't Let Go', 'Just One Look', 'I Can't Tell The Bottom From the Top', 'Bus Stop', 'Another Night', 'Fourth of July, Asbury Park (Sandy)', 'Star', 'My Island', 'I'm Down', 'Stop, Stop, Stop', 'Long Cool Woman (in a Black Dress)', 'Carrie Anne', 'The Air That I Breathe', 'Too Young To Be Married', 'He Ain't Heavy, He's My Brother'.

A Crazy Steal

Personnel:
Allan Clarke: lead vocals
Terry Sylvester: vocals, guitar
Tony Hicks: vocals, lead guitar
Bobby Elliott: drums, percussion
Bernie Calvert: bass guitar, keyboards
plus Jimmy Jewel: alto and soprano sax
Hans-Peter Arnesen: piano, clavinet
Pete Wingfield: Roland synthesizer and keyboards
Produced at Basing Street Studios by The Hollies, 1 March-26 August 1977,
plus Alan Parsons, producer for 'Boulder to Birmingham', 8-9 January 1976.
Released: 1 March 1978, Polydor 2383 474, with American edition Epic JE 35334
Running time: 44:50
No chart placings.

Funk, Punk, Glam, Glitter and Disco were erupting in the music world
outside, and although there's the occasional nod at such transient modernity,
The Hollies now existed in their own separate continuum where they were
knocking down £25,000 for a week's cabaret! With just a glance back over his
shoulder, 'fans don't want way-out songs,' Allan told journalist Gordon Coxhill.
'While Graham was with us, there was a tendency to experiment more with
singles', adds Tony. 'But not anymore. We will bring out what we think will
sell.' Which is fine, as far as it goes. But even high-gloss formula pop needs
a level of commitment for it to be convincingly honest. The Hollies sound is
now as distinctive and comfortable as an old friend; they hardly need to try any
more, the harmonies are instinctive and effortlessly exact.

Photographer Martyn Goddard's cover-shot shows the band queued-up for
a Dalek-like soft-drink dispenser spotted in the Stadthalle theatre during a
German tour, with Allan Clarke, Tony Hicks, Terry Sylvester, Bernie Calvert,
Bobby Elliott, plus add-on musicians including Pete Wingfield. As well as
playing with the Alan Parsons rhythm section, and on several Colin Blunstone
albums, Pete had scored his own pastiche pop-referencing transatlantic hit with
'Eighteen With A Bullet' in 1975

'Writing on the Wall' (Clarke, Hicks, Sylvester)

From the opening weary harmonica, this has something of the classic 'He
Ain't Heavy' feel, enforced by an Eagles wide-horizon expansiveness. A
wounded heartbreak Clarke-Hicks-Sylvester 'such a sad story' composition,
there's Sol Amarfio playing congas, and two smooth Jimmy Jewel sax breaks,
before it effectively fades back to Allan's poignant voice against simple
mouth-harp and plangent piano. This was issued as a Canadian single b/w
'Burn Out' (Columbia C4-8199), and in New Zealand b/w 'Clown Service'
(Parlophone NZP 3566).

'What Am I Gonna Do' (Clarke, Hicks, Sylvester)
Piano and high near-falsetto vocal lines as the slow, laid-back mood continues, ascending into supernatural highs with repetitions of the title. At a full 4:31-minutes, there's a middle-eight at the 1:46-mark sweetened by razor-honed harmonies, then a nicely flanged guitar-break at 2:15, before the self-pitying lyric resumes. 'Another lonely night' lies ahead, 'I suppose that I'll survive,' building into a big dramatic piano-sprinkled climax.

'Let It Pour' (Clarke, Hicks, Sylvester)
Nice tinkling electric piano, before Pete Wingfield's synth curls and curlicues in around the sophisticated Steely Dan rhythms, with a treated vocal on their most un-Hollies-like track, but it pours as it soars. The melody line vaguely resembles 'Devil Woman', which could be the result of a close brush with Alan Tarney, who plays on the Cliff Richard hit, and the synth can be overheavy at times, but it's a cool groove. 'You ain't mine, I ain't yours,' he croons, but it doesn't matter, 'we get on with the action.'

'Burn Out' (Clarke, Hicks, Sylvester)
Tony takes vocals with just a Springsteen-tinge to his story of street-car races on Highway Nine, with guitar distortion to add auto atmospherics against Pete Wingfield's eloquent organ passages. The Motorvatin' Rebel has always been part of the Rock 'n' Roll iconography, lifted from the Marlon Brando biker of *The Wild One* (1953) and James Dean's surly sneer, celebrated by Chuck Berry through to Steppenwolf's 'Born To Be Wild' even before Springsteen reconfigures it through a Spectoresque soundscape into 'Born To Run'. So 'Burn Out' is part of a long tradition. Although the rebel was never a natural Hollies fit – he warns 'I'd be a rebel when I'm good and ready' – yet this freewheelin' highway 'burn on rubber' is pedal-to-the-metal all the way and cruises like a cool breeze...

'Hello to Romance' (Clarke, Hicks, Sylvester)
It's goodbye to the crazy steal of one-night stands, with jazzer Tony Coe playing late-night cruising soprano sax, as the Rock 'n' Roll changes to a symphony ... well, maybe. Terry ghosts Allan's voice on the verse, until a three-way Allan, Terry and Tony chorus catches wing and flies. The track shifts through a series of moods, including a jazzy guitar break. Coe's impressive curriculum vitae takes in spells with Humphrey Lyttelton, John Dankworth and Georgie Fame as well as modernists Michael Garrick, Ian Carr (Nucleus) and Norma Winstone.

'Amnesty' (D. Doumas)
No matter where the music takes them, there is no Hollies album without at least one song to touch the spirit. This anthem to the solace of love has both purity and clarity. 'Love is the sweetest amnesty/ floats like a cloud between

the sky and the sea' it opens tastily a cappella and ascends angelic. Originally a contender for the album title, it was issued as a 29 July 1977 single (Polydor 2058 906), flipped with 'Crossfire', a non-album track from the Basing Street sessions, displaying all the professionalism that their years of studio expertise guarantees. Opening with gunshot-like drumming, and a storyline from the criminal underworld, it was later collected onto the *Head Out of Dreams: The Complete Hollies August 1973-1988* compilation. An expertly-tailored product of 'The Hollies Self-Service Machine' shown on the album cover.

'Caracas' (Clarke, Hicks, Sylvester)

Jim Jewell's atmospheric sax, Disco guitar, and Sol Amarfio's busy congas set a tropical loose, blue-eyed Funk feel, for a tasty cocktail of exotic rhythms simmering in a warm sunshine inspired by the South American city. 'Knocked together' by Allan, Terry and Tony and recorded 11 July – according to Bobby, in preparation for a September trip to Venezuela on the Air France Concorde. So it's more their anticipations of Caracas rather than their experience of playing there. The reality proved less enticing! Hans Peter Arnesen joins on cool piano, and 'Tony's driving guitar solo rounded off the picture-postcard production.' It's a Club Tropicana where drinks aren't free but attractively priced, a gift to the nation's tourist board.

'Boulder To Birmingham' (Danoff, Harris)

The single from two years previous, with one-off production input from Alan Parsons, plus Pete Wingfield on Fender Rhodes electric piano (see singles review). The basic track was recorded at Richard Branson's 'The Manor' studio in Shipton-on-Cherwell in Oxfordshire, during an 8-9 January 1976 session. The rest of the album was done at the London Basing Street Studios between 1 March and 26 August 1977.

'Clown Service' (Clarke, Hicks, Sylvester)

No relation to Graham's 'Clown' on *For Certain Because* in long time-lost 1966. This is an unusual melancholy country jog-along, lit by Allan's haunted harmonica and Pete Wingfield's truck-stop piano. The Tears of a Clown has been a useful metaphor for much quality pop – as in 'Harlequin' on the next Hollies album, who is another 'broken clown' – but here Allan pours out his broken heart to the phone operator, as he calls the hotline for losers in love. In the days when they had real live human phone operators...

'Feet on the Ground' (Clarke, Hicks, Sylvester)

Each of the great harmony sounds of the era was built around an unique chemistry of voices. An instantly identifiable DNA that marks out the Beatles, The Beach Boys, The Mamas & The Papas ... or The Hollies. This big dramatic ballad closer is hung up on indeterminacy, but the frontline vocals are never in doubt. Where will tomorrow take us? A new love or a sad parting? Reflective piano with sensitive strings, Allan's solo voice builds towards harmony choruses that blend immaculately into a shifting instrumental arrangement. Undeniably Hollies.

Related Releases
'Hello to Romance' (Clarke, Hicks, Sylvester) b/w **'Forty-Eight Hour Parole'** (Clarke, Hicks, Sylvester) (May 1977, Polydor 2058 880)
Two tracks we've already talked about as part of the last two albums. It's goodbye to those one-night stands in a smooth blending of Hollies-branded harmonies with expansive MOR sweep, both sides collected onto the 2014 3CD fifty-track *Hollies At Fifty* album (Parlophone 825646223541).

The Hollies: Twenty Golden Greats (July 1978, EMI EMTV 11)
Highest chart position: 2
For every determined step forward into new album ventures, there was the immense gravitational force exerted by the attractions of their back catalogue. Well-exploited by their previous label, there'd already been a vinyl double-album, *The History Of The Hollies* (November 1975, EMI EMSP 650). Now – soon on CD too (EMI CDP7 46238-2) – these 'twenty great sounds that grew out of the North', heavily advertised by a high-profile TV campaign, take them all the way to number 2 on the album chart, which focuses attention relentlessly on the past while the band remain increasingly marooned in the present. Even the press is less than sympathetic, with *NME* calling The Hollies 'one of Britain's longest-running Soap Operas' and *Melody Maker* asking 'why are they getting into the artistic-stroke progressive-stroke intellectual-stroke serious side of rock' while these old hits are 'darned great pop, cheap and rubbishy and marvellous':

'The Air That I Breathe' (licensed from Polydor for inclusion on the album), 'Carrie Anne', 'Bus Stop', 'Listen to Me', 'Look Through Any Window', 'I Can't Let Go', 'Long Cool Woman (in a Black Dress)', 'Here I Go Again', 'I Can't Tell The Bottom From the Top', 'I'm Alive', 'Yes I Will', 'Stay', 'Sorry Suzanne', 'Gasoline Alley Bred', 'We're Through', 'Jennifer Eccles', 'Stop, Stop, Stop', 'On a Carousel' 'Just One Look' (reissued as a March 1984 single b/w 'Her I Go Again' (EMI GG11), 'He Ain't Heavy, He's My Brother' Reissued as an August 1982 single b/w 'Cos You Like To Love Me' (Parlophone PMS 1001), then again in October 1983 b/w 'Bus Stop' (Old Gold OG 9386).

The Other Side of the Hollies (August 1978, Parlophone PMC 7176)
Compiled by Colin Miles, and deliberately shadowing the initiative established by the success of *Twenty Golden Greats*, the twenty tracks here were taken

from the old singles' corresponding B-sides. It was followed by *The Best of the Hollies EPs* (August 1978, Parlophone PMC 7174), and by a reissue programme of original albums, *Evolution* (August 1978, Parlophone PMC 7175), *Butterfly* (PMC 7177), and *Confessions of the Mind* (PMC 7178). Licensed to the Beat Goes On label, there was a series of reissues in beautiful new editions of *Stay With the Hollies* (October 1987, BGOLP 4), *In The Hollies Style* (March 1988, BGOLP 8), *For Certain Because* (April 1988, BGOLP 9) and *The Hollies* (July 1988, BGOLP 25). While rewarding, these albums were increasingly pushing The Hollies towards the nostalgia circuit. The full tracklisting for *The Other Side of the Hollies* is:

"Cos You Like To Love Me', 'Everything Is Sunshine', 'Signs That Will Never Change', 'Not That Way At All', 'You Know He Did', 'Do the Best You Can', 'So Lonely', 'I've Got a Way of My Own', 'Don't Run and Hide', 'Come On Back','All The World Is Love', 'Whole World Over', 'Row the Boat Together', 'Mad Professor Blyth', 'Dandelion Wine', 'Baby That's All', 'Nobody', 'Keep Off That Friend of Mine', 'Running Through the Night', 'Hey What's Wrong With Me'

I Wasn't Born Yesterday by Allan Clarke (May 1978, Aura) No chart placings.

The *NME* headline yelled 'Clarke Leaves Hollies – Again' (25 March 1978). Well, not exactly. With his own separate management, Allan's solo career continued parallel to The Hollies' latest releases. But the fifteen years of relentless global touring that had elapsed since the release of The Hollies' first record was taking something of a toll. Where there's the tedium and boredom of endless travel, the increasing time taken with soundchecks prior to a performance, as the sophisticated demands of sound technology complexity, there are always distractions. 'I nearly died from hospitality' The Climax Blues Band sing on 'Couldn't Get It Right', because there's always complimentary wine in the Hotel chiller and a free record company tab at the bar. It's easy to slip. And there were occasions when he slipped. With 'Dandelion Wine', or maybe that lyric he voices about drinking beer from an empty can?

Allan sang 'Breakdown' on the second Alan Parsons Project concept album, based around the Isaac Asimov *I, Robot* books (June 1977, Arista SPARTY 1012). His own single, 'I Don't Know I'm Beat' b/w 'Passenger' (January 1978, Polydor) was followed by this album which includes both sides of the May 1978 single ', I'm Betting My Life On You' b/w 'I Wasn't Born Yesterday'. Another track lifted from it '(I Will Be Your) Shadows In The Street' b/w 'No Prisoners Taken' plus 'Light Brigade', did well as a US chart single.

Each release was politely well-received. None of them provided the response necessary to decisively rechart the course of his career. He would always be 'Allan Clarke, singer with The Hollies.' But what a wonderful thing that was! For the 1979 album *Legendary Heroes* (aka 'The Only One'), he switched to Elektra. There was also a one-off single for Forever Records, 'Someone Else Will' b/w 'Castles In The Wind'.

Reasons To Believe followed in 1990; eleven new tracks issued on German Polydor with a bonus track 'That's What Dreams Are Made Of' on the CD edition – the title is not taken from the Tim Hardin song, but is a strong rock-heavy original written by Allan with some-time Hollie Alan Coates. It was initially unreleased in either the UK or the USA. (UK Polydor 847 036-1). This was to be Allan's final solo venture until the well-received come-back album *Resurgence* (2019).

Five Three One, Double Seven O Four

Personnel:
Allan Clarke: lead vocals, guitar, harmonica
Terry Sylvester: vocals, guitar
Tony Hicks: vocals, lead guitar, banjo, mandolin, keyboards
Bobby Elliott: drums
Bernie Calvert: bass guitar, keyboards
plus Pete Wingfield: keyboards
Hans-Peter Arnesen: keyboards
B.J. Wilson: drums
Gary Brooker: keyboards, vocal on 'Harlequin'
Tony Hymas: string and horn arrangements, keyboards
Produced at Abbey Road Studios by Ron Richards, 16 August 1978-18 January 1979.
Released: March 1979, Polydor 2442-160
Running Time: 44:33
No chart placings.

By all the laws of pop, The Hollies should no longer even exist, let alone be engaged on album twenty. Many sixties one-two-&-three-hit-wonders were resurrected from has-been obscurity by the endlessly touring revival packages, from which a good living could be made, sometimes gathering around the nucleus of a single surviving member, or two opportunistically-reconciled erstwhile feuding members who'd been slagging each other off in the press for a decade. The Hollies never did that. Nor did they need to. They could play cabaret. They could headline theatres in their own right.

What is it audiences want from The Hollies? People listened and applauded politely to a selection of titles from 'our new album,' but they reserved the real enthusiasm for the hits, 'Carrie Anne', 'I'm Alive', 'The Air That I Breathe', 'Jennifer Eccles' and the rest. That is the bedrock that makes the rest possible. But to the band itself, there was always the thought that they were still in the game. Still contenders. All they need is that one song.

This time the CD takes its name from an inverted reading of the digital numbers, which appear to spell 'Hollies'. Allan Clarke had returned after another brief spell of absence, although Tony had contingency plans in place in case he didn't. Dave Cousins of The Strawbs tells how he'd bumped into Tony while walking down the Chelsea Kings Road. 'I asked Tony if they'd found a singer yet, and he asked if I was interested. I said one word: 'Yes'... I immediately went out and bought a Hollies album and started to sing along. The lead vocals were in a higher range than I was used to, but I could manage.' Negotiations got to the point of agreeing that Cousins could sing his own song 'Benedictus' as part of The Hollies set – then Allan returned (as told in *Exorcising Ghosts* by Dave Cousins).

Ron Richards settled back into the producer's chair for the last time. He retired following the completion of the album to concentrate on his photography and gardening. He died on 30 April 2009. Terry Sylvester, Tony Hicks, Bobby Elliott and Bernie Calvert were reinforced by Pete Wingfield (keyboards), B.J. Wilson (drums) and Tony Hymas, who not only contributed keyboards, string and horn arrangements but co-writes three tracks with poet-lyricist Pete Brown. But there was also Procol Harum's Gary Brooker, who added vocals to Terry Sylvester's voice on his song 'Harlequin'. Terry also takes the lead vocal on 'Boys In The Band'. Allan co-writes 'Satellite Three' with Gary Benson, a writing partnership that features heavily on Allan's solo LP *I Wasn't Born Yesterday*. But for this Hollies album, there was no US edition.

'Say It Ain't So, Jo' (Head)
This is one of a number of 1970s and 1980s tracks that, with the correct alignment of the planets, could have been the hit single The Hollies were searching for. That they didn't happen has less to do with the material or the performance as it is to do with the complex infrastructure paraphernalia of promotion, media opportunity and image. There's no logic or reason. When you're hot, you're hot, when you're not, you're not. It's a much-covered song of denied disillusionment from actor-writer Murray Head's second album, with another version by Roger Daltrey, but Allan's impassioned delivery – less rock-forceful than the Who frontman, more plaintive, lifts The Hollies interpretation, with chorus-lines of shattering intensity. The Hollies also drop the 'e' from Joe. Gary Brooker heard the song while he was playing The Hollies session, and cut his own version, produced by George Martin, for his debut solo album later the same year.

'Maybe It's Dawn' (Hymas, Brown)
Pete Brown had written the lyrics for Cream's 'White Room' and 'I Feel Free' in partnership with Jack Bruce, and 'Sunshine Of Your Love' with Eric Clapton, as well as fronting his own bands Battered Ornaments and Piblokto! As a result, this is a pleasantly poetic 3.55-minute excursion into balladry, with tasteful keyboard and subtly scored strings. They've gone their separate ways, but even within his darkness, he finds signs of optimism, 'somewhere the light shines bright along the highway.'

'Song of the Sun' (Hymas, Brown)
Steamy crawling swamp-beat, 'head into the sun, you ain't the only one.' Tony Hymas had previously composed the *Mr Men* theme for the TV kids' animation and would later join vocalist Jim Diamond as PhD for the hit single 'I Won't Let You Down'. Allan effortlessly takes the clear vocals as the lyrics fly higher and the instrumentation burbles and sizzles around him, into the molasses-thick Tony Hicks solo and long-simmering fade.

'Harlequin' (Brooker, Reid)
Terry and Gary Brooker himself sing, while Procol drummer B.J. Wilson sits in for an ill Bobby Elliott, effectively fusing the ethereal whiter shades of Procol Harum poetry with an elaboration of Hollies harmonies. An exquisite track. There's a story that Brooker laid down what he intended to be guide-vocals only, and that he was surprised to discover himself there on the last verse of the completed record. It's also said that Gary's liquid ornamentation outshines Terry's more pedestrian reading of the song. But when the final guitar overdubs were added on 18 January 1979 at Abbey Road, the album was done.

'When I'm Yours' (Head)
Also taken from Murray Head's 1975 *Say It Ain't So, Joe* album, this power-ballad has classic piano configuration combined with a cleverly-constructed build polished by hallmark Hollies vocal-harmony perfection. There's also a finely regulated Tony Hicks guitar solo. If this calculated level of emotionally-moving pop has become almost predictable for Hollies albums, something we take for granted, that still makes it an extraordinary thing to assume.

'Something To Live For' (Hymas, Brown)
Travelling, touring, 'so many towns where the trains don't ever stop.' Nothing but changes, with the melody carried on thoughtful stately electric keyboards. What to do? Just 'keep pushing tomorrow' in the hope of finding that 'elusive something.' Did The Hollies ever find it? They come pretty damn close to that elusive something. Previously done by Jack Bruce on his 1977 *How's Tricks* solo album – the same Jack who'd previously stood in as Hollies bass player during Eric Haydock's absence during 1966! The track was issued as a March 1979 single b/w 'Song of the Sun' (Polydor POSP35) with the bonus 'The Air That I Breathe' on the twelve-inch edition (POSPX 35), when *NME* described it as 'more of a comedown than a comeback', although its release was supported by three consecutive nights at the Wembley Conference Centre (27-29 March).

'Stormy Waters' (White)
An enticing nautical sway, with no sheltering harbour in view, Allan's harmonica adds eloquent, wordless comment. Maybe they're still searching for the next 'He Ain't Heavy, He's My Brother' or 'The Air That I Breathe' ... but if so, with tracks as strong as this, the search process must be considered hugely rewarding. Recorded 14-15 December 1978, a take without the added harmonies remains unissued.

'Boys In The Band' (Brown)
From Mr Soul to King Creole, the boys in The Hollies all live in harmony, don't they? Life is a poem, isn't it? Why can't the outside world of Mr Politic, where pushers push and hookers hook, work in the same way as the simple

melody that frees your soul? Terry Sylvester takes vocals with a lilting tilt on an undemanding easy-rocking excursion. It's lyric-dense until the splintery guitar interlude, followed by a close-harmony close.

'Satellite Three' (Clarke, Benson)
An eerie space oddity, with twinkling electric keyboards scattered with a stardust of spatial relativistic effects, although it's also an effective metaphor for isolation. Electronic constellations percolate and glimmer around Allan's alien desolation, towering into coronas of light, protesting 'I've endless fuel to burn' yet falling into the bleak gravity-well of the closing phrase 'don't let me die, don't let me die, don't let me…' The Hollies never quite lost the capacity to spring surprises.

'It's in Everyone of Us' (Pomeranz)
For the final song to be recorded for the album, engineer Mike Jarrat linked a 16 to a 24-track machine in order to achieve depth. Allan sings the first verse virtually a cappella with full gospel intensity before the subtle instrumentation fades in behind him. It follows the arrangement of the original David Pomeranz version on his 1975 album, which was picked up as an inspirational quasi-religious Christmas song for John Denver's appearance on *The Muppet Show*. One of Freddie Mercury's final live performances was to duet this song with Cliff Richard at the Dominion Theatre (4 April 1988). The Hollies version stands easily alongside other interpretations and makes a powerful album closer.

Related Releases
'Soldier's Song' (Batt) b/w 'Draggin' My Heels' (Clarke, Hicks, Sylvester) (April 1980, Polydor 2059 246)
They rehearse a Mike Batt song called 'Can't Lie No More' with Mike in the producer's chair at Wessex Sound Studios and Bobby playing along to a click-track for the first time. It would remain unissued until 2003. Shortly afterwards, they commenced work on this epic 4:03-minute tale written and produced by Batt at Lansdowne Studios (19 November 1979), with ghosted wordless vocals fading into the shivering dramatic strings of eighty-five members of the London Symphony Orchestra recorded live, in order to tell the dramatic story of a young infantryman who rides out at seventeen to join his first brigade. He shelters in a farmhouse where he meets the woman who 'makes a man' of him on the eve of war. The complex arrangement sets Allan's powerful lead vocal against swirling orchestral peaks strengthened by martial horns. Yet it peaks no higher than a UK number 58, with the B-side lifted from *Russian Roulette*, produced by The Hollies, written by Clarke-Sylvester-Hicks. Much later, when Carl Wayne assumed The Hollies' vocal role, he recorded a more bombastic 'Soldier's Song' as a one-off side-project with Et Cetera, issued only in Germany (2003, Major Oak Records AKA 200306-2/ 181.547).

Graham Nash

While The Hollies story continued, the Graham Nash discography was becoming increasingly complex. There were solo albums, duo albums (with David Crosby), trio albums (with Crosby, Stills & Nash), and four-piece albums (with Crosby, Stills, Nash & Young), as well as guesting appearances on other people's records, including Jefferson Starship's *Blows Against the Empire* (November 1970), on Joni Mitchell's *For the Roses* (November 1972) and with Pink Floyd's David Gilmour for *On an Island* (March 2006).

Songs For Beginners (May 1971, Atlantic 7204)

A reflective debut solo album packed with West Coast session 'friends' including Jerry Garcia, Neil Young, Rita Coolidge, Chris Ethridge, Dallas Taylor, PP Arnold, David Crosby and others, with stand-out songs 'Military Madness', 'Simple Man', 'I Used To Be A King' and the charting 'Chicago' (*Billboard* number 35) about the Democratic Convention riots. The album reached number 15 and was certified gold. Track four on side two, 'Sleep Song', had been offered to The Hollies, but the lyric 'when you awake I'll kiss your eyes open and I'll take off my clothes and I'll lie by your side' had evoked horrified reactions from Allan, 'Bloody 'ell – can't say that lad ... no!'

Wild Tales (January 1974, Atlantic SD 7288)

Recorded in a darker tone following his split with both Joni Mitchell and Rita Coolidge, and during a period of group inactivity, with Crosby, Stills and Neil Young unwilling to reunite for new recordings. There are nevertheless guesting appearances by Crosby, Dave Mason, 'Joe Yankee' (Neil Young) and Joni Mitchell for ten new Graham Nash-penned songs including 'Prison Song', 'And So It Goes' plus 'Another Sleep Song'. The album reaches a *Billboard* number 34. It is also the title of Graham's autobiography (Penguin, Jun 2014).

Earth and Sky (February 1980, Capitol Records TC-EA-ST 12014)

With Jackson Browne, David Crosby, Joe Walsh, Nicolette Larson and Stephen Stills in the mix, and ten new songs, it was to be followed by *Innocent Eyes* (March 1986, Atlantic 781-633-1) and *Songs for Survivors* (July 2002, Artemis), taking him into the new millennium, and new adventures.

Graham Nash and David Crosby (April 1972, Atlantic SD 7220)

Following the mega-success of *Déjà Vu*, Graham and David Crosby tour as an acoustic duo, resulting in this album which not only reaches number 4 on the chart, but spawned the Graham-penned 'Immigration Man' single, which climbs to 36. *Wind on the Water* (September 1975, ABC Records ABCD –902) followed and peaked at Number 6, with guest musicians James Taylor, Russ Kunkel, Carole King and David Lindley. A third duo album *Whistling Down the Wire* (June 1976, ABC Records ABCD-956), made number 26 and produced two singles with Graham sharing writing credits, 'Out Of The Darkness' and 'Spotlight'. A live duo LP (October 1977) and a Crosby & Nash *Best Of...* compilation (1978, ABC Records) took them towards the end of the century. There would be more collaborations.

CSN (June 1977, Atlantic K 50369)

This book is about The Hollies and only really concerns Graham Nash's subsequent work peripherally – until his brief Hollies 1983 rapprochement. There was a period during which the individual members of the CSN&Y collective embarked on solo projects and in various combinations. Graham had produced two solo albums and three duo albums with David Crosby before this triumphant return to the original three-piece line-up. And it was worth the wait. With its Wooden Nickel amplified acoustic sound, it's an incredibly good album with two hugely powerful Graham Nash songs, 'Just A Song Before I Go', which became the trio's highest-charting hit at a *Billboard* number 7, and 'Cathedral' written about an LSD trip he'd taken in Winchester Cathedral. The album reached Number 2 and eventually qualified quadruple platinum.

Lifted from the album *Daylight Again* (June 1982, Atlantic K 450-896), Graham's 'Wasted On The Way' – about the time the group spent in arguments, rifts and diversions rather than concentrating on their music – was also its biggest single, number 9. Then Neil Young rejoined in time for *American Dream* (November 1988, Atlantic 781-888-2).

Into the 1980s
Buddy Holly

Personnel:
Allan Clarke: lead vocals, guitar, harmonica
Terry Sylvester: vocals, guitar
Tony Hicks: vocals, lead guitar, banjo, mandolin, keyboards
Bobby Elliott: drums
Bernie Calvert: bass guitar, keyboards
plus Pete Wingfield: keyboards
Hans-Peter Arnesen: keyboards
Don Harper: violin
Dave Caswell, Howie Casey, Reg Brooks, John Mackswith: horns
Recorded at Odyssey Studios, a Hollies Production.
Released: 1 October 1980, Polydor POLTV 12, Polydor 2383 593
Running Time: 58:53 (Extended edition, 1998)
No chart placings.

The Hollies took their name from Buddy Holly. They'd first witnessed him play on the black-&-white BBC-TV *Six-Five Special* in 1958, and were mesmerised by what Graham Nash calls 'the simplicity and unbelievably clear structure' of his songs. After their *Hollies Sing Dylan* album, this project was not only logical but almost inevitable, one which, to *Q* magazine, 'successfully takes them back to their roots while expanding with harmonies the possibilities of Holly's simple song structures' (May 1995). Despite a TV-advertising campaign, the album fails to chart. The Hollies revisit 'Take Your Time', and add others from the Charles Hardin Holley catalogue. Allan's vocals on 'Heartbeat' and the harmonies work very effectively. Pete Wingfield and Hans-Peter Arnesen add occasionally intrusive synth keyboards. Sometime later, in a unique fusion of talents The Hollies – with Graham this time – get to overdub the original Buddy Holly demo of 'Peggy Sue Got Married' for inclusion on the *Not Fade Away: Remembering Buddy Holly* compilation (1996, MCA MCD11260). The 2007 edition of *Buddy Holly* is re-mastered and expanded:

'Peggy Sue' (Holly, Allison, Petty)
Taken with nagging electro-backing and gathering momentum, this had been Buddy's first major UK hit under his own name, number six on 25 January 1958, on a chart that also included Elvis 'Jailhouse Rock' (number 1), 'Great Balls Of Fire' by Jerry Lee Lewis (number five) and The Crickets – with Buddy – at number four with 'Oh Boy!' Holly academic John J Goldrosen claims that the song's polyphonic effect has its roots in bluegrass music, in that it 'does not rely on sudden shifts between loud and soft passages to create excitement; instead, tension is built through the conflict of rhythmic patterns and the varying blend of voices and instruments' (*Buddy Holly: His Life and*

Music, Charisma Books, 1975). This is a lesson that The Hollies learned and demonstrated effectively. For in Manchester, schoolboys Allan and Graham were listening in awe to the music that would change and determine the course of their lives.

'Wishing' (Montgomery, Holly)
Recorded at the album's first session, 2 May 1980 at Odyssey, with long upfront guitar play-in, The Hollies make Buddy's fragile, delicate acoustic composition a more up-tempo harmony rush of merged voices, pushing the song's original two minutes to double its length, then punching out key-words 'wishing' and 'dreaming' emphatically into the fade. There's no point in simply replicating what has already been done, yet something of Buddy's wistful, plaintive yearning is still there intact.

'Love's Made A Fool Of You' (Montgomery, Holly)
Incongruous Tijuana horns stomp out the corners around Allan's lead and the harmony choruses – right through to a long effective slow-down instrumental fade. Originally penned by Buddy with his Lubbock schoolfriend Bob Montgomery in 1954 and cut as a demo intended for, but never used by, The Everly Brothers, it was first released on Buddy's posthumous *Showcase* album (1964), by which time a Crickets (with Sonny Curtis) version had been issued. Among other covers, The Bobby Fuller Four, Bobby Vee and Tom Rush had also recorded this song prior to The Hollies.

'Take Your Time' (Holly, Allison, Petty)
The Hollies had anticipated the Holly tribute album by making this song the side two opening track of *Would You Believe* in long-ago 1966. It's a song with the same chordal pattern as Buddy's 'Look At Me', with a refrain that follows the country music formula of juxtaposing humour and word-play with seriousness – 'take your time, and take mine too, I have time to spend.' This remake ditches the jingle-jangle guitars, and comes wrapped in swirling synths and personalised by a newly elongated vowel delivery. It works fine.

'Heartbeat' (Montgomery, Petty)
Piddly-pat. A charming slowed-down version of Buddy's iconic 1958 song, with soft sax solo, issued as a September 1980 single b/w 'Take Your Time' (Polydor POSP 175). It's difficult to get a new spin on such a familiar song, especially as UK revivalists Showaddywaddy had had a more clunky number seven hit with it as recently as 1975, following earlier covers by Tommy Roe, Herman's Hermits, Skeeter Davis, Bobby Vee and others. But The Hollies remake it into shiny newness. The song would be used to title a light-hearted nostalgia TV series, with the show's photogenic star, Nick Berry, taking a rather more blandly routine version as high as number two in the UK in June 1992.

'Tell Me How' (Holly, Allison, Petty)

The song that closed the first side of Buddy's 1957 *Chirping Crickets* album, and despite soft synths The Hollies retain the song's essential rockabilly simplicity. A keyboard fades in to gentle strings before the tripping rhythms intensify, with pleasing shifts between solo voice and harmony lines, and an uncluttered guitar solo. When the *Music Week* reviewer wrote 'TV-advertised LP featuring Hollies covering Buddy Holly tracks. Can't really fail', this is probably what he was thinking about.

'Think It Over' (Holly, Allison, Petty)

Begins with a heavily percussive drum-stomp before opening out into the pleading, insinuating lyric, 'a lonely heart grows cold and old.' Whereas Holly's nuanced 1958 vinyl lasted just 1:45-minutes, The Hollies less subtle interpretation adds Bobby Elliott's drum-solo and celebratory horns as it heads towards the 3:27-minute mark. P.J. Proby and Ringo Starr later had a stab at recording the song. Some insist that the original's still the greatest.

'Maybe Baby' (Holly, Petty)

An effectively sensitive reworking of Buddy's wistful yearning song of imagined possibilities. It succeeds in retaining the essential quality of the song, while treating it to a sympathetic new arrangement. Even the synth-break is not entirely distracting. The March 2017 six-CD box-set *Head Out of Dreams* (Parlophone 0190295892333), gathers tracks from August 1973 to May 1988, with liner notes by Uli Twelker; it includes the full content of the *Buddy Holly* album.

'Midnight Shift' (Lee, Ainsworth)

It sounds like this was a fun track to record, a slap-echo rockabilly rocker from 1956, with a lyric that might just be about a 'working girl'. The album cover art shows the iconic black-framed spectacles with a single tear suspended from the rim, superimposed over boiling cloud; it catches the idea of ghosting the Holly memory, yet this track is less about reverence and more about celebration, with boogie-woogie piano and horns, rising to Bobby's staccato drum climax.

'I'm Gonna Love You Too' (Mauldin, Sullivan, Petty)

There's much academic quibbling over who actually wrote this song. Despite the credits bracketed beneath the title, drummer Jerry Allison quite reasonably suggests that it was actually Buddy's song all along. Whatever, another feller took you, but he still can't overlook you. A minor 1964 US hit for British Invasion band The Hullaballoos from Hull, then revived by Blondie in 1978 on their *Parallel Lines* album, The Hollies respectfully return it to Buddy in a smoother, tighter mood, with complex mid-point changes.

'Peggy Sue Got Married' (Holly)
Buddy's own playful answer-disc to the 'girl that's been in nearly every song,' a sequel that works in subtle quotations from the earlier record, this is also one of my own personal favourite Buddy Holly songs. From the pitter-pattering drum intro of The Hollies' restructuring, 'please don't say. Don't say that I told you so' – but maybe the reggae setting doesn't quite work? Or maybe it injects a note of variety into this otherwise respectful album? Listen and discuss.

'What To Do' (Holly)
A heartbreak lavished in synth strings, with deep-voice doo-wop interjections from when rock was young. The Hollies retain the sense of poignant restlessness that Buddy invests in the song. One of Holly's private home recordings taped with just acoustic guitar in apartment 4H of the Greenwich Village 'Brevoort' building, and released posthumously, it's a song that remembers record hops, soda shops and walks to school. A composition that makes you realise just how much we lost in the snows of Clear Lake, Iowa.

'That'll Be The Day' (Holly, Allison)
In a kind of arc of separation, Buddy lifted this title from John Wayne's dialogue in the Western movie *The Searchers* (1956). The Searchers took their name from the same movie, while The Hollies took their name from Buddy. The Searchers recorded Buddy's 'Listen To Me', which The Hollies sneak into the fade of 'Everyday'. The Hollies take 'That'll Be The Day' as a kind of jogging boogie, with a bar-room piano break. The song was arguably the first track The Beatles ever recorded on a privately recorded disc in the summer of 1958. The Crickets' breakthrough hit, 'That'll Be The Day' displaced Paul Anka's 'Diana' from the UK number 1 spot in 1957. The same Paul Anka who would write the next track.

'It Doesn't Matter Anymore' (Anka)
Buddy's first single to be released posthumously, this took him comfortably to the UK number 1 for three weeks during April 1959. With Rock n' Roll still a fledging music, what Don McLean called 'the day the music died' was a generational seismic event with lasting formative impact. Golly-Gee, I remember it. So did young Allan Clarke and Graham Nash in drab Manchester. The Hollies largely interpret the song straight, without unnecessary embellishments, dispensing even with the string-section orchestration of the Holly original.

'Everyday' (Hardin, Petty)
'Charles Hardin' was a flag-of-convenience pseudonym adopted by Buddy for contractual reasons, and this song features a chord pattern not found in his other compositions. As John J Goldrosen explains 'the chords in the refrain are

built on a new tonic, the flattened seventh of the tonic in the body of the song (i.e., if the song is in C, the chords in the verses are C, F, and G, while those in the refrain are Bb, Eb, and F)'. Whereas Buddy had used celeste, Allan's vocal lines are framed by keyboards and sax, which capture the mounting expectation of that love roller-coaster he's about to ride. The track closes at the 2:47-minute point, when it resumes into a mélange of the entrancing 'Words Of Love', 'Love Is Strange' (the Mickey & Sylvia 1956 classic which later became a 1965 UK number 11 hit for The Everly Brothers) and the appealing 'Listen To Me'.

'Reprise'

A 2:47-minute collage of the album highlights, weaving strands from earlier tracks into a medley, a neat summing up, and an anticipation of 'Holliedaze' to come. Patrick Humphries calls the album 'an undistinguished tribute to one of rock's seminal figures, adding little or nothing to the originals' (*Melody Maker*, 1 November 1980). Yet, to this listener, it seems to be honest, without veering into the over-reverential.

Related Releases
'Holliedaze (Medley)' b/w 'Holliepops (Medley)' (14 August 1981, EMI 5229)

In May 1981, Terry Sylvester and – days later – Bernie Calvert quit The Hollies. The split followed troubled studio sessions produced by former Shadow Bruce Welch. There'd been escalating ego-conflicts and a dispute concerning The Hollies' separation from long-term manager Robin Britten. Bernie quit music to open a delicatessen in Nelson. Terry, who had been a vital part of The Hollies' post-Graham Nash regeneration, as writer, musician and voice – he sang lead on 'Long Cool Woman' during Allan's occasional absences – went on to form a duo with Jimmy Griffin, releasing the Polydor album *Griffin & Sylvester* (1982, Polydor 5063).

With The Hollies effectively reduced to a trio, Alan Coates, formerly of Broken English (who had a Stones-inspired 1987 New Wave hit with 'Comin' On Strong'), joined on rhythm guitar (as a full member 1983 to 2004). Meanwhile, The Hollies revisited their own history in a kind of 'Stars-On-45' format edited together from the original tapes by Tony Hicks – assisted by studio tech-guy Mike Day – with 'Just One Look', 'Here I Go Again', 'I'm Alive', 'I Can't Let Go', 'Long Cool Woman', 'Bus Stop' and 'Carrie Anne' sequenced with a unifying Linn-drum clap-track.

For a BBC *Top of the Pops* slot on 10 September 1981, introduced by that same Jimmy Savile who had hosted their very appearance on the show on New Year's Day 1964, Graham Nash and Eric Haydock temporarily returned to the fold, which helped take them back into the lower reaches of the chart for seven weeks, reaching a high of number 28. Even *NME* was forced to concede that 'age shall not wither Tony Hicks, and Graham Nash looked a lot happier than with SC&N (sic).' The B-side, from a title originally coined by George

Martin, works the same remix trick with 'Stay', 'Yes I Will', 'Look Through Any Window', 'On A Carousel', 'Jennifer Eccles', 'Listen To Me' and 'He Ain't Heavy He's My Brother'.

'Take My Love and Run' (Chatton, Black) b/w 'Driver' (Clarke, Hicks) (13 November 1981 Polydor POSP 379)

The Hollies' final Polydor single, recorded around a nucleus of Clarke-Hicks-Elliott, was written and produced by keyboard player Brian Chatton (with Barry Black), who had recorded his own 1981 version of the song on his *Playing for Time* album, and who appeared as a group member during its promotion. There's a thumping drum track overlaid with twinkling electro, leading into a catchy chorus. They promoted it with an appearance and a brief interview on the Russell Harty chat show. The Hollies would rerecord the song with Graham Nash for *What Goes Around*. The B-side is a previously-unissued Clarke-Hicks instrumental recorded 6 June 1981, based around a guitar riff, almost a studio jam with free improvisation, prominently featuring organ and synthesizer, and a good, punchy bassline supplied by Alan Jones (of The Shadows).

What Goes Around...

Personnel:
Alan Clarke: vocals
Graham Nash: vocals, guitar
Tony Hicks: lead guitar, vocals
Bobby Elliott: drums
plus Andy Brown, Steve Stroud: bass
Joe Lala: percussion
Alan Tarney: rhythm guitar (on 'Something Ain't Right'), keyboards
Frank Cristopher: rhythm guitar (on 'Having A Good Time')
Bran Chatton, Mike Batt, Paul Bliss: keyboards
Produced by The Hollies, Graham Nash, Paul Bliss, Stanley Johnston.
Released: June 1983, WEA 25-0139-1
Running Time: 32:09
Highest chart position: US: 90, UK: did not chart

The cover photo emphatically shows Graham Nash, Allan Clarke, Tony Hicks and Bobby Elliott reformed for this one-off album for Atlantic. However, Graham's writing and vocal talents weren't used to full advantage; in a great missed opportunity, there's no new Graham Nash song. No new Nash-Clarke song. No new Nash-Clarke-Hicks song. Not even a 'Marrakesh Express', which might have been nice. After all, they'd demoed the song on 2 April 1968 but failed to complete it. Instead of sitting down around that Hollies round table and planning out new strategies together, Graham merely added to a song selection already compiled. There are various production credits going to Nash, Paul Bliss, Stanley Johnston and The Hollies themselves, as well as the vocal harmonies of Graham with Allan and Tony. Bobby Elliott is there in the drum-chair, and Tony Hicks' guitar is just as distinctive. The basic tracks were laid down at Abbey Road's Studio Two between March and May 1982, to be completed with Graham in his L.A. Rudy Records studio, with final overdubs in February 1983. There were promising omens when their revival of The Supremes' 'Stop In The Name Of Love' provided their final US hit, reaching number 29. And they revisit 'Just One Look' less convincingly, softened with synth, but Graham's voice-breaks stand out. Other album participants were Alan Tarney (bass and keyboards), familiar from the hits he'd written for Cliff Richard, including his only US number one, 'We Don't Talk Anymore'. Mike Batt is probably best known for his Wombles hits, but he also produced for David Essex and Katie Melua.

There was a curious addition as track 15 to a German CD reissue of *What Goes Around* (2000, Rock-In-Beat-Records RB203), a 3:17-minute 'I Don't Understand You (Anymore)' – written by Steve Thompson (and featured on his website), this is the contentious work-in-progress attempted with producer Bruce Welch, and recorded in Brian Bennett's Hertfordshire studio. The former Shadow 'cruelly sidelined' Bernie Calvert – who he considered 'inadequate' (according to Bobby Elliott). Bernie had been a Hollie since 'Bus Stop' in June 1966, and no one had ever questioned his competence before. The session instead used bassist Alan Jones, and drafted in Cliff Hall on keyboards. Labi Siffre added harmonies to ongoing re-takes. What were intended as Allan's guide-vocals stand up well, because even rejected Hollies sessions were slick and professional.

There was a US edition of *What Goes Around* issued through the Wounded Bird label in July 1983, which reached a *Billboard* number 90. A live 'Reunion' album recorded during the American promotional tour, with the Clarke-Hicks-Nash line-up, was issued as *Archive Alive* in 1997, then reissued with two bonus tracks as *Reunion* in 2004 (see separate entry).

'Casualty' (Bliss)
Of course, bands must evolve. But these thumping electro-pop drums and synth ventures were doomed to be ignored by Indie youth, while they failed to meet the expectations of long-term Hollies followers. Here, with Paul Bliss taking writer and producer credits, he's a 'casualty, a victim of my own circumstance,' with Allan confidently riding the rhythms of a pleasant bouncy route map to gatecrash the changing times. Some claim to detect trace elements of Laura Branigan's 'Gloria' in its stabbing synth riff. Performed on Dick Clark's ABC-TV *American Bandstand* during the promotional tour, this is one of a handful of recent tracks they valued highly enough to play live on the *Reunion* album.

'Take My Love and Run' (Black, Chatton)
The time is here; the moment's right. This is an essay in pure pop, with the appliance of science. Around the early eighties, the music press was busy debating the thorny issue of what exactly constitutes 'Perfect Pop', in terms of cute *Smash Hits* bands such as Haircut 100 or ABC – while perfect pop was simply what The Hollies had been purveying all along. With twinkling Human League instrumentation, this is a re-dubbed version of the earlier single, which tackles the problematic equation of balancing band-continuity with innovation, and pulls it off.

'Say You'll Be Mine' (Bliss)
A perfect slice of sweet summer pop, with scorching lead guitar work from Tony Hicks. Voices glide on swells of electro-strings around a melody as light and disposable as Kleenex, 'you don't have to tell the truth', but sometimes beguiling lies can be as enticing. Soft-focus voices blend and merge on catchily melodic ripples. Suspend your disbelief, and simply enjoy this track for the moment.

'Something Ain't Right' (Tarney, Snow, Spencer)
Following the 'Holliedaze' reunion, Graham Nash subsequently 'tagged along' to join the group in the Audio International studio for this session, 10

133

September 1981. 'The two Salford pals, Harold and Willy, were having fun again', recalls Bobby Elliott, he 'caught glimpses of the original Two Teens, as Allan and Graham became Ricky and Dane again.' The three-part harmonies still work, Tony's guitar work falls perfectly into place, and the electro flourishes are sensibly kept to the minimum. The pleasing results lead to a full reunion and the rest of this album.

'If the Lights Go Out' (Batt)
The sky might be falling down, the world might be ending, but while we have each other, we'll go down together. Again the emphasis is on the traditional strengths of guitar-driven harmonies, with only a single tasteful synth-riff, and the track is better because of it. An alternate take further reduces the synth figure. The rest of the album should have been as confident. Although they perform this song on the tie-in American tour, it is omitted from the live album.

'Stop In The Name Of Love' (Holland, Dozier, Holland)
There's a persistent story that, during the sixties, The Hollies considered covering Holland-Dozier-Holland's 'Reach Out, I'll Be There', before the Four Tops' original Motown recording took off spectacularly and dominated the airwaves. Since then, Phil Collins scored a massive hit by rejigging The Supremes' 'You Can't Hurry Love' in December 1982, and Kim Wilde would take her interpretation of 'You Keep Me Hanging On' up to number 2 in 1986. Maybe that magic would work for The Hollies? Using an Alan Tarney arrangement, they delete the compulsive Motown pulse in favour of a smoother appeal for their lover to Stop Stop Stop, unobtrusively gender-switching the lyric from 'run to her, leaving me alone and hurt' into 'go to him, leaving me alone again.' The Supremes original Tamla Motown single was climbing the UK chart just as The Hollies' 'Yes I Will' was sliding down. This track was issued as a July 1983 single b/w the non-album 'Musical Pictures' (WEA U9888), which is a slow piano-led paean to the power of music to paint moods, and to be carried away by the melody.

'I Got What I Want' (Bliss, Kipner)
As brightly tight and as slickly professional as we've come to expect, doing what The Hollies do. Once the bad, bad go-getter of 'Would You Believe', now he's found her, there's nothing more to be desired. It's lightweight catchy, dance-jumpy – if inconsequential, with a slower middle-eight. 'I never settled for second best,' well – maybe. But it's no more than an economical 2:29-minutes, with Tony's attractive guitar solo set off by electric keyboard embellishments.

'Just One Look' (Payne, Carroll)
The energy rush of 'Just One Look' constituted one of The Hollies' first career breakthroughs. They'd probably performed it 10,000 times since, in venues

across the world. How can they recapture that freshness? The answer is, they can't. This remake effortlessly pulls the fangs from the 1964 version, with synths dancing around the chorus, even Graham's 'thought I was dreaming, but I was wrong' takes it on a more relaxed, stress-free mode. This is a rather pointless exercise in rewriting the group's personal history. A measure more of what they've lost than the compensating gains they'd achieved elsewhere.

'Someone Else's Eyes' (Bliss)
Introduced by Graham on the tie-in live album as 'a slightly slower tune, a very beautiful song,' with soothing keyboard subverted by an excess of synths where a dose of Tony's guitar would have been more rewarding, but full evocative Allan-Graham-Tony three-part harmonies too. 'If I never seem to reach your expectations, I'll make it up to you somehow.' A pledge that this plaintive track, and this album, almost delivers. Issued as the B-side of 'Casualty' as a single (Atlantic 7-89768), it is this track that actually registers on the *Billboard* AOR chart.

'Having a Good Time' (Bliss, Kipner)
She reads her stars in the morning papers and believes every word they say. But love is difficult to predict. There are no certainties. Why not simply enjoy the here and now? The punchy vocal admits, 'I can't guarantee a happy ending,' with its stomping undistinguished radio-friendly smoothness, just maybe 'the story is always unwinding.' For The Hollies, that unwinding story still has some unexpected turns that will lead them who knows where?

Related Releases
'Too Many Hearts Get Broken' (Clarke, Leeson, Vale) b/w **'You're All Woman'** (Clarke, Hicks, Vale), with bonus track **'Laughter Turns to Tears'** (Will Birch, William Murray Bremner) on the twelve-inch edition. (10 May 1985, Columbia DB9110)
President Ronald Reagan was facing Mikhail Gorbachev, incoming leader of the USSR, as in the UK, the National Union of Mineworkers capitulated to the Thatcher government after a divisive year-long strike. The world was changing. While – following their temporary reunion – Graham went back to America 'to make some real money', and normal Hollies business resumed. With Allan, Tony and Bobby re-signed to EMI, rhythm-guitarist Alan Coates and bassist Steve Stroud, who'd played backup on the *What Goes Around* tour, were promoted to become full members. Denis 'Francis' Haines also joined The Hollies on keyboards from 1983-1991; born in Barnet, Middlesex, in September 1957, he'd previously worked with Gary Numan. After his time with The Hollies, he would work on TV and movie music, including *The Return Of The Living Dead* (1997), and collaborate with Allan Clarke on his solo *Resurgence* album (2019). Meantime, this single has a slow harmony build,

with curling synth figures and strong drum-breaks, although the song itself – by Allan with Mike Leeson and songwriting partner Peter Vale – is weak. The bonus track was recorded at the Matrix Studios (5-6 February 1985). In June 1986, Ray Stiles, formerly of the Glam-Glitter band Mud, replaces Steve Stroud on bass.

'This Is It' (Pope) b/w 'You Gave Me Strength' (Clarke, Hicks, Vale), with bonus track 'You're All Woman' on the twelve-inch edition (26 January 1987, Columbia DB9146)

Written by Maldwyn Pope, responsible for the TV *Fireman Sam* theme, and recorded at the Maison Rouge studio during September 1986, this is a tight, snappy soft-Rock performance. There's slightly-phased guitar and a handclap-driven chorus, which Allan performs in animated style, in a leather jacket and cropped-back hair. 'You're All Woman', written by Alan and Tony with Peter Vale, was recorded at Abbey Road (23 November 1984). It plays in with glassy, staccato electric keyboards, and just a teasing guitar ripple of 'Long Cool Woman'; she is smooth as silk, sharp as a knife, hotter than hell, but cooler than ice.

'You Gave Me Strength' is an appealing ballad with faultless production sheen, from the same team of Allan Clarke & Tony Hicks, with Peter (Benson) Vale – whose biggest songwriting success came with 'Would I Lie To You' a number 1 hit for the Charles & Eddie duo. Although he's also written for Sheena Easton and Jim Capaldi, his writing for The Hollies tends to the bland and predictably proficient – as though, in striving for a more sophisticated grown-up pop, they've omitted the necessary guts. It's listenable but forgettable, leaving no aftertaste or lingering impression.

'Reunion of the Heart' (Pope) b/w 'Too Many Hearts Get Broken' (Clarke, Leeson, Vale), with bonus track 'Holliedaze (Medley)' on the twelve-inch edition (23 March 1987, Columbia DB 9151)

'A brand new start' for this smooth Maldwyn Pope song – well, maybe. Slow-paced, carried into a surging crescendo by emotive synths with back-up girl voices mixed low, Allan makes the most of an essentially slight composition, while Tony adds fine high guitar lines, but why does the lyric claim Allan was living in Egypt? The B-side offers a second time around for the May 1985 single.

'Stand by Me' (Klaus-Dieter Gebauer, Hans Juergen Fritz, Tony Hendrik, Juergen Brinckmann) b/w 'For What It's Worth, I'm Sorry' (Clarke, Benson) (January 1988, Germany-only single Coconut 109-664)

Not the Ben E King classic, but an upfront drum-fronted number with sax break, programmed drums and an extended twelve-inch 'Dance Version' edition. He's lying awake at 3 a.m. wondering why he falls in love 'with a girl like you'? If she will only 'stand by me', the good times will roll. It was helped up to number 59 by being used as a theme-tune for a German TV show. The B-side is a reflective ballad written by Allan and Gary Benson, with vague 'He Ain't Heavy' strings in the instrumental break. It was recorded at The Hollies' home studios.

'Shine Silently' (Lofgren, Wagner) b/w 'Your Eyes' (Henrik, Van Haaren) (June 1988, Coconut 109-981)

A strongly evocative song written by Nils Lofgren and Dick Wagner and included on his fifth solo album *Nils* (1979), The Hollies give it a vaguely electro treatment – 'I don't need no light in the darkness' – with backing tracks recorded in Hennef, West Germany, and vocals mixed at Abbey Road (9 May 1988). Lofgren is a hugely respected musician who had worked with Neil Young in Crazy Horse and later in Bruce Springsteen's E-Street Band. His 2006 *Sacred Weapon* album features guest appearances by David Crosby and Graham Nash. The Hollies always displayed exquisite taste in their selection of covers, and this is no exception. The B-side, written and produced by T Hendrik and K Van Haarwen, swoops on synth strings, broken by Tony's cutting guitar solo.

'He Ain't Heavy, He's My Brother' b/w 'Carrie' (Miles, Marshall) (August 1988, EMI EM 74, with a 12" single adding 'The Air That I Breathe')

Meanwhile, in a separate continuum, The Hollies 1969 hit is reissued to coincide with its use in a Miller Lite lager TV-ad, and to compete with a new recording of the song by Bill Medley – recorded for the film soundtrack of *Rambo III*. By 3 September, the Bill Medley version enters the top 40 higher, but the following week The Hollies vault into the top ten – and sit at number one for three straight weeks (preventing Phil Collins' 'A Groovy Kind of Love' from making the top slot), twenty-three years after 'I'm Alive' gave The Hollies their first number one. Its success pushes the song, and The Hollies, back into the media spotlight, back onto *Top of the Pops*, with the tabloids devoting column-inches to exploring the song's provenance and interpreting it as a metaphor for internal family dynamics, and for the interdependence of social groups within the wider community, across races and creeds. Truly, 'the road is long, with many a winding turn, that leads us to who knows where? Who knows where...?' It makes for a wonderful chart return. But one that emphasises again that The Hollies' future lies in their past. In 1995 The Hollies joined the cast of TV-Soap *Coronation Street* for a special revival of 'He Ain't Heavy'! The B-side is not the old 'Carrie Anne' single but a new song recorded 6 June 1981 during a session with singer-songwriter John Miles – 'one of The Hollies' unsung heroes.' At Abbey Road, with Peter Bown overseeing the session, Alan Jones on bass and John Miles on piano, John Miles adds his own high harmony voice to his hopeful lyric 'you see my sad old days are over, never need to hide away, gettin' stronger every day, Carrie Carrie.'

The Hollies: Rarities (November 1988, EMI EMS 1311)
A generous seventeen tracks compiled by Bobby Elliott and Mike Heatley, this album features Peter Doggett liner notes and includes:

1. 'Carrie', not 'Carrie Anne', but the John Miles, Marshall composition.
2. 'Mexico Gold', see *Out on the Road*, April 1973. A trip to Mexico City where customs demand 'do you carry a gun, take drugs or are you communist?'
3. 'If It Wasn't for the Reason That I Love You' (Cooke, Greenaway) recorded 14 September 1972 with complex guitar interplay and Mikael Rickfors vocals. It's the kind of light hair-blowing-in-the-breeze radio-friendly confection that Cooke & Greenaway specialise in, but although he sings it well, perhaps it's not exactly Rickfors' forte. It remained unissued until now. The song was also recorded by Miki Antony – for whom it was a number 27 hit in February 1973, and by Wayne Newton, also in 1973.
4. 'Louisiana Man', after the Graham Nash line-up had performed this Doug Kershaw song as a duet with the host of the BBC-TV *Bobby Gentry Show*, they began work on an aborted 'Hollies Sing Country' album. This laid-back song about a fishing line strung across the river is the only track that survives.
5. 'She Looked My Way', recorded in July 1969 and also included as a *Hollies Sing Hollies* bonus track, at 2:43-minutes – it opens with heavy piano, leading into a lyric about a glance above the 'noisiest' (or maybe 'nauseous'?) crowd during an otherwise tedious dance where he's 'sick and tired of the same old scene,' but the glance remains a sad and regretted missed opportunity.
6. 'Eleanor's Castle' from the *Hollies Sing Hollies* sessions, and included as a bonus track on the 1996 remastered CD edition. It opens with a tinkling harpsichord and a dancing cheekiness of innuendo; Allan's lyric uses the metaphor of breaching her turrets tall, but 'I can't win if you won't let me in.' Huge fun, but maybe a last-minute loss of nerve led to the track being withheld.
7. 'Here in My Dreams', taped in July 1976 but left off the *Russian Roulette* album. An idealistic ballad written by Colin Horton Jennings with Peter Arnesen, carried on keyboards, with a smooth sax break. Allan does his best with limply inadequate material, 'we can go where wishes go.' Although outtakes can become the grail of fans' obsession, there are examples of some remaindered tracks that were left on the shelf for good reason.
8. 'Sanctuary', written by Allan's occasional co-writer Gary Benson; he walks the twilight zone beyond the city lights in a histrionic drama that can't even be saved by Tony's excoriating solo.

9. 'Relax', Graham Nash's good-timey 1:31-minutes – complete with yawns – salvaged from axed post-*Butterfly* sessions (26 and 27 March 1968). Slightly phased as he watches the world go 'heltering-skeltering by.' It's the first of two previously unissued tracks that would justify inclusion on those 'Nuggets' rare-psychedelia compilations.

10. 'Tomorrow When It Comes', written by Allan and Graham, strident pop-psych with phased guitar and a rapid drum shot hail, Graham's voice rides high in the falsetto bridges. Recorded across 26 and 27 March 1968, on this evidence, it would have been a great album.

11. 'Open Up Your Eyes' – the neglected B-side of 'Jennifer Eccles', recorded 9 and 11 January 1968.

12. 'The Times They Are A-Changin'', the live version.

13. 'Look Through Any Window' sung in French as 'Regardez Par Des Fenetres', recorded at two sessions 20 December 1965 and 4 January 1966.

14. 'After the Fox', the movie single with Peter Sellers.

15. 'Non Prego Per Me', as performed in Italian at the 26-28 January 1967 'San Remo Festival'.

16. 'Like Every Time Before', a Nash-Hicks-Clarke song in classic beat-group style, recorded in mono in 1966 as a demo for The Everly Brothers album – given a 1968 Tony Hicks twelve-string guitar overdub, and issued as the German B-side of 'Do The Best You Can' (Parlophone SD 6042).

17. 'Wings', recorded during January 1968, and originally released as part of the eco-charity LP *No-One's Gonna Change Our World* (December 1969, Regal Starline SRS5013) for the World Wildlife Fund.

'Find Me a Family' (Clarke, Beson) b/w 'No Rules' (Clarke, Hicks) (13 February 1989, EMI EM86)

The theme for the Wendy Nelson ITV show *Find a Family*, which promotes fostering and rehousing disadvantaged children. It leads in with simple acoustic guitar figures into a touching, yearning message-song written by Allan with Gary Benson, 'I take my life one day at a time,' it peaks at number 79. A desolate note of world-weary resignation adds authenticity. Oddly, there's an effective instrumental version included on the German *The Hollies Up Front: The Coconut Collection*, which works pretty well too. The B-side is a 3:05-minute Clarke-Hicks original, with a snap sharp drum track. Both sides are later collected onto *The Hollies At Abbey Road 1973-1989*.

'Baby Come Back (Single Version)' (Hanno Harders, Holger-Julian Copp, Gerald Heinemann, Mary S Applegate) plus 'Hillsborough' (Tony Hicks) b/w 'Baby Come Back (Long Version)' (1989, WEA 246 786-2)

A Germany-only single, in a 2:48-minute edit with an extended 5:47 mix, strongly electro with sweeping synths driven by Bobby Elliott augmented by programmed drums, but saving space for a Tony Hicks guitar solo. Allan throws in the curious line 'my baby's a cat,' while the long fade is strewn with sampled snippets of the vocals. An attractive single that climbs number 22 on the German chart, and stands its ground against the China Crisis and Blancmanges of the time. The 3:06-minute 'Hillsborough' is a touching song of separation written by Allan and Tony, 'go on your way, little angel, there'll be friends who greet you down the line'. With Tony's lead vocals and a plinky-plonk keyboard hook, the only clue to the Hillsborough disaster is the title itself. It prefigures their later involvement with The Justice Collective, dedicated to the ninety-six victims of the human crush at the FA Cup semi-final match between Liverpool and Nottingham Forest at the Sheffield Hillsborough Stadium, 15 April 1989.

The 1990s and into the 21st Century

The Hollies Up Front: The Coconut Collection (1990, Coconut Studios 260448000)
No chart placings.
A tie-in album, gathering the various mixes of their work, issued through the label:
'Stand by Me (Special Dance Version)' 07:11, 'Stand by Me (Abbey Road Version)' 04:03, 'Stand by Me (Radio Dub Version)' 03:48, 'Stand by Me (Instrumental Version)' 04:26, 'Shine Silently (Special Twelve-Inch Version)' 07:16, 'Shine Silently (Seven-Inch Mix)' 03:57, 'Your Eyes (Special Twelve-Inch Version)' 04:32, 'Your Eyes (Seven-Inch Mix)' 03:40, 'For What It's Worth, I'm Sorry (Seven-Inch Mix)' 04:13, 'Long Cool Woman (Twelve-Inch Mix)' 05:51, 'Find Me a Family (Instrumental Version)' 03:42, 'Draggin' My Heels (Special Disco Version)' 06:27

'The Woman I Love' (Kershaw) b/w 'Purple Rain (live)' (Prince) (8 March 1993, EMI CDEM 264)
To mark the band's thirtieth anniversary, a twenty-six track compilation album *The Air That I Breathe: The Very Best of the Hollies* climbed to a UK number 15. It included this previously unissued single, a cheerfully jog-a-long song written by electro-popper Nik Kershaw, which gets no higher than number 42. The CD-single edition adds 'The Air That I Breathe' and '(Ain't That) Just Like Me'. The contrast is clear. Where The Hollies started out ravenous for success, the itchy motivation to recapture that lost success does not burn with the same hungry urgency. A German CD single is made up of 'The Air That I Breathe', 'Two Shadows', a live 'Another Night' and a new track, a percussive 4:16-minute 'Naomi' written by Tony with his son Paul, capturing a tropical Caribbean sway with party horns (1992, EMI 560-7243-8-80155-2-3). For the unlikely 5:03-minute cover of Prince's 'Purple Rain', Steve Stroud briefly returns alongside keyboardist Dave Carey, who was soon replaced by Ian Parker of Clannad (born 26 November 1953 in Irvine, North Ayrshire). The single passed virtually unnoticed, which is sad in that it represents Allan Clarke's last time around as Hollies lead singer.

Reunion

Personnel:
Allan Clarke: vocals, guitar, harmonica
Graham Nash: vocals, guitar
Tony Hicks: lead guitar, vocals
Bobby Elliott: drums
plus Steve Stroud: drums
Paul Bliss: keyboards
Released: 2005, Snapper Music SMACD 919/ Fuel 2000
Running Time: 01:08:39
No chart placings.

Recorded live at the at the Ohio 'Kings Island Amusement Park' in Cincinnati, 2 September 1983 with original members Allan Clarke, Tony Hicks, Graham Nash, Bobby Elliott, augmented by Steve Stroud (bass) and Paul Bliss (keyboards), with a Henry Diltz cover photo. They run through the classic hits, a sprinkling of more recent titles, plus a few of Graham's Crosby, Stills & Nash titles. The acoustic 'King Midas in Reverse' is stand-out, and while it's good to hear Allan's harmonies on 'Teach Your Children', it's strange that Graham's opening lines on 'On A Carousel' are also sung by Allan, until Tony works some quotes from 'Shakin' All Over' into the extended closer 'Long Cool Woman (in a Black Dress)'. The full track-listing is:

'I Can't Let Go', 'Just One Look', 'Bus Stop', 'Casualty', 'On A Carousel', 'Someone Else's Eyes', 'Look Through Any Window', 'King Midas In Reverse', 'Wasted On The Way', 'Teach Your Children', 'Soldier's Song', 'Stop, Stop, Stop', 'The Air That I Breathe', 'Carrie Anne', 'Stop In The Name Of Love', 'He Ain't Heavy, He's My Brother', 'Long Cool Woman (In A Black Dress)'

What Goes Around (2003, Magic Records 3930370)

The extended French CD reissue adds bonus tracks to the original ten, including the beautifully Folksy 'Let Her Go Down' – a dramatic tale of a doomed nautical wreck, originally recorded by the song's writers, Steeleye Span, on their *Sails of Silver* (1980) album. The track was issued as the New Zealand B-side to 'Stop In The Name Of Love', and was also rescued onto *The Long Road Home 1963-2003* compilation. The bonus tracks are:

'Musical Pictures' (the B-side of 'Stop In The Name of Love'), 'Baby Come Back', 'Baby Come Back (Long Version)', 'Hillsborough' (featured on the 'Baby Come Back' single), 'Take My Love and Run (First Version)', 'Driver' (B-side of 'Take Your Love and Run'), 'If The Lights Go Out (First Version)', 'Carrie', 'Let Her Go Down'

Staying Power

Personnel:
Peter Howarth: vocals, acoustic guitar
Tony Hicks: guitar, banjo, mandolin, electric sitar
Bobby Elliott: drums, percussion
Ray Stiles: bass, vocals
Steve Lauri: guitar, vocals
Ian Parker: vocals, keyboard
Produced by Ian Parker and Ray Stiles.
Released: 7 February 2006, EMI 0946 355983 2 2
Running Time: 47:31
No chart placings.

Dedicated, polished and professional. How could it be otherwise? For their forty-third year, with six figures framed in the cover-photograph, The Hollies on this album are mainstays Tony Hicks on guitar and backup voice (plus banjo, mandolin, sitar), plus longtime drummer Bobby Elliott holding the rhythm section together (drums, percussion). Allan Clarke was gone. When he stepped down for health reasons, Carl Wayne became Hollies vocalist, debuting in June 2000 on the Isle of Wight. Born Colin David Tooley in Birmingham's Winson Green, 18 August 1943, he'd name-switched to 'Carl Wayne' in time to become vocalist for The Move on their 1967 hits 'Night Of Fear', 'I Can Hear The Grass Grow', 'Fire Brigade' and the rest. He fronted The Hollies from February 2000, adding 'Blackberry Way' and 'Flowers In The Rain' to the band's already extensive repertoire, until he played his final Hollies gig in Egersund, Norway on 10 July 2004, before being diagnosed with oesophageal cancer, from which he subsequently died on 31 August.

He was replaced, in turn, by Peter Howarth, a former Cliff Richard and Kylie Minogue backing singer. Having assumed frontman status that same October 2004, he carries the vocals here, and plays acoustic guitar. Ian Parker had played Roland JV1080 and Korg SGID Digital Grand Piano with The Hollies since 1991, filling in the body of the songs. He'd also recorded a 1996 solo album *Count The Waves,* on which Tony Hicks co-writes and adds guitar and vocals. To complete the line-up, there's the harmonising of guitarist Steve Lauri, who also joined in October 2004. Born 26 April 1954 in London, Steve was a session player who had also toured with Cliff Richard's band. Bassist Ray Stiles joined in 1986, leaving in 1990 only to rejoin a year later. Ray part-owned Pelican Studios, where Steve Lauri had played sessions. This proved to be the stable line-up that persists from 2004 on. Ian Parker and Ray Stiles also get producer credits. The online allmusic.com claims 'the songwriting is also very strong throughout most of the album, and with the energy levels much higher than one expects from a band in its forty-third year, *Staying Power* seems a triply appropriate title – indeed, this is the album they should have released for that 1983 reunion when they had all of the press attention on them.' Well, maybe…

'Hope' (Davis, Mac)

There are radio-friendly cruising American-style affirmative harmonies and the positive anthem of 'hope' that can't really disguise the limitations of the jog-along material. Issued as a blandly slick September 2005 CD-single b/w 'Shine On Me' (EMI 0946-340623-2-9). The Hollies make the best of the slight and inadequate song, with counter-harmonies playing against the lead voice, uniting to punch out the single-word title message.

'So Damn Beautiful' (Stack, Read)

A showcase track in which Peter Howarth's yearning voice takes the verse until the close-harmony chorus recalls something of the band's earlier distinctive power. It was issued as a sweetly melodic February 2006 CD single b/w the non-album Rob Davis-Tom Nicholls song 'Too Much Too Soon' (EMI 094635-40642). Although it's so smooth, there are no rough edges to snag the attention.

'Prove Me Wrong' (Stack, Read)

With programmed rhythms to reinforce Bobby's drum track and quivering synth-stabs to illuminate a pleasantly inoffensive ballad, Peter Howarth delivers the lead voice with confident sincerity. As it fades into a mid-point instrumental pause, he resumes in a fine showcase for his vocal range and emotive control. It closes with Bobby's trademark cymbal shimmers.

'Break Me' (Iglesias, Alexander, Davis)

More up-tempo with strong guitar and handclaps, a slight revision on Enrique Iglesias' own version, which is titled 'Break Me, Shake Me (You Can't Make Me)'. From his 2003 album 7 – his seventh studio album – which made the son of slick crooner Julio Iglesias one of the music industry's biggest-selling Latin artists. The Hollies started out doing Chuck Berry and Buddy Holly songs; now they're 'Livin' La Viva Loca'…? Actually, that's Ricky Martin, who opened the door for the global breakthrough of Latin music, from which Enrique would reap the benefit. But you get the drift?

'Shine on Me' (Masterson, Read, Hart)

Big dramatic flourishes with sweeping guitar figures, 'look at us, we've come so far.' This otherwise homogenised mid-Atlantic soft rock. He's been through so many changes; worlds collide until the truth of her love saved him. Peter narrates the verse into the uplifting group harmony chorus and brief inspirational guitar break. It's seamless, with all evidence of quirky individuality efficiently smoothed away, despite a 'you were right there in front of me' interjection that could almost have come from musical theatre.

'Suspended Animation' (Davis, Nicholls)

With submerged sample voices deep in the mix, the melody carried on a strong soft-rock tempo, and guitar offset by a slight autotune vocal-ripple, the surges of synths never overstay their welcome. Intended as a device to correct or disguise vocal imperfections, what phasing had been to 1967, so the autotune audio processing software had become to pop since Cher's 'Believe' made it a global number 1. The Hollies' use of the effect is restrained and tasteful.

'Touch Me' (Iglesias, Alexander, Davis)
A promisingly heavy guitar riff, which soon loses its way, as Peter Howarth competently protests that he's more than just a one-night stand, over a busy celebratory arrangement that dips into a slow-down intermission before picking up its energies to resume the catchy invitation to intimacy. For Iglesias, it was thumped out more emphatically as 'The Way You Touch Me'. This is the second of the album's three Enrique songs. Perhaps The Hollies were missing the stimulus of Terry Sylvester's creative input?

'Emotions' (Dozier, Davis)
As well as being one-third of the sixties' most prolific songwriting teams, Lamont Dozier was part of the quintessential Motown writing machine responsible for – among countless others – The Hollies' almost-hit 'Stop In The Name Of Love'. Yet this is just another burnished mid-paced sweet power ballad. 'I'm out of control', he protests, but it could be argued that too much control is what undermines the album. Although the songs renew The Hollies repertoire with new material to punctuate TV shows and live performance with a pretence of relevancy.

'Weakness' (Braide, Davis)
Lit by three-part harmony choruses, allmusic.com considers that when Howarth's powerful voice is 'focused properly, with the right quality lyrics,' it does recall Allan Clarke, and that together 'they generate a lean and powerful pop-rock sound, with lots of guitar and vocal hooks.' The triad harmonies lift the song into a swaying sing-along chorus which they perform to a receptive audience on the German *Hit Gigantem* TV show. Despite the changes inflicted by time, when it works, The Hollies' on-stage magic still retains considerable power.

'Live It Up' (Iglesias, Davis and 'Alex Ander', who is Gregg Alexander of the New Radicals)
A positive message, 'we are straight, we're gay, we're bi. We are black, we're white'. We celebrate our diversity with a catchy 'da-da-dat' background vocal riff that is more pronounced on Enrique Iglesias' more strident original 'Live It Up Tonight', the third song that The Hollies took from his 2003 album 7. Are three covers from the same source-album too much?

145

'Yesterday's Gone' (Twigg, Read, Topham)

Tis song has an attractive ticking guitar riff with spacey but unobtrusive synth swirls, and a lyric that reminisces about the long lost days. They'll never get it back. Let it go. Strummed guitar, with Steve Laurie and bassist Ray Stiles adding harmonies, while Ian Parker's keyboard fleshes out the soundscape. Tony's distinctive fuzz-tone solo makes for a pleasing surprise. One of the album's stronger songs.

'Let Love Pass' (Braide, Davis)

Don't look back. Don't turn around. Keep straight ahead. A pleasing enough synth-strewn break-up ballad. Peter Howarth has the vocal range and power to deliver. And yes, there's Tony Hicks and Bobby Elliott here to provide unarguably clear lines of continuity from the very earliest Hollies days, but the band sound on this album bears little resemblance to the creative energies that ignited it all. When Terry Sylvester replaced Graham Nash, the group sound became more consistent, less extreme. When Peter Howarth replaced Allan Clarke, that process was taken further. The sound is smoother still, pureed down into an undifferentiated oleaginous sheen. What's gone has gone.

Related Releases

Radio Fun (May 2012, EMI 440 7702). No chart placings.

During the mid-sixties, if you weren't on the BBC, you weren't on the radio. The Beatles gathered *The Beatles at the Beeb*, so The Hollies replied with a compilation of their own many appearances on various BBC radio and TV shows, taking live sessions from *Saturday Club*, *Top Gear* and the *Top of the Pops* TV show. There are 32 previously unreleased pieces of 1964-1971 audio history, rescued from the archives, with Bobby Elliott providing background anecdotes in the eight-page liner notes booklet. The title of the album is an affectionate glance back to the weekly comic paper of the same name, in which the comedy exploits of radio stars of the day were told in comic strip form. The tracks are:

1. 'Here I Go Again' (*Saturday Club*, 28 September 1964)
2. 'Jennifer Eccles' (*David Symonds*, 25 March 1968)
3. 'Bus Stop' (*Saturday Club*, 28 June 1966)
4. 'I've Got a Way of My Own' (*Saturday Club*, 13 December 1965)
5. 'Wings' (*David Symonds*, 25 March 1968)
6. 'Step Inside' (*David Symonds*, 25 March 1968)
7. 'Wishyouawish' (*Saturday Club*, unknown, late 1968)
8. 'Shake' (*Saturday Club*, 28 June 1966)
9. 'Put Yourself in My Place' (*Saturday Club*, 6 September 1965)
10. 'Ride Your Pony' (*Saturday Club*, 6 September 1965)
11. 'I Take What I Want' (*Saturday Club*, 23 March 1966)
12. 'Little Bitty Pretty One' (*Saturday Club*, 25 January 1966)
13. 'Away Away Away' (*Top Gear*, 13 October 1967)

14. 'Charlie And Fred' (*Top Gear*, 13 October 1967)
15. 'I Can't Let Go' (*This Must Be the Place*, 14 January 1966)
16. 'Hard Hard Year' (*Saturday Club*, 28 June 1966)
17. 'If I Needed Someone' (*Saturday Club*, 13 December 1965)
18. 'That's How Strong My Love Is' (*Saturday Club*, 23 March 1966)
19. 'To You My Love' (*This Must Be the Place*, 14 January 1966)
20. 'So Lonely' (*This Must Be the Place*, 28 September 1965)
21. 'Something's Got a Hold on Me' (*Saturday Club*, 29 September 1964)
22. 'Nobody' (*Delaney's Delight*, 26 January 1965)
23. 'Set Me Free' (*Saturday Club*, 28 September 1964)
24. 'She Said Yeah' (*Delaney's Delight*, 26 January 1965)
25. 'You Must Believe Me' (*Top Gear*, 19 February 1965)
26. 'Lawdy Miss Clawdy' (*Saturday Swings*, 28 July 1965)
27. 'Too Many People' (*This Must Be the Place*, 28 September 1965)
28. 'Look Through Any Window' (*Saturday Swings*, 28 July 1965)
29. 'Too Young To Be Married' (*Top of the Pops* (TV), 3 March 1971)
30. 'I'm Alive' (*Saturday Club*, 24 May 1965)
31. 'The Games We Play' (*Top Gear*, 13 October 1967)
32. 'He Ain't Heavy He's My Brother' (*Top of the Pops* (TV), 2 October 1969)

Then, Now, Always

Personnel:
Peter Howarth: vocals, acoustic guitar
Tony Hicks: lead guitar, vocals
Bobby Elliott: drums, percussion
Steve Lauri: rhythm guitar, vocals
Ray Stiles: bass, vocals
Ian Parker: keyboards
Recorded in Ray Stiles Studio.
Released: 4 October 2010, EMI 5099991750228
Running Time: 42:57
No chart placings.

They'd come a long way since '(Ain't That) Just Like Me'. Name another
straight-up British rock-pop band as long-lived as The Hollies, with their
consistency, slick, professional performance and taste in material. You can't.
Whatever audiences wanted from them, those distinctive harmonies, plain
good music, or nostalgia, they got it. But when is a band no longer the same
band? The Rolling Stones survived the loss of Brian Jones and the defection of
Bill Wyman, but they continue. Roger Daltrey and Pete Townshend still perform
as The Who. Fleetwood Mac have gone through enough changes to baffle even
the most dedicated rock academic, yet are still Fleetwood Mac. Even Queen
persisted after Freddie Mercury's passing, with Paul Rodgers or Adam Lambert.
  In a sense, The Hollies had become an entity in its own right, greater than
any of its component parts. It never became Allan Clarke & The Hollies – or
even Tony Hicks & The Hollies, in the way that it became Eric Burdon & The
Animals, Diana Ross & The Supremes or Smokey Robinson & The Miracles. The
Hollies was a brand, and no individual member was bigger than the band itself.
As early as 1964, Allan's intention to marry created a rift that almost led to him
being forced out of the group. Pop stars were seen as surrogate boyfriends;
marriage was bad for their image. John Lennon tried to conceal his marriage
to Cynthia for the same reason. Although Allan married – to no perceptible
detriment to the group's popularity – it's indicative that they'd even considered
continuing without him. The Hollies survived the loss of Graham Nash, and
went on to even greater things – 'The Hollies, after I left in 1968, had the
audacity, the gall, to have three number one records' he jokes, 'thanks a lot,
guys.' There was the Terry Sylvester period, Allan Clarke came and went, then
returned. He finally quit for good when, as he told me, 'I was going on stage
and singing those songs, and it didn't feel comfortable, it no longer felt right
for me to be doing them that way. There is a time for everyone to say 'that's
it'!' He played his last Hollies gig in Stoke-on-Trent on 27 November 1999, to
quit music when his wife Jennifer was given a second cancer diagnosis, and he
decided that spending time with her took priority.
  'I don't even know who's in The Hollies these days' he told me.

While for Graham, 'The Hollies were a great band' he told me wistfully, 'a great band'.

But the third face of that 'L Ransford' triangle – Tony Hicks – and drummer Bobby Elliott had been constant through all the post-1963 changes, a continuity through the Mikael Rickfors period, through the later Carl Wayne vocal era, until *Then, Now, Always* with lead vocals handled by Peter Howarth. And, naturally, there had been style changes too. Yet it was still The Hollies, even though the sound had the smoother, more mid-American AOR style of Foreigner, Toto, Air Supply...

'Then, Now, Always (Dolphin Days)' (Elliott, Nelson)
Sung by Tony, co-written by Bobby, the lyric affectionately delves back to the very beginning of the long Hollies career arc, recalling how 'we came down from the hills, the land of millstone grit' as illustrated by the cartoony album cover-art showing terraces of *Coronation Street* houses, railway arch and towering gasometer, then 'escaping from tradition where our faces didn't fit' before referencing the 'Bus Stops and Carousels' of success. The Dolphins in question, of course, were Tony and Bobby's pre-Hollies band.

'If You See Her' (Read, Soervaag)
Sharp drum punctuation throughout, promising rippling guitar, although the vocals lack character and the melody is unexceptional. 'Nothing left but an empty space' indeed. This album was initially released in March 2009, available only through The Hollies website, until it was picked up and given an official EMI release. *Record Collector* magazine concedes, 'there are still some fine examples of the rich harmonies and melodies that have kept the group in our hearts.'

'One Touch' (Olsson, Johansan, Read)
With a welcome return of Tony's unique sitar-tuning, there's a solid drum-thump and tight harmony back-up to Peter Howarth's lead vocal. Polished with a production sheen as clean and superficial as a Eurovision entry, the song carries the affirmative message 'one touch, one kiss ... one life, one soul ... trust in what your heart knows', yet it fails to deliver anything resembling the killer punch it needs.

'Passengers' (Davis, Poole)
Nothing in life is for keeps; we are simply temporary residents on this planet. Life is so precious and wasted. Everything we have can melt away. Celebrate the moment. Peter's lead voice is answered by backup responses, which then break into full wrap-around chorus harmonies. There's nothing here to actively dislike. But again, the potential power is neutered by a certain vocal and instrumental blandness.

'I Would Fly' (Read, Stack)

From the frozen reflective keyboard notes of the play-in, through the warning 'they say be careful what you wish for' because he's been wishing all his life, this power-ballad has moments of very attractive build, and a perfect Tony Hicks guitar solo. Keeping The Hollies dream alive. So it's interesting, if a little churlish, to conjecture how Allan Clarke could have delivered this song.

'Coming Home' (Mullins)

That novelty skanking rhythm was never a very convincing Hollies guise, although the slight guitar distortion and reverse-tape noodling give bonus substance. 'He ain't a rebel, we knew he was cool', but this playful excursion, this 'supernova in a universal sigh', adds a playful twist to the album. Behind the writer credits, Michael J Mullins had been vocalist with charting Modern Romance before going on to creative interactions with The Alan Parsons Project, and with Peter Howarth in Cliff Richard's vocal back-up crew, as well as closing another node of connection by contributing session voice to 'Cold', the last song The Everly Brothers recorded together.

'I Lied' (Diamond, Masterson, Read)

This song begins with Morse blips and an effective squeal of guitar noises, then a nagging minimalist riff, as Bobby pins the rhythm with rock-hard precision. Only the song is something of a let-down; he's 'been burned and found out the hard way,' he swore off romance, but he relents and lets her under his skin. The instrumental break allows the attractive dissonance to momentarily flow back in around the pleasantly acceptable harmonies.

'One Way Ticket' (McCarthy)

Exotic Santana guitar curls in around an attractively upbeat singalong chorus. There's little to provide a strong aftertaste, but it's an enjoyable trifle. Writer Kevin has an interesting career in his own right extending back to sixties also-rans The London Beats. He'd demoed a cover of The Hollies 'You Know He Did' for solo artist Mary McCarthy, before he joined cult prog-rock band Cressida for two albums for Vertigo.

'Too Much Too Soon' (Davis, Nicholls)

A celebratory paean to love, is he crazy to fall? Is he taking it all too fast? Only time will tell. Twittering synths smooth out into the appealingly signature lushness that permeates the album. The unique DNA of The Hollies, sufficiently malleable to adapt to the changing times through the preceding decades, has flattened and broadened out into an immaculate big concert-friendly Sensurround proficiency. Although maybe here it's more a case of too little, too late.

'Unforgivable' (Masterson, Read)

A nagging little guitar riff leads into another dramatic designer love ballad. A former member of boyband A1, writer Mark Read had already contributed songs to *Staying Power*, and had a reliable track record of writing for reliable AOR names such as Michael Bolton, Boyzone, Paul Carrack ... and Charlotte Church! Although The Hollies had featured in various pop pin-up magazines in their heyday – they were good-looking boys – they could never have been considered a boyband. The guise does not a good fit make now.

'Hearts Don't Lie' (Hart, Masterson, Read)

They're running fast and getting nowhere. But where hearts collide, everything is going to work out fine. Hips don't lie either. Although Peter emotes competently enough, there's very little of such anatomical energy here. The show is over, so bring the curtain down. Don't read too much into these lyrics. The Hollies will continue. It will take the global Covid-19 pandemic to pause their never-ending tour.

'She'd Kill for Me' (Elliott, Nelson)

A faint distant 'it's a long road home when you've gone' three-voice a cappella introduction. Then lushly rippling Tony Hicks guitar play-in, with a promising passionate straight-from-the-heart performance that almost succeeds in making it. A tango in the dark. A last-minute addition to the EMI official release, this is one of the album's better tracks, with a catchy chorus, strong guitar soloing and an effective wind-down back to a three-voice a cappella close. Stop the clock. Rewind the hands of time.

Related Releases

'He Ain't Heavy, He's My Brother' by The Justice Collective
(December 2012, Metropolis 506500-1566387)

Following the precedent set by Band Aid, every catastrophe brought forth a fund-raising charity single. If that record also helped raise the media visibility of those involved, well – so be it! Organised by Peter Hooton of The Farm in aid of the Hillsborough Justice Campaign, and produced by Guy Chambers, the participants include Gerry Marsden and Paul McCartney, with Holly Johnson, Robbie Williams, Melanie C, Shane MacGowan, comedian John Bishop, and footballer Kenny Dalglish as well as Tony Hicks and Bobby Elliott. When it entered the reconfigured UK chart of mp3, digital download and streaming at number 1 (29 December 2012), it made Bobby – aged 71, the oldest chart-topper to date!

This Path Tonight by Graham Nash

Released: 15 April 2016, Blue Castle Records
Personnel:

Graham Nash: lead vocals, acoustic guitar
Shane Fontayne: guitars, backing vocals, production
Jennifer Condos: bass
Todd Cladwell: Hammond organ
Patrick Warren: piano
Jay Bellerose: drums, percussion
Running Time: 41:43
Highest chart positions: UK: 41, US: 93

This was Graham's first solo record of new music in fourteen years, produced by Shane Fontayne, who also plays guitar and adds backing vocals. This is a meditative album that reflects on the changes in his life, long-term and over recent years, with a new relationship following his divorce from wife Susan, as well as the much-publicised bust-up with long-time friend and co-writer David Crosby, which was revealed during the media interviews promoting this album. The songs 'Myself At Last' and 'Target' are highlights, while 'Golden Days' is a moody dream of the sixties Hollies past. The tracklisting is:

'This Path Tonight', with Graham still wondering where are we going, 'where will it lead me…?', 'Myself At Last', 'Cracks in the City', 'Beneath the Waves', 'Fire Down Below', 'Another Broken Heart', 'Target', 'Golden Days', Graham sings how 'I used to be in a band, made up of my friends'.'Back Home', the lyrics tell how 'Mother Earth will soon be calling you'. 'Encore'. Plus bonus tracks: 'Mississippi Burning', 'Watch Out for the Wind', 'The Fall'

Resurgence by Allan Clarke
Personnel:
Allan Clarke: vocals, guitar, harmonica, producer
Alex Albrow: guitars
Sam Clarke: guitars
Francis Haines: keyboards, programming, guitar, backing vocals
Phil Haines: drums, engineer
Lydia Stables: violin
Howard Martin: guitars
Jake Hook: backing vocals
Released: December 2019, BMG
Running Time: 43:02
No chart placings.

His real name is Harold. The title of his first solo LP, in 1972, told us so. But 47 years later, the voice of The Hollies returned, and was as distinctive as ever. 'For many years, people would ask, 'why don't you go back to singing?' Well, what I couldn't do was perform Hollies songs anymore' he confided to me. 'When I recorded those hits with The Hollies, they were really high songs. But later, my register changed. But what I should have said was, there may come a time when I'll be able to sing, because I'll be doing songs I've written myself. Because, well, I never stopped. I jot lyrics down. It was always on the back-burner.' His neatly-combed short iron-grey hair is combed into a fringe across his forehead, a slightly pained expression on his face to denote the seriousness of his intent. But when he grins, it's that same *Top of the Pops* smile from all those hit records.

There's a strong Classic Rock spine, name-checking one of The Hollies' biggest US hits with 'Long Cool Woman's Back In Town', Allan's voice slightly echoed as his cutting harmonica works that same lethal femme fatale strut – 'sometimes the right way is the wrong way to go'. An obvious focal point, 'Hearts Of Stone', co-written with Carla Olson, also takes its fang-and-claw riff from the same source, eighties-style soft-rock leaning heavy on the bass. But there's more than just that, Allan's 'The Door Is Slowly Closing' has an unobtrusive 'Om' meditative chant to counterpoint a slinky southern 'Black Velvet' feel, giving its restless lyrics an edge, 'nowhere to run, nowhere to hide.' And a slow-paced acoustic interplay on a premature burial image for 'I'm Only Sleeping'. Then gnawing electro-pulse with guitar slap-back on 'I Don't Know The Reason', its lyric 'they say Rock 'n' Roll is over' answered by a stinging guitar solo as if to prove the doomsayers wrong.

'But I'm never going out on tour or anything like that', he told me. 'I did that for over forty years. And though I miss it ... slightly, I wouldn't want to go out and do the tours that I did with The Hollies. I wouldn't want to be a part of that sort of circus again. I'm not really ready for that yet. But I've had lots of offers by lots of people, so who knows...?'

As on the album, 'It's the start of a new day, I'm going to jump and hope to fly, I'd be a fool if I didn't try.' The tracklisting is:

'Journey of Regret', 'You Broke My Heart', 'The Door Is Slowly Closing', 'I'll Just Keep On Walking', 'I'm Only Sleeping', 'Heart of Stone', 'I Don't Know the Reason', 'Don't Let Me Down', 'Long Cool Woman's Back in Town', 'I'm Comin' Home'

Hollies Compilations

The Hollies Greatest Hits (May 1967, US Imperial 9350-12350)
US: 11.

Hollies Greatest (November 1972, Parlophone PCS 7148) UK: 1.

Hollies Greatest Volume Two (November 1972, Parlophone PCS 7148)

The Hollies Greatest Hits (April 1973, US Epic KE32061)

The History of The Hollies: Twenty-Four Genuine Top Thirty Hits (November 1975, EMI EMSP 650, double-vinyl)
The sleeve-notes by Toby Mamis claims that 'of all the groups that exploded onto the pop music scene in the halcyon and hectic days of the early sixties group explosion that proved to the world that Britons could rock in the same league as Americans, The Hollies are among the few that had distinctive talent. That explains their longevity.'

Clarke, Hicks, Sylvester, Calvert, Elliott (April 1977, US Epic PE-34714)

Twenty Golden Greats (July 1978, EMI EMTV11) UK: 2.

The Best of The Hollies Eps (August 1978, Parlophone PMC 7174)
Later reissued as *The EP Collection* (See For Miles SEE CD94), it includes a rare remix of 'I'm Talking About You' from 1964. All tracks are mono except 'Whatcha Gonna Do 'Bout It'.

The Other Side of The Hollies (August 1978, Parlophone PMC 7176)

The Best of The Hollies (October 1980, Polydor Australia)

Nothing But the Very Best (October 1982, Australia, Hammard)

The Hollies (1985, Music For Pleasure MFP 4157271)
Seventeen hit songs including three previously-unissued archive tracks: 'Zip-A-Dee-Do-Dah (Song of the South)', the 1946 Disney film song given renewed relevance by Phil Spector's Bob B Soxx & The Blue Jeans, recorded with three-part beat-group harmonies 15 May 1963.

'Poison Ivy' (Jerry Leiber & Mike Stoller) originally done by The Coasters, then subsequently by The Rolling Stones and by The Paramounts (early Procol Harum line-up), recorded raw 11 October 1963

'Little Bitty Pretty One', written by Bobby Day and a 1957 hit for Thurston Harris, recorded in thin mono 30 June 1965.

The Hollies: Their Forty Greatest Hits (1986, EMI TP9, New Zealand double-vinyl)

The Hollies Collection (1986, EMI 4346462, N Z double-CD)

All The Hits And More: The Definitive Collection (September 1988, EMI EM 1301)
A UK number 51 in the wake of the renewed chart success of 'He Ain't Heavy He's My Brother'.

Rarities (November 1988, EMI EMS 1311)
See detailed listing.

Epic Anthology: From the Original Master Tapes (June 1990, US Epic EGK-46161, CD)

Thirtieth Anniversary Collection 1963-1993 (EMI Music Distribution E2-99917)
Remixed by Ron Furmanek, much to Allan Clarke's disapproval, this three-CD 57-track Box-Set includes previously unissued songs:
'I Understand' recorded 15 July 1963 in a jaunty strutting 6/8-time – not the Freddie & The Dreamers song.

'Nothing Else But Love', a big emotive power-ballad with shimmering sweeps that elaborate the contours of the Richard Marx original.
There are also three tyro 'L Ransford' tracks recorded during their prolific 1965 run, demo-quality songs that could easily have been worked up into B-sides or album cuts:

'She Gives Me Everything I Want' (2:22-minutes, 14 September) a fast Beatles-paced song with stinging guitar and Graham solo voice-lines.

'I Can't Get Nowhere With You' (1:51-minutes, cut at the New York Roulette Studios, 22 September) with engagingly simple beat-group structure.

'You in My Arms' (2:02-minutes, 13 October), nimble Tony Hicks guitar and appealing harmonies, with Graham taking the high-voice middle-eight.

The Air That I Breathe: The Very Best of The Hollies (March 1993, EMI EMTV/CDEMTV 74)UK: 15.

The Hollies: Four Hollies Originals (May 1995, EMI 7243-8-322232)

The full albums *Another Night*, *Buddy Holly*, *Russian Roulette* and *5317704* which *Q* magazine deems 'The Hollies trapped in a sixties-based style which was no longer very profitable'.

The Hollies at Abbey Road 1963-1966 (October 1997, EMI CDABBEY 103)

Features the 'Alternative Arrangement' of 'We're Through' recorded 16 August 1964.

The Hollies at Abbey Road 1966-1970 (February 1998, EMI CD 493-4502)

Compiled by Bobby Elliott with Tim Chacksfield, it features previously unreleased tracks:

'Schoolgirl', a Graham Gouldman song recorded at two dates on 22 February and 8 March 1967 during the *Evolution* sessions. Tony garnished the acetate with additional guitar during final production and mixing by Paul Hicks at Abbey Road 16 November 1997. It's a strong dramatic song with serious forceful delivery that tells the story of a teenage pregnancy – 'she was a schoolgirl with seven GCE's and one ambition was to collect degrees' until she met a student with smiling eyes who 'taught her subjects of which she'd never heard.' With the supposed Permissive Society on the horizon and its attendant perceived decline in moral standards, the song was exposing social hypocrisy and gender double-standards, 'all is pure to the pure,' but it was perhaps this potential controversy complicated by nervous expectations of a BBC radio ban that delayed its release, until Graham Gouldman produced an inferior version with The Mindbenders, issued as a November 1967 single (Fontana TF 877). Despite prefiguring The Hollies' own 'in the passion of the Spring, came the Baby,' and with the subject of unplanned pregnancy also covered by The Troggs on their February 1968 hit 'Little Girl' and Gene Pitney's April 1968 'Somewhere in the Country', The Hollies 'Schoolgirl' was nevertheless indefinitely shelved.

'Man With No Expression (Horses Through a Rainstorm)', another major track, written by Graham together with Terry Reid and recorded at Abbey Road, 14 and 15 August 1968. A beautifully complex composition rich with psychedelic imagery, it features Graham singing the middle-eight and maybe taking a parting shot at The Hollies with 'there are many things I'd like to turn you onto, but somehow I feel you're safer where you are.' Although Bobby describes it as 'one of the finest tracks we ever laid down,' Ron Richards was unimpressed, and it remained unissued. There was also an outtake version of this song done by Crosby, Stills & Nash, recorded during the *Déjà Vu* sessions (28 December 1969) and eventually issued as part of the *CSN* box-set (1991).

'Sign of the Times', a Clarke-Hicks composition that was recorded November 1969 at Abbey Road, with a swirling Hammond organ sound and stinging guitar solo that shines through the 'unfinished' demo sound-quality, 'don't be hurt' pleads the lyric, 'we love you, still.' It was later collected as part of the *Changin' Times* box-set.

The Hollies At Abbey Road 1973-1989 (August 1998, EMI CD 496-4342)

The Hollies: Orchestral Heaven (June 2000, EMI UK 526-0912)
Eighteen tracks taken from all points in the story, united only by orchestral arrangements from Johnny Scott, Chris Gunning, Mike Batt, Tony Hymas, Mike Vickers or Pete Wingfield, includes 'Butterfly', 'Heartbeat', 'Say It Ain't So, Jo', 'Boulder To Birmingham' and others.

The Hollies: Super Hits (April 2001, US Sony BMG 85349)

Greatest Hits (March 2003, EMI UK 582-0122)
UK number 21. 'Carrie Anne' had been featured in TVs *The Sopranos* episode 'Down Neck' (Season 1 Episode 7) during one of Tony's flashbacks. This 47-track 2CD set also includes an easy-swinging new Paul Bliss composition 'How Do I Survive' sung by Carl Wayne. This undistinguished mid-paced track is his only entry in The Hollies discography.

The Long Road Home (October 2003, EMI 02743-584856, six-CD box set)
With original tracks, B-sides, foreign-language versions and several previously-unreleased recordings, including three 'L Ransford' songs demoed at the New York Bell Studios 27 April 1965:

'Listen Here to Me', 2:04-minutes with a catchy 'Mystery Train' rhythm back-up and a high Graham Nash middle-eight solo. 'It's a crime, it's a shame' that they never developed this promising composition further.
'Bring Back Your Love to Me' a fast-paced handclap-driven L Ransford song with a masterful Tony Hicks guitar solo and Allan inflicting his deepest soul voice on the lyric. It was first issued as a bonus track on the 1997 extended Rhino edition of The Hollies (1965).
'So Lonely', an early try-out of the plaintive B-side of 'Look Through Any Window'.
'She Said Yeah', there's also this brief 1:41-minute track cut 10 November 1964, which proves that The Hollies don't really do raucous. Originally a Larry Williams B-side with Sonny Bono (as 'Don Christy') & Roddy Jackson writer-credits, it was done in a more fierce R&B style by The Rolling Stones on their

Out Of Our Heads album, as well as by The Animals, and was later revived by
Paul McCartney for his 1999 LP Run Devil Run.

'Can't Lie No More', another previously unissued gem on Disc Five, a
Mike Batt song recorded November 1979 with final strings dubbed during
the 'Soldier's Song' session. Faint strings and piano notes build into Allan's
mournful big-ballad mode, kicked uptempo into a collective voice chorus.
Memories aren't enough; he can't pretend to love anymore; this is the moment
'when the laughing has to stop.'

Midas Touch: The Very Best of The Hollies (February 2010, EMI 6082272)

A UK number 23. A 48-track collection that includes a digitally remastered 'Bus
Stop', the song that Allan Clarke joins Crosby & Nash to sing onstage at the
Royal Albert Hall, 8 October 2011. Graham announces it as 'a personal thrill
for me' to sing again with 'my dear friend.' Issued the year The Hollies were
inducted into the Rock 'n' Roll Hall of Fame, this album brings the story up to
date with 'Then, Now, Always (Dolphin Days)' and 'I Would Fly'.

Clarke, Hicks And Nash Years: The Complete Hollies April 1963-October 1968 (May 2011, EMI 5099909624221, 6CD Box Set)

Eric Haydock, who plays bass on the April 1963-July 1963 tracks here, died 5
January 2019.

The sixth disc includes eight tracks recorded at the Lewisham Odeon, 24
May 1968, intended for the live album that never happened. With walls of
screams between the tracks Graham introduces 'King Midas In Reverse' as a
song which 'wasn't too popular with a lot of people,' and he takes the 'Mothers
and Fathers throughout the land' verse on 'The Times They A-Changin''. They
are tight professional performances of familiar material, with a string-section
interlude added to 'Carrie Anne'.

'Stop Stop Stop', 'Look Through Any Window', 'The Times They Are
A-Changin'', 'On a Carousel', 'King Midas in Reverse', 'Butterfly', 'Jennifer
Eccles', 'Carrie Anne'

The Hollies Essential (March 2012, DE EMI 5099964402222, CD)

The Hollies: Fifty at Fifty (2014, Parlophone 825646223541, 3CD)

All the regular expected hits, with first studio cuts of 'If the Lights Go Out' and
the tinkling electro-Pop synths of 'Take My Love And Run', live versions of 'On a
Carousel', 'Too Young To Be Married' and 'Then, Now, Always (Dolphin Days)',
plus one previously-unreleased track, 'Skylarks' written by Bobby Elliott, Peter
Howarth and Steve Vickers, a big emotive power-ballad asking 'what happened
to romance, what became of love and respect?', immaculately-arranged with

piercing guitar and soaring orchestration strewn with evocative images of 'skylarks, church bells, white cliffs.'

Head Out Of Dreams: The Complete Hollies August 1973-May 1988 (March 2017, Parlophone 0190295892333, 6CD box-set)

It takes its title from the opening lines of 'I'm Down', with liner-notes by Uli Twelker, and gathers familiar material alongside the snappy electro-pop 'You're All Woman' and 'You Gave Me Strength' – two mid-eighties B-sides previously unissued on official CD (see January 1987, 'This Is It'), both versions of 'Take My Love And Run', plus 'Crossfire' (neglected B-side of 1977 single 'Amnesty') from the *A Crazy Steal* period.

Changin' Times (The Complete Hollies: January 1969-March 1973) (July 2015, Parlophone 0825646336111, 5CD box-set)

92 tracks sequenced in session order, with Tony Hicks and Bobby Elliott's 'Elucidating Observations' comments in the 24-page booklet. It includes the full *Out on the Road* German album, plus two remastered versions of 'Oh Granny' – one with Allan Clarke and the other with Terry Sylvester vocals. The rare tracks content includes:

'Indian Girl', the American B-side of 'Magic Woman Touch', written and sung by Terry Sylvester, operating around a simpler acoustic guitar setting than his own solo version. Denny Doherty of The Mamas & The Papas issued his version of this song as a 1973 single (Columbia 4-45779).

'If It Wasn't for the Reason That I Love You' the Greenaway-Cooke song already described as part of the *Rarities* album.

'Papa Rain', a sensitive Colin Jennings song with Mikael Rickfors rich soul vocals offset by hallmark Hollies harmonies, taken from the *Romany* sessions and issued as a bonus track on the 2007 remastered CD edition.

'Witchy Woman', written by Don Henley and Bernie Leadon and issued as the second single from the Eagles debut album. Although it was an American Top Ten hit it failed to register in the U.K, hence The Hollies tentative but ultimately unissued cover from the *Romany* sessions. Closely following the hard-edged Eagles arrangement, Mikael Rickfors standing in for Henley's vocals, this is a 2007 remastered version. It's a strong track. But does it sound like a Hollies track? I think not.

'I Had a Dream', Terry Sylvester's B-side of the German 'Jesus Was A Crossmaker' single.

'He Ain't Heavy, He's My Brother' is track one on CD2...

The road is long, with many a winding turn, that leads us to who knows where? Who knows where?

Bibiography

The Road Is Long: The Hollies Story by Brian Southall (June 2015, Red Planet Publishing, ISBN 978-1-9059-5976-1)

It Ain't Heavy, It's My Story: My Life In The Hollies by Bobby Elliott (2020, Omnibus Press, ISBN 978-1-91317-220-6)

Wild Tales: A Rock & Roll Life by Graham Nash (June 2014, Penguin, ISBN-13 978-0241968048)

Record Collector: 100 Greatest Psychedelic Records by David Wells (2005, Diamond Publishing Ltd, ISSN 1746 8051)

Lillian Roxon's Rock Encyclopedia by Lillian Roxon (1971, Grosset & Dunlop).

Exorcising Ghosts by Dave Cousins (September 2014, Witchwood Media Ltd, ISBN 978-0956588715)

RnR magazine, for setting up the Graham Nash and Allan Clarke interviews www.rock-n-reel.co.uk

The Hollies: Look Through Any Window 1963-1975 (2011, Eagle Vision DVD, Reelin' In The Years Productions LLC), with ten minutes of rare footage from 1967 of the Hollies recording in the EMI Abbey Road Studios, and colour home movies filmed backstage and on tour during the 1960s.

The excellent Hollies discussion website: https://elevatedobservations. proboards.com/
The discographical resource website: https://www.discogs.com/
The Manchester music website: www.manchesterbeat.com/index.php/groups1/ hollies

The Billboard Book Of US Top Forty Hits by Joel Whitburn (1983, Billboard Publications, ISBN 0-8230-7511-7)

The Guinness Top Forty Charts by Paul Gambaccini, Tim Rice, Jonathan Rice (1992, GRR Publications ISBN 0-85112-541-7)